Mathematics OF MONEY

FROM DECIMALS TO DERIVATIVES

MARY BETH RUDIS

innovativeink
PUBLISHING
A Division of Kendall Hunt

innovativeink PUBLISHING
A Division of Kendall Hunt

www.kendallhunt.com
Send all inquiries to:
4050 Westmark Drive
Dubuque, IA 52004-1840

Print ISBN: 979-8-3851-1290-6
eBook ISBN: 979-8-3851-1291-3

Published in the United States of America

DEDICATION

In memory of Dr. Paul Perdew, who believed in me

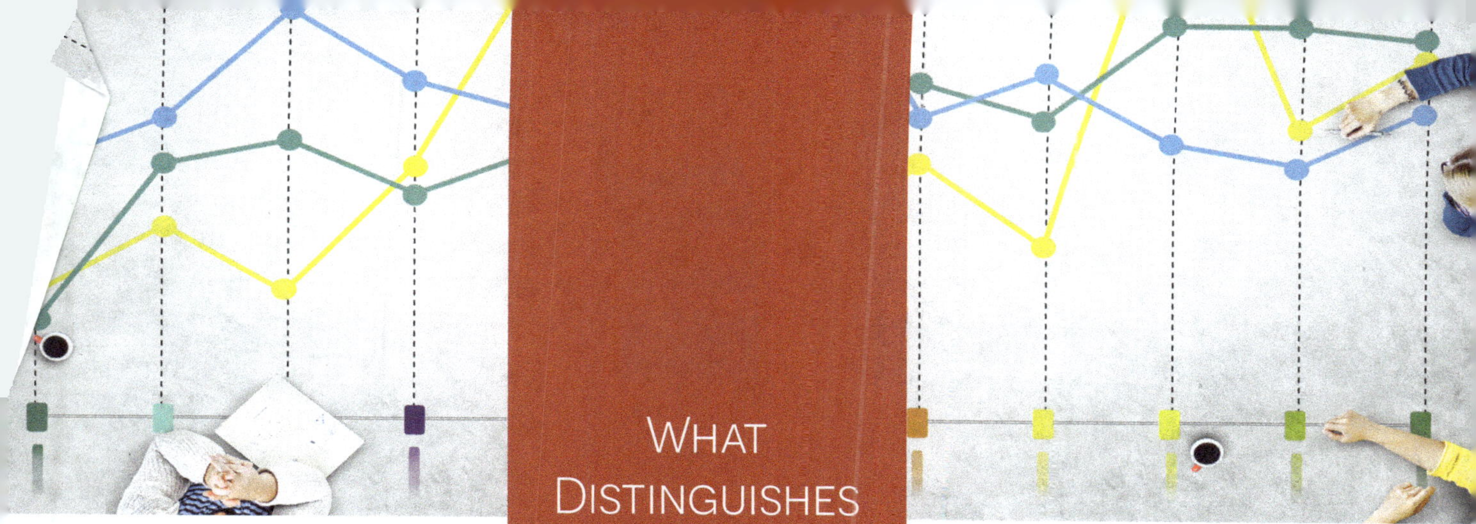

What Distinguishes This Text from Others

1) It employs universal design principles in how information is presented. Some examples of this are: simplicity and consistent use of common notation, careful explanation of mathematical 'jargon', vertical rather than horizontal arrangements of visual or tabular information, and avoidance of symbols with multiple meanings.
2) Develop marketable skills applicable in a business environment – whether it be a company or organization comprising of one individual, 50 individuals, or a thousand. Many of the lessons include applicable spreadsheet activities that enable the student to visualize the mathematical principles which help to answer meaningful questions.
3) With practice, the student will develop confidence toward being able to communicate accurately using mathematical models, formulas, and data tools. Instead of emphasizing procedures, the emphasis is on extrapolation, interpretation, analysis, and critical thinking.
4) With the emergence of large language models and intelligent systems, the need for computation and algebraic manipulation will be less relevant. Online graphical and algebraic solvers are constantly improving as the training data and prompt engineering improves. Since these automations are still developing and still are prone to errors, it is even more necessary to be able to assess and evaluate information that is presented. Citizens of the 21st century need the skills to determine AI solutions' reliability, and to assess its practical application (when, how, and by whom).
5) The inclusion of the introductory chapter is missing from other texts; it offers the student more than just elementary mathematical concepts. These foundational concepts are put in context which enriches and broadens the learner's perspective. Numbers are not just objects to be plugged into a formula. They mean something contextually. A fraction isn't just a fraction, but a means to engage meaningfully with numbers as information.

CONTENTS

CHAPTER 1: FOUNDATIONS OF MATHEMATICAL REASONING AND EXPRESSION 1

CHAPTER 2: FUNCTIONS OF TWO VARIABLES 21

CHAPTER 3: LINEAR MODELS AND EQUATIONS 39

Chapter 4: Systems of Linear Equations 63

Chapter 5: Quadratic Functions and Polynomials As Models 81

CHAPTER 6: EXPONENTIAL AND LOGARITHM FUNCTIONS AS MODELS 103

CHAPTER 7: FINANCE – INTEREST 119

CHAPTER 8: FINANCE – SPECIAL TOPICS 141

1 Foundations of Mathematical Reasoning and Expression

Section 1.1 The Real Number System

Number, numeral, digit, decimal, fraction, and ordinal are all words we use when describing the quantity, order, value, size, or amount of something. Why do we have so many words for essentially the same thing? What is the difference between a number and a numeral? There are also different families of numbers. What are they all about? The formal rules of mathematics have been developed so that people can communicate with each other in precise ways. We often take precision for granted, but the precision of mathematics is necessary in many situations; advanced manufacturing, microsurgery, space exploration, and computerized financial systems are all situations where exactness matters. An architect's drawings contain lines and measurements that the builder can understand and translate that into the practical details of materials and labor required for the building project. Here are some informal definitions of commonly used words which we often take for granted. Each of these vocabulary words refers to a number or part of a number and how it is used in our language.

Definition: A ***number*** is a measure or a count of something. It refers to the value of something using a standard way of quantifying information. "There were 10 ducklings in number." If the word ***number*** can be replaced with words like ***quantity***, ***count***, ***value***, or ***size*** in a sentence, then the correct word is being used.

Definition: A ***digit*** is one of the unique characters or symbols that are used in the writing of a number. Hindu-Arabic numerals are base 10 which means 10 unique digits: 0, 1, 2, 3, 4, 5, 6, 7, 8, and 9.

The formal term for a number that can include digits to the left or right of the decimal point, as well as fractions, is numeral.

Definition: A ***numeral*** is the written form of a number. It refers to the written expression as a series of digits, and sometimes includes a decimal point as well as commas (to aid in reading). "What is the *value* of 7 in the numeral 472.15?" Answer: 7x10 or 70

Numerals can involve fractions as well. Another example of a numeral that can involve a fraction is this: the price of a gallon of gasoline is $3.45 $\frac{9}{10}$ or $3.459.

The above example is what mathematicians call a ***mixed expression*** because it uses decimal notation as well as fraction notation. The word notation literally means "the way something is written."

When a number is used to refer to the position of something, such as finishing a race behind two other competitors, we use ordinals.

Definition: An ***ordinal*** is the expression used to describe the order or placement of a thing. Here is a partial list of ordinals: first, second, third, fourth, fifth, sixth.

Everything in modern mathematics has a basis in our decimal numeral system. We will start with the simplest numbers: the whole numbers. The word "decimal" comes from a Latin root word meaning *a tenth*. Our number system is what we call a ***positional*** number system. This means that numbers have digits (represented by 0 through 9) and each digit has value that is a multiple of a power of ten. Nine is the largest value of a power of ten. Anything past that goes to the next power of 10.

Example: Write the number 452 in ***expanded form*** using digits and powers of 10.

Solution: The number 452 is written in expanded form as $(4 \times 100) + (5 \times 10) + (2 \times 1)$ where $100 = 10^2$, $10 = 10^1$, and $1 = 10^0$. Note: any number raised to the 0 power = 1.

The position of each digit in a numeral matters because we need to understand that 452 is not the same number as 524, or 245. The set, or collection, of numbers that represent the kinds of numbers we use to count things (not including 0) is what we call ***natural numbers***. These are the first numbers that humans learned to use. Then by including the number 0 we refer to the "natural numbers + 0" as the ***whole numbers***. By including all the negatives of these, we have the ***integers***. Each of these sets of numbers has a fancy Roman-style letter for its name.

We will now describe all the special collections of numbers, show what numbers are included in each, and what designation we give to them. We call collections of things ***sets***. A ***set*** is a well-defined collection of numbers or objects. We can easily determine if something belongs to a set, or not.

Example: The set of ***counting numbers*** can be seen as a list inside {}:
{1, 2, 3, 4, 5, 6, 7, 8, 9, …, ∞} and is denoted N

These are the ***whole numbers***:
{0, 1, 2, 3, 4, 5, …, ∞} is denoted W (not as common)

These are the ***integers***:
{…, −5, −4, −3, −2, −1, 0, 1, 2, 3, 4, 5, …, ∞} is denoted Z

These are the ***rational numbers***:
{numbers that can be expressed as a ratio of two whole numbers} is denoted Q. Why Q? It comes from the word "quotient" which is the result of a division of two whole numbers.

These are the ***real numbers*** (informal definition):
{all numbers that can be *approximated* by a rational number} is denoted R. We sometimes will write R = (-∞,∞) meaning numbers that extend infinitely far in both positive and negative directions.

Because numbers can be ordered and used to measure, we have a visual representation of the real numbers using the number line.

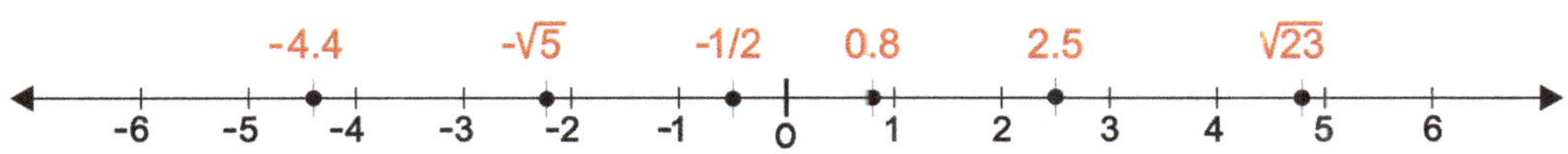

Do they belong? If a number is a member of one of these sets, is it also in some of the others as well? How do they overlap? Membership gets more exclusive as the requirements are more restrictive. Here is a way to visualize belonging to these sets of numbers. Think inheritance. The more inclusive sets (those that are larger in size and scope) inherit all the properties of the smaller sets. Let us describe this belonging in another way.

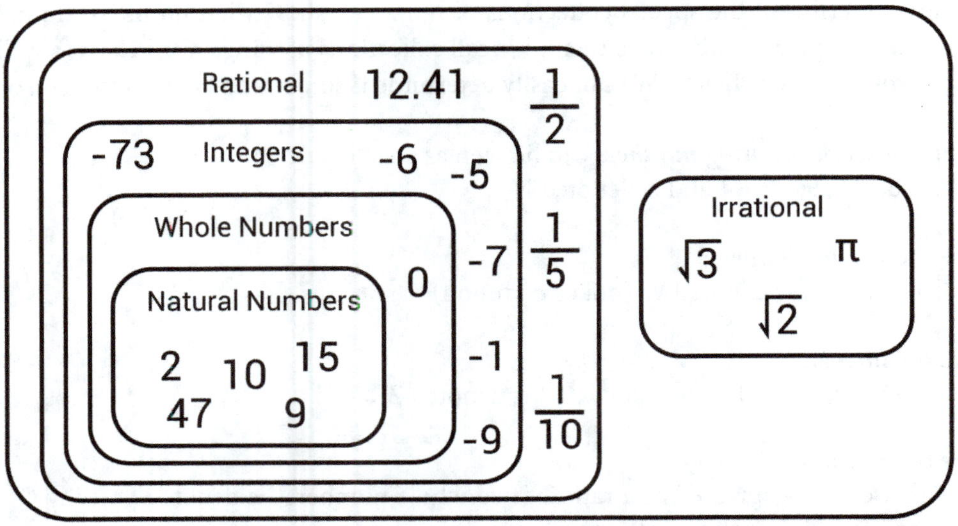

Dream01/Shutterstock.com

Conversation Starter: Why do you think there are so many vocabulary words for numbers?

Conversation Starter: Can you think of number systems that are not decimal (base 10) systems? If so, what are some ways other number systems are different? the same?

Try This: Using this word bank: **whole, integer, rational, real** (W, Z, Q, or R), write an "is ___ but is not ___" sentence about each number shown that reads as follows:
Example: Make a sentence for the number *e* "The number *e* is **real** but is not **rational**."
Try to use each word at least twice! By the way, $e \cong 2.72$.

2.015 -3 $\frac{5}{3}$ 0 6001 π $\sqrt{2}$ $-\sqrt{4}$

SECTION 1.2 ABOUT FRACTIONS

In September of 1978, the rock band Styx released its eighth studio album. The album was cleverly named Pieces of Eight. The title track was about the human pursuit of wealth and the consequences that often come with the relentlessness of it. What exactly is a "piece of eight" and why mention it here?

Yaroslaff/Shutterstock.com

For over 300 years in the western world, when Europeans were expanding to North and South America, one of the most widely used currencies was the Spanish *Reale de ocho*, which was minted from silver and imprinted as official currency backed by the government of Spain. One "cob" or piece of silver was worth 8 reales = 1 peso and depended on weight and composition rather than shape. The value was in the silver content (93%). It does not take much of an imagination to see how this may have led to global levels of fraud, and scandal. Silver is a soft enough metal that these cobs could be clipped or shaved, then could be hammered, or combined with a common metal like tin to restore the weight. The reduced cobs could contain as little as 65-75% of the original silver. To combat fraud, eventually the world saw rounded coins which were harder to clip (no corners!); these replaced the irregular-shaped cobs.[1]

For an exercise, let us assume that an early 1700s traveler could purchase a week's stay at an inn for one of these silver coins, but the traveler only wanted to stay one night. All the traveler has for currency are these silver coins (in English "dollar"). Well, it turns out the traveler is in luck. The town has a blacksmith who happens to have a tool used to cut one of these coins in half. Since this is an acceptable practice for currency in the early 1700s, the traveler visits the blacksmith and asks for the

1. Allan, John, et al. "coin." *Britannica Money*, Encyclopaedia Britannica, 27 May 1999, https://money.britannica.com/money/coin.

coin to be cut into 8 "bits". Why eight? Well think about the math involved, as well as the physical constraints. Here is an object about 1 ½ inches in diameter that needs to be divided up into smaller pieces. The simplest thing to do is to cut it in half. Cut something in half and now there are 2 half-moon-shaped pieces. Cut each of those in half and there are now 4 wedge-shaped pieces. Now cut each of those in half. There are 8 roughly equal-sized pieces. In the early 1700s and into the 1800s each of these slim wedge-shaped pieces was called a "bit" which were worth the same as a 1-reale coin in trade. Sound familiar? It should. Fast forward to the 20th century and a bit is an eighth of a byte, the binary code upon which computers are based.

Returning to the inn, the traveler can pay 2 bits for the room for one night and both the evening and morning meal. In mathematical terms the traveler paid $2/8$ peso which is also ¼ peso. The fraction is the word mathematicians came up with when describing pieces of a whole. The root of the word is the same that we use in the word fracture.

At first, all fractions were what we call ***unit fractions***, in that the numerator was always 1. In a ledger from the 14th century, one might see written /4 which literally means ¼. The slash was used interchangeably with a horizontal fraction bar. The choice of how to express a fraction was often due to limitations of printing and typography. Historically fractions were used before the printing press, which meant making copies by hand – using ink or a stylus (like a chisel) in leather or parchment.[2]

> **Conversation starter:** Can any fraction be decomposed as a sum and/or difference of unit fractions? Why not try it with the fraction ⅜ without resorting to the obvious ⅛ + ⅛ + ⅛?

In geometry, the ratio of the circumference of a circle to its diameter is always the same, regardless of the size of the circle. This ratio is one of the most famous ***irrational*** (real but not rational) numbers in mathematics. Since it cannot be written as an exact decimal, or as a repeating decimal, the number instead has been given a name – π which is a letter of the Greek alphabet pronounced "pie"). π can be approximated using the fraction $22/7$. Sometimes the decimal approximation 3.14 is used. A grassroots effort began in 1988, then officially designated by the U.S. Congress in 2009 to mark March 14th as "Pi Day" celebrating the famous number.

> **Conversation starter:** $22/7 = 3\,1/7$. Can you think of any reason this combination of numerals and digits might appeal to some people? Is there a cultural connection we can make?

2. Miller, Jeff. "Earliest Uses of Symbols for Fractions." *MacTutor History of Mathematics*, University of St Andrews, Scotland, April 2015, https://mathshistory.st-andrews.ac.uk/Miller/mathsym/fractions/

Here is another application of the fraction in our everyday life. This is a tale as old as time, or at least as old as humans were tracking the number of days in a solar year. Talk to an astrophysicist or astronomer and they will tell you that the solar calendar year is decreasing. It is happening very slowly, because of the changing gravitational forces of the solar system in which the Earth is one planet among eight. When we say the phrase "one year" talking to a physicist we may be referring to the "tropical year", that is the length of time in days, hours, minutes, and seconds from one *vernal equinox* to the next. The solar year measures the year from a different vantage point. The length of our solar year 2023 for example is 365 days 5 hours 48 minutes 46 s. Each year will be slightly different. Our calendar calculations require some estimate, like an average, on which the days are based.[3]

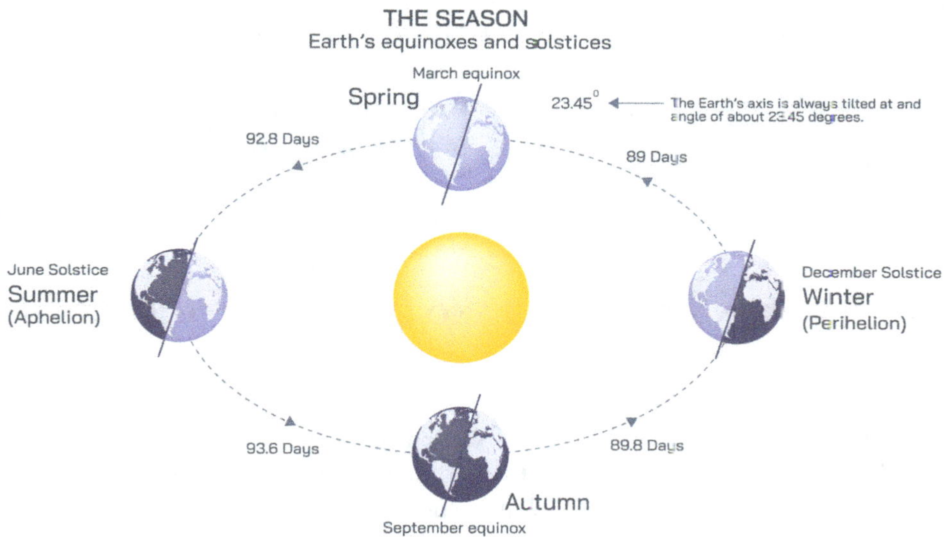

Anshuman Rath/Shutterstock.com

This explains the need for a ***leap year***, but it does not exactly explain why we include an extra day every *four years*. Until we do the math, that is. Also, we do not *always* insert an extra day every 4 years. There are some exceptions. But we are getting ahead of ourselves. At the time of Julius Caesar, emperor of Rome, calculating the length of a solar year to be about 365.25 days was a pretty big deal. It is worth noting that 6 hours out of 24 hours in a day is exactly 0.25 day. Leap year calculation was based on the length of a year = 365 days and 6 hours. This was a remarkable achievement at a time when sundials were high tech.

$$6 \textit{ hours} = 0.25 \textit{ day} = \tfrac{1}{4} \textit{ day}$$

The fraction ¼ informs the decision to add a day every 4 years. The denominator measures how many years to wait before adding an extra day.

3. The Editors of Encyclopaedia Britannica. "year." *Britannica*, Encyclopaedia Britannica, 20 July 1998, https://britannica.com/science/year.

But the length of a solar year is *not* 365 days and 6 hours. The difference between that and 365 days, 5 hours + 48 minutes may not seem like a big deal when calculating the length of an entire year. It is not in the short term. But historically as time went on, adjusting by too many leap days began to be noticed around the 16th century. To put it in perspective, after two thousand years, our seasons would be off by nearly 2 weeks. Instead of 20th June being the longest day of the year in the northern hemisphere, the longest daylight day would be more like 7th June (day 158 in a nonleap year by Julian calendar measurements).

Pope Gregory XIII, a 16th-century head of the Roman church, instituted a new calculation for leap years that was based on a more accurate measurement of the length of a solar year. This calculation is in use today. The Gregorian year is 365 days + 5 hours + 49 minutes + 12 s.

Conversation starter: Length of a solar year $\cong 365 + 1/4 - 1/100 + 1/400$. What is that in decimal form? How do these fractions determine leap year calculations?

Section 1.3 From Fractions and Decimals to Percents

Our journey into numbers takes us to a unit of measure that we call the percent. More than just a symbol next to a number, the % even has its own key along with the number 5 on computer keyboards. The symbol itself looks like *0 divided by 0*, where the slash means to divide. Division of a nonzero number by smaller and smaller numbers, approaching 0, yields larger and larger results. When we try to divide 0 by 0 the result is something we call *indeterminate*. This is one of the oddities in mathematics, and something we can experiment with as well. Let us unpack what is meant by indeterminate. In words, we mean to say *cannot be determined without further analysis*. Let us see why that is.

Weird things can happen when numbers get close to 0. Some of the more interesting areas of research involve objects or phenomena that measure infinitesimally small. In biology, much of medicine occurs at the microscopic and cellular level. In chemistry, some of the most destructive forces on earth involve the smallest atom – the hydrogen atom. In physics a whole area of study involves what happens to things moving at high speed but whose mass is virtually indetectable. In finance, infinitesimally small interest rate changes have dramatic effects when the prime lending rate is already below 0.5% or 0.005.

Since we do not have a way to divide 0 by 0, let us choose a number that is close to 0 , then move the decimal point to get smaller, and see what happens in 3 situations, all involving a calculation that would be 0 divided by 0, if $x = 0$.

Start with $x = 0.01$. Calculate these 3 expressions using 0.01 in place of x and increasing the number of decimal positions, making x smaller and smaller each time. Each time we get a different *approximation* of 0 ÷ 0.

	$2 \cdot x \div x$	$x^2 \div x$	$3 \cdot x \div (x^2)$
$x = 0.01$	2	0.01	300
$x = 0.001$	2	0.001	3000
$x = 0.0001$	2	0.0001	30,000
$x = 0.00001$	2	0.00001	300,000
seems to be 'approaching'....			
$x = 0$	2	0	∞

Conversation starter: What do you notice? What do you wonder? Compare and contrast the results you see in the table above. Each of the 3 calculations should give us insight about 0 divided by 0. Summarize your findings and what can you infer?

Clearly % is not 0 divided by 0. Instead, the symbol can be better explained in terms of other symbols that have been used for the same thing. We can deduce how the symbol % came to be. In the box below, every symbol is another version of % seen in writings from about the 14th century onward. The *p* is the abbreviation for the Latin word *per* and *c* represents *cento*.[4]

p/c	/100	*pc*^{o}	*per* $\frac{0}{0}$	%

The fact is % is a ***unit of measure*** that forces us to make a correction when performing calculations with other numbers. It is really that simple.

In practical terms, suppose a customer at a restaurant wants to leave a 15% tip on a food order that totaled $32 without sales tax. 15% literally means 15 cents for every 100 cents, or $1 spent. We do not need a calculator for this.

- Take 10% of $32 first, by moving the decimal point one place to the left. 10% of $32 is $3.20.
- Another 5% is half of that. $1.60 is half of $3.20.
- Add them up. $3.20 + $1.60 is $4.80.
- If the customer is in a hurry, they can simply leave a $5 bill. Keep the change.

4. Houston, Keith. "Miscellany No 59: the percent sign." *Shady Characters*, Keith Houston, 17 March 2015, https://shadycharacters.co.uk/2015/03/percent-sign/

If someone had their smart device, and forgot how to use the special % key, the tip could be calculated by multiplying 32 x 0.15. Converting 15% to the ***number equivalent*** allows it to be multiplied by $32.

We will avoid referring to the number equivalent as "decimal form" because what if there is already a decimal point in the %? This can lead to confusion. Here is another example to illustrate that point. Suppose an individual wants to know how much interest they will be charged on their next credit card bill, when their balance is $431.87. Finance charge is calculated by taking the annual percentage rate (APR) and dividing it by 12 (because there are 12 months, payment periods, in a year).

Example: Suppose the APR (Annual Percentage Rate) is 17.99%. How much finance charge will there be on this month's bill if the end of month balance is $431.87?

Solution: Take the APR (%) and divide by 12, and then divide that by 100. We could also save time by dividing by 1200. Do it both ways and see:
$17.99 \div 12 \cong 1.49917$ *Then* $1.49917 \div 100 = 0.0149917$

Alternatively:
$17.99 \div 1200 \cong 0.0149917$

Pro tip: When rounding decimal numbers in financial calculations, either do not round until the very end OR make sure to include as many decimal places as possible until the final calculation is made.

Now multiply by the balance: $431.87 \times 0.0149917 = 6.4745 \cong \$6.47$

If the credit card holder wants to see their balance go down, the payment will need to be greater than $6.47, and they will need to avoid using this card on any more purchases unless they are prepared to make a larger payment every month.

Section 1.4 How Big or Small; High or Low; Near or Far

Now that we have developed some notation concerning numbers and types of numbers, let us discuss how we measure things in mathematics. If we want to know how big or how small something is, we quantify it. This means using the **decimal system** to assign a numeric value, and the **real number system** to understand how to place numbers relative to other numbers. The problem with mathematicians is that we sometimes forget that context matters. Numbers mean different things when we assign units to them, or when we compare them to other numbers, such as the size of something relative to the whole.

For example, let us start with a number; it will be **negative**: –68. Now we ask a mathematical question: ***How big is –68?*** Or perhaps it is not big at all. Perhaps it is very small. How big is anything really? Why does it matter? Honestly these questions are meaningless without context. But in math we often must solve problems that do not seem to have any real purpose because we are simply "doing the math." We are left to wonder what the purpose might be. What could –68 represent, then? It might be 68 ft below sea level. It might be 68° below freezing on a Celsius scale. It might be a weight loss of 68 lb. It might be a payment of $68.00. It might be a drop of 68 ft. It could be 68 miles south. 68° rotation (pivot) in a negative direction.

Conversation starter: Name two other possible uses and meanings for the number –68 that are not mentioned here.

All these involve a ***size of 68*** and a value that indicates either something negative in direction or negative in how something reduced or went down:

DESCRIPTION	CONTEXT	INTERPRETATION
68 ft below sea level	Depths range from sea level (0) to 1 mile below sea level (–5,280 ft)	Given the context this depth is relatively shallow (low)
68° F below zero	Temperatures vary from –70 to 120° F	Temperature is on the extreme low end compared with other temperatures in the range
Weight loss of 68 lb	Blue whales weigh around 400,000 lb	Small as a portion of the weight of a blue whale
Payment of $68.00	What was paid to the babysitter for 2.5 hours	Big compared with typical pay for 2.5 hours babysitting
Drop of 68 ft	Plane flying at an altitude of 36,000 ft	Very small compared with overall altitude
68 miles south	Works anywhere from 5 miles away to 75 miles away from home each day	Big (far) compared with other distances traveled each day for work
Rotate 68° down	Scope can be pivoted between 85° upward and 85° downward	Fairly steep angle compared with the range that the scope can be tilted down or up

Measuring the **difference** between two numbers is another way we decide how big something is, or how small something is, how close or how far. One might also suppose that calculating the difference between two numbers tells how far apart they are. Yet a lot of what we do in math depends on numbers always being positive or always being negative. We will see this come up again and again

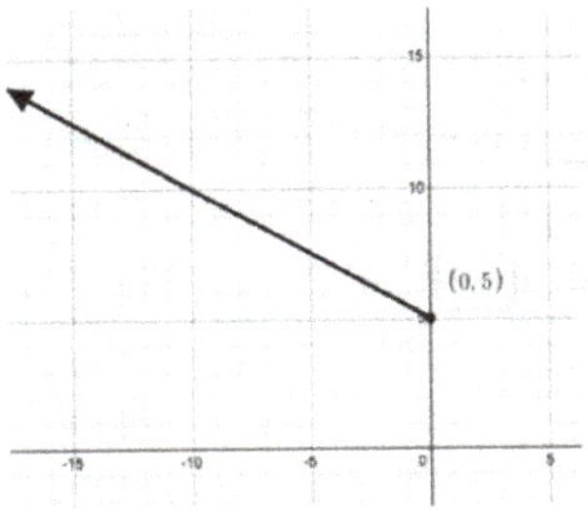

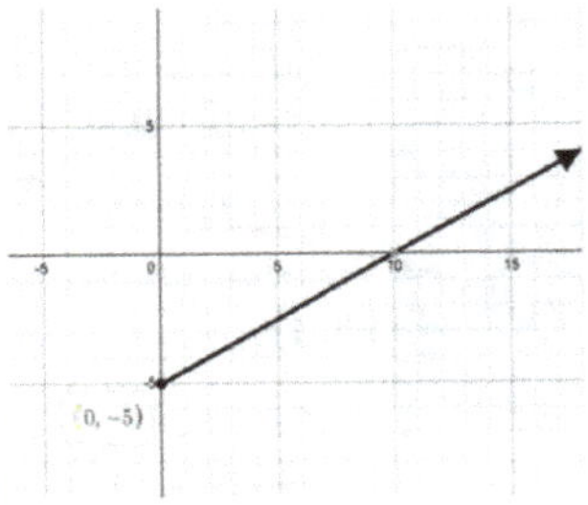

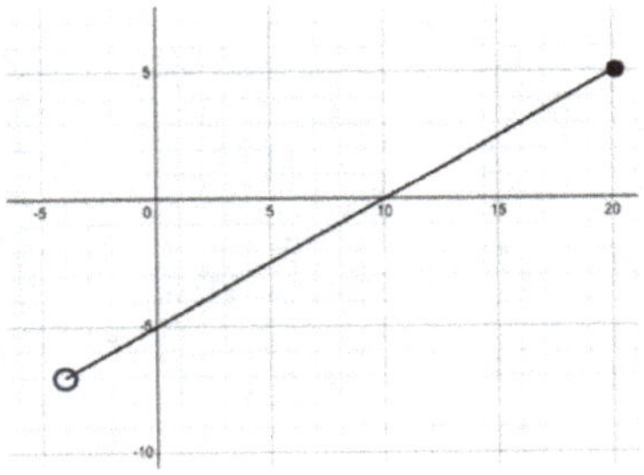

Domain		
$(-\infty, 0]$	$[0, \infty)$	$(-4, 20]$
$-\infty < x \leq 0$	$0 \leq x < \infty$	$-4 < x \leq 20$
Range		
$[5, \infty)$	$[-5, \infty)$	$(-7, 5]$
$5 \leq y < \infty$	$-5 \leq y < \infty$	$-7 < y \leq 5$

The use of a square bracket [or] signifies that the end point is included in the interval. The use of a curved bracket, or parenthesis symbol, (or), signifies that the endpoint has been removed, or there is no endpoint; in the event of a finite interval the endpoint sometimes is and sometimes is not included.

On the graph, endpoints are either open o or solid •. Open means the endpoint is excluded. Solid means the endpoint is included.

We use functions of one variable, or many variables, to predict outcomes or to place someone or something in terms of geography, age, species, or other attribute. For example, can we predict how many cookies will be made from a recipe that uses 180 grams of flour? Yes, but there are many factors that determine this. What kind of cookie? What size are the cookies? What are the other ingredients? If we were referring to a specific cookie using a known recipe, how much more likely could we predict the number of cookies? How much better are we at predicting when we can eliminate most of the unknowns? These questions are all part of "doing the math."

What do we need to know about a fossil to determine its age?
A storm is making its way across the Atlantic Ocean. Can we tell where it will be in one hour? In 8 hours? In a day? Two days?
A person graduates with a degree in psychology. What more do we need to know if we want to predict their salary a year from now? Two years from now? Five years? Ten?

Researchers at Harvard University, in cooperation with the U.S. Census Bureau, sought to identify factors at birth that are strong indicators of a person's future success. Over 20 million Americans were part of the study, based on voluntary responses to the Census Bureau survey that happens every decade.

These Americans would have been born in 1975, grown up into the 1980s, and reached the age of 35 in 2010. The data included their self-reported status as an adult compared with household information from childhood. The results were aggregated into a map of the United States showing median income, incarceration rates, marital status, and a list of other outcomes solely based on where these people were born. The project is called The Opportunity Atlas.[1] https://www.opportunityatlas.org/ All reported outcomes represent the "middle" of a range of outcomes, so individual results will not necessarily be reflected in the numbers. What we see there is a representation of what is typical for that region, county, or zip code. We have one predictor variable— one's place of birth. Then several outcome or response variables—income, marital status, incarceration status, graduation status, wages, and other socioeconomic data—have been studied. The concept of equal opportunity for all is something many democracies continue to strive toward, but it is necessary to be objective about identifying what is wrong before society can fix it.

When trying to answer complex questions involving many variables and many possible predictors, analysts will look at a graph of dozens, sometimes hundreds of variables, looking for strong correlations. Then, they cook up a recipe that attaches weights to each predictor variable. Weights are like the portion of an ingredient in a recipe. The sum of all those weighted variables produces an outcome called the response.

Conversation Starter: Name the predictor variables for the perfect chocolate chip cookie. Be specific (for example, not just sugar, but granulated or brown sugar). If a batch of cookie dough weighs 1,000 grams or 1 kg, how many grams of each ingredient is included?

SECTION 2.3 RATES OF CHANGE AND INCREASING/DECREASING PATTERNS

Functions show us the relationship between one quantity and another: given an input value x, we can identify the associated value of y that goes with it. That is a very static arrangement. But suppose we have an input that is changing from one value to another. One of the attributes we study is rate of

1. Chetty, Raj, et al. "The Opportunity Atlas: Mapping the Childhood Roots of Social Mobility." *Opportunity Insights Neighborhoods*, Opportunity Insights, October 2018, https://opportunityinsights.org/paper/the-opportunity-atlas/.

change of the y quantity with respect to the x quantity. How much, or how little, the outcome changes when the input changes from x = a to x = b, is where we go next. To illustrate this, we will look at annual gasoline prices in the United States from 1994 to the present time. Here we see the table from which we will make a graph, and then we will consider what it means to track rate of change.

eia Data source: U.S. Energy Information Administration

This series is available through the EIA open data API and can be downloaded to Excel or embedded as an interactive chart or map on your website.

U.S. All Grades All Formulations Retail Gasoline Prices (Dollars per Gallon)

Decade	Year-0	Year-1	Year-2	Year-3	Year-4	Year-5	Year-6	Year-7	Year-8	Year-9
1990's				NA	1.078	1.158	1.245	1.244	1.072	1.176
2000's	1.523	1.460	1.386	1.603	1.895	2.314	2.618	2.843	3.299	2.406
2010's	2.835	3.576	3.680	3.575	3.437	2.520	2.250	2.528	2.813	2.691
2020's	2.258	3.100	4.059							

- = No Data Reported; -- = Not Applicable; NA = Not Available; W = Withheld to avoid disclosure of individual company data.

Release Date: 9/11/2023
Next Release Date: 9/18/2023

Year (x)	Price (y)
0	1.078
1	1.158
2	1.245
3	1.244
4	1.072
5	1.176
6	1.523
7	1.460
8	1.386
9	1.603
10	1.895
11	2.314

First, we will measure time in years after 1994, since that is the first year we have data. On this table, next to decade we have the year, so 1990's Year-4 is really 1994. For our purposes, 1994 will be x = 0. Then 1995 will be x = 1, 1996 will be x = 2, and so on. The y values will be the prices in $. Converting all this data into an ***xy-table***, let us start with the first 11 years, ending with 2005. We also will highlight the lowest price and highest price using orange text.

For the purposes of our calculations and investigation, the domain of our graph is [0,11] and the range is [1.072, 2.314].

Notice that the upper and lower limits of the range do not always occur at the endpoints. If the graph consists of ups and downs, then we must be careful to observe the lowest point and the highest point. In the first year, we see the gasoline price went up from 1.078 to 1.158, for a change of $0.08 or 8 cents. In the second year, the price went up from 1.158 to 1.245, for a change of $0.087 or 8.7 cents a gallon. The increase in the price of a gallon of gasoline from one year to the next at least starts out almost constant. Let us add a column to our table and calculate the amount of increase from one year to the next for all the data. We can find the ***average rate of change*** between year 0 and year 11 as the mean, or average, of all the increases. On the table we simply add up the increase amounts, keeping the signs intact, and then dividing by the number of values we just added up. From our calculation at left, we can conclude that the average rate of change of a gallon of gas per year *during the period of 1994 to 2005* was $0.1124. In other

Year (x)	Price (y)	Amount of Increase
0	1.078	-
1	1.158	0.08
2	1.245	0.087
3	1.244	-0.001
4	1.072	-0.172
5	1.176	0.104
6	1.523	0.347
7	1.460	-0.063
8	1.386	-0.074
9	1.603	0.217
10	1.895	0.292
11	2.314	0.419
	Sum	1.236
	÷ 11	$0.1124

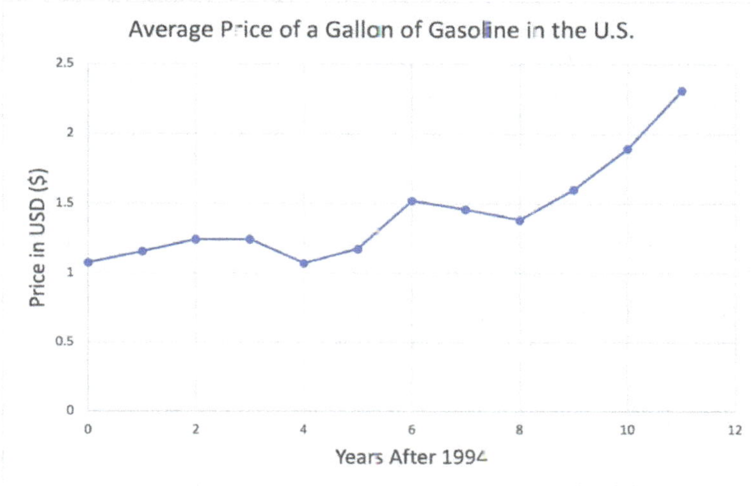

words, if we start with the initial price of $1.078 and add $0.1124 each year we should end up with something very close to $2.314 in 2005 (year 11).

But it cannot be that difficult to find the average rate of change of y with respect to x. In fact, there is an easier way to do it. We can simply use the **first** and **last** data values, subtract the y's and the x's, and divide. We call this the difference quotient. The word quotient means the result of a division problem. But before we do this, we will show that our average can be used to estimate gas prices all the way down to $2.314.

Try This: Use the average rate of change = average increase/decrease to estimate the price of a gallon of gas each year and complete the table here. The first few values are given. (**Just keep adding $0.1124**) If our calculations were correct, we should see $2.314 in the last row of the table when x = 11. This may be the most important formula or calculation we use because it leads directly to so much more that is useful in answering questions about how things change.

Year (x)	Price (y)	Amount of Increase	Estimate Price
0	1.078	-	1.078
1	1.158	0.08	1.1904
2	1.245	0.087	1.3028
3	1.244	-0.001	
4	1.072	-0.172	
5	1.176	0.104	
6	1.523	0.347	
7	1.460	-0.063	
8	1.386	-0.074	
9	1.603	0.217	
10	1.895	0.292	
11	2.314	0.419	
	Sum	1.236	
	÷ 11	$0.1124	

Definition: The average rate of change of a function with outputs y and inputs x over an interval $[a,b]$ is $f(b) - f(a) = \Delta y$ divided by $b - a = \Delta x$.

$$f_{avg} = \frac{\Delta y}{\Delta x} \text{ also written as } \frac{f(b) - f(a)}{b-a}$$

Let us use this formula to find the average change in the price of gasoline:

1) [a,b] is [0,11] which means $\Delta x = 11 - 0 = 11$
2) $\Delta y = f(b) - f(a) = f(11) - f(0) = 2.314 - 1.078 = 1.236$
3) Divide $\Delta y \div \Delta x = 1.236 \div 11 = 0.1124$

Note that the average rate of change has nothing to do with 2.314 being the highest gas price. That was coincidental. Calculating the average rate of change has only to do with the y values at the endpoints of the interval in question. Here is what the calculation would look like using the vertical calculation technique.

Vertical Calculation: Start with ***final point***, but instead of **x, y** write it as **y, x**. Underneath, place the ***initial point*** y , x

2.314 , 11 ↓
1.078 , 0

Subtract in each ***column***

2.314 , 11 ↓
−1.078 , −0

This is Δy ***and*** Δx 1.236 11 →→ 1.236 ÷ 11 = 0.1124
$\Delta y \div \Delta x$

But what if we do not have the list of (x, y) data? Instead, suppose all we have is the formula, or equation that defines y in terms of x. The only extra step involved is to calculate the two y values from the formula.

Example: For $f(x) = 3x^2$ calculate the average rate of change of f(x) for x in [−2,5].

Solution: First it is important to recognize that −2 and 5 are both x values. We will need to calculate the y values from the formula, since y = f(x).

$$f(-2) = 3(-2)^2 = 34 = 12$$

Ordered pair number one: (−2,12)

$$f(5) = 35^2 = 75$$

Ordered pair number two: (5,75)

y	x
75	5
12	−2
75	5
−12	−(−2)
63 ÷	7
Δy	Δx
9	

We will use the *vertical calculation approach* because it helps to avoid many of the common errors, since order matters. Keeping numbers in a table helps to organize, then we can do the subtraction top to bottom and division left to right.

First we will put y first, then x (because y is over x) (5, 75) switch so the y coordinate is in the left column. With (-2, 12) we will do the same and line them up.

Now make it a subtraction problem. Shown here »
Subtract each column of numbers and divide. »
The result is $\frac{\Delta y}{\Delta x}$ or average change in y with respect to x.

What this means is that on average, every time x increases by 1 unit, y increases by 9 units. Remember it is an ***average*** rate of change. It does not represent the *actual* rate of change at a specific point on the curve. We will talk about that in a later chapter. Visually, we can see the graph of the curve, which is f(x), and a straight line between the two endpoints that represents average rate of change. The scale has been changed for clarity. Normally this curve would be very tall and thin in appearance, when the x and y scale is the same.

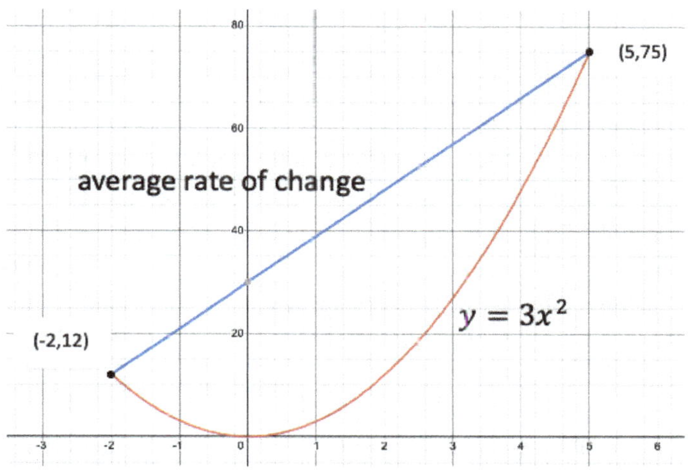

Notice that the y values are displayed as multiples of 20, whereas the x values are single digits.

Conversation Starter: When confronted with a situation or problem involving functions, what are some of the facts that should be determined, even if they may not be directly needed to solve the problem? What is worth knowing before even attempting to answer the question?

Let us look at an example where the average rate of change happens to be a negative number. Is this even possible? Yes, it means that something is decreasing rather than increasing. Let us look at this example:

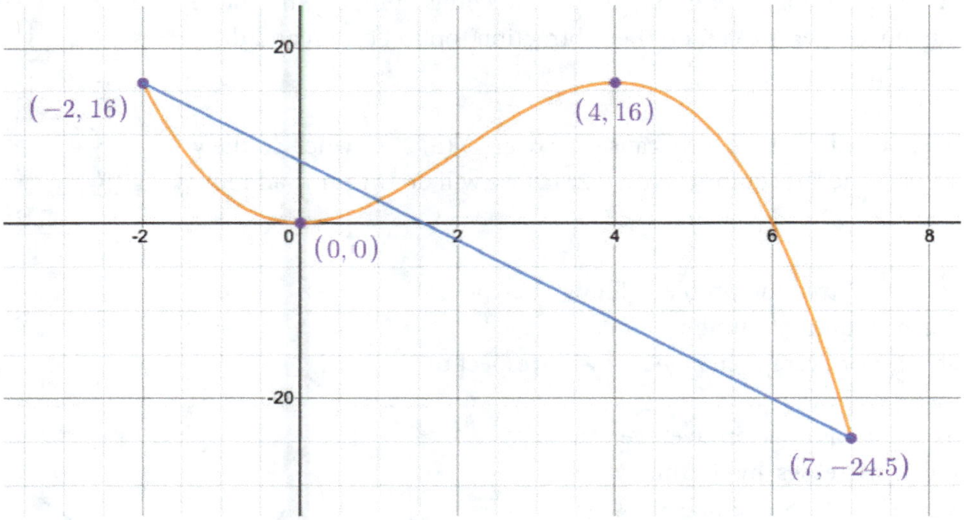

The curve shown here is decreasing, then increasing, then decreasing again. We always go left to right when discussing increasing/decreasing behavior. Also, we need to be specific about where a function is increasing, and where it is decreasing. We do this by referring to the interval on the ***x* axis** that ***corresponds*** to the increase or decrease. Take note that no mention is made of the actual y values. We are only interested in whether there is an increase or decrease, and for what inputs (x) this occurs. In words and numbers, we can describe the curve. But first we need a definition.

> **Definition:** When a function is continuously trending downward on an interval [*a*,*b*], we say that *f(x)* is decreasing between x = *a* and x = *b*. When a function is continuously trending upward on an interval [*b*,*c*], we say that f(x) is increasing between x = *b* and x = *c*.

Note that usually *a, b, and c* are specific numbers. Every situation is different, so here we are being general. On the graph shown above, *f(x)* is decreasing between $x = -2$ and $x = 0$ and again between $x = 4$ and $x = 7$. *f(x)* is increasing between $x = 0$ and $x = 4$.

> **Definition:** When a function transitions from increasing to decreasing on a path that is not broken, this occurs at a point that appears as a "peak" or "valley". The mathematical term for this point of transition is a turning point, or also called a critical point.

We will revisit that definition again in a later chapter when there is more to be said. For now, all that matters is that the function is ***neither increasing nor decreasing*** at one of its turning points.

This is why we must be careful here about intervals of increasing/decreasing. What we need to say about this graph is that at $x = -2$, $x = 0$, $x = 4$, ***and*** $x = 7$, on the graph these four points are either endpoints or they are turning points. The turning points are points of transition from increasing to decreasing, or vice-versa.

> **Try this:** The graph above has endpoints (–2, 16) and (7, –24.5). What is the average rate of change for the function on this interval?

Check your work. Answer: –4.5

SECTION 2.4 OPERATIONS WITH FUNCTION EXPRESSIONS

We have seen how to create new functions by composing two existing functions, chaining them together. New functions can be created by adding, subtracting, multiplying, and dividing existing functions.

Definition: Let f(x) and g(x) be functions with a shared (common) domain. Then we can create four new functions using operations

$$\text{SUM } [f+g](x) = f(x) + g(x)$$
$$\text{DIFFERENCE } [f-g](x) = f(x) - g(x)$$
$$\text{PRODUCT } [f\cdot g](x) = f(x)\cdot g(x)$$
$$\text{QUOTIENT } [\tfrac{f}{g}](x) = \frac{f(x)}{g(x)} = f(x) \div g(x)$$

In each of these the domain will remain the same, except the last one. For $f(x) \div g(x)$ we need to remove any x values for which $g(x) = 0$.

There are several examples that easily come to mind in business. One involves **revenue** as a **product** *quantity × unit price*. Another is that **total cost** is a **sum** *fixed cost + variable cost*. Lastly, **profit** as a **difference** *revenue – cost*. From now on, we will use the names

R(x) for revenue, *C(x)* for cost, *P(x)* for profit

Whenever we are dealing with price over quantity, revenue, cost, and profit, the input variable will consistently represent quantity of goods made/sold.

Example: Let x represent the quantity sold/produced. If the unit price of a book trilogy is given by $price = 38 - 0.15x$, write the function for revenue from sales of the book sets.

Solution: It is necessary to know that $revenue = quantity \times price$
Since we know $quantity = x$ and $price = 38 - 0.15x$ then we can write revenue by multiplying the two function expressions. IMPORTANT: Whenever performing operations with expressions, use ( ) around each expression. The only exception to the ( ) rule is if an expression consists of only one term. Here we have one that qualifies. As we can see here:

$$revenue = R(x) = (x) \cdot (38 - 0.15x)$$

If this looks a bit awkward, it is because we do not need ( ) around x. It is not incorrect, but it does look strange. Instead, we will write

$$R(x) = x \cdot (38 - 0.15x)$$

Simplifying we get $R(x) = 38x - 0.15x^2$

Example: The fixed cost for designing the book trilogy is \$150 and the variable cost for printing/boxing it is \$2.50 per item. What is the total cost function?

Solution: Fixed cost = 150, and total variable cost = $2.5 \cdot x$. For the total cost $C(x)$ we add the two: $total\ cost = C(x) = 150 + 2.5 \cdot x$

Example: If $R(x) = 38x - 0.15x^2$ and $C(x) = 150 + 2.5x$, write the profit function, $P(x)$.

Solution: We need to use $P(x) = R(x) - C(x)$.

$$profit = (38x - 0.15x^2) - (150 + 2.5x)$$

When subtracting like this, we can arrange the terms in columns with like terms lined up, *filling in 0's when terms are missing* and remember to subtract everything on the bottom row.

$$\begin{array}{ccc} 38x & -0.15x^2 & +0 \\ -2.5x & -0 & -150 \\ \hline 35.5x & -0.15x^2 & -150 \end{array}$$

$$P(x) = 35.5x - 0.15x^2 - 150$$

§

Even though we were not asked to graph any of these functions, it can be helpful to have a visual representation of the situation. Here is what the graph of the profit function looks like:

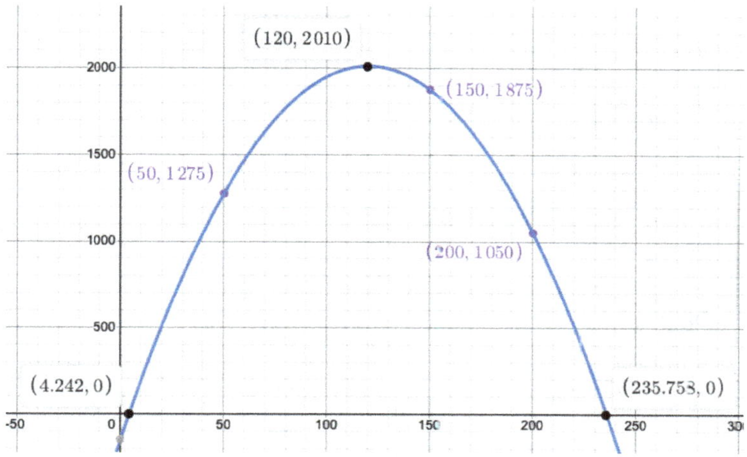

Conversation Starter: Was this graph a surprise in any way? Since the y axis is profit, and the x axis represents quantity made/sold, what can we tell from this graph?

Try this: Between the points (4.242, 0) and (120, 2010) what was the average rate of change of profit? Express your answer using a complete sentence and units.
Example: The car sped up by 10 mph per second.

Solution: $\Delta y = 2010$ and $\Delta x \cong 115.8$ When we divide we get *Profit increases* ≅ $17.36 *per unit sold/produced*

As a complete statement, we would say "For sales between 4 book sets and 120 book sets, profit increases an average of $17.36 per book trilogy sold."

Practice Exercises

1. List the ordered pairs of the function

x	2	5	6	10
y	2	8	10	18

2. Suppose $f(x) = (x - 5)^2$. Create a table of (x,y) values for x in {2, 3, 4, 5, 6}. What is $f(4)$ = ? For what x is $f(x) = 4$?

3. Given the table what is $f(3)$ = ? What is x when $f(x) = 6$?

x	0	1	2	3	4	5	6	7	8	9
$f(x)$	64	3	6	16	47	65	56	60	40	72

4. The total cost to produce x sets of earbuds is given by the equation $C(x) = 7.5x + 40{,}000$ what is the total cost to produce 2200 sets of earbuds?

5. State the domain and range of the function in the graph below.

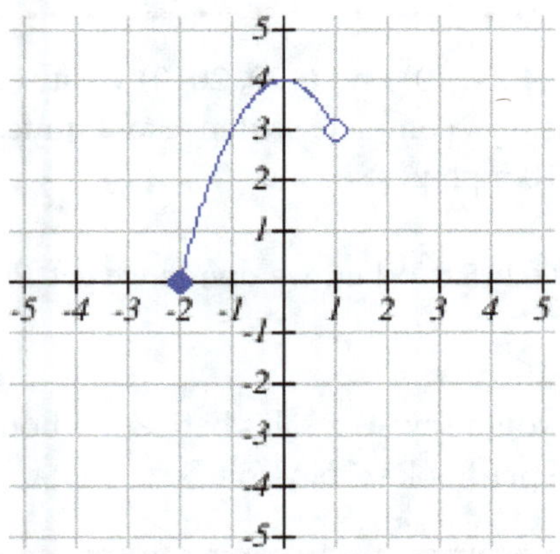

6. Given the graph of a function, f(x), what is the average rate of change of f(x) for x in [−2,0]? for x in [0,4]? for x in [4,7]? for x in [0,6]?

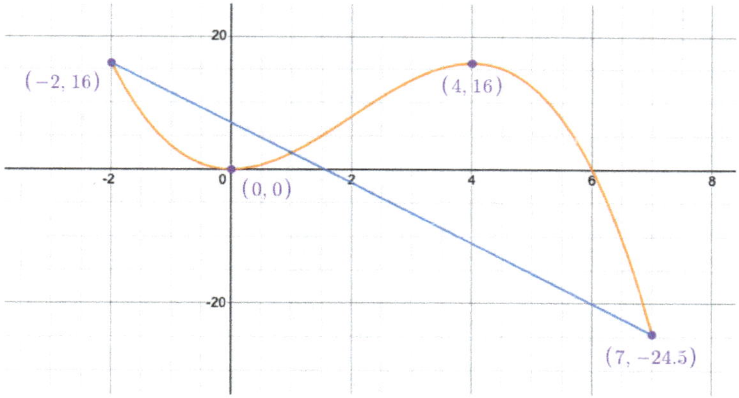

7. Write the profit equation if $R(x) = 50x - 0.3x^2$ and $C(x) = 4x^2 - 8x + 175$.

8. Name the intervals (of x) where this graph is increasing and decreasing.

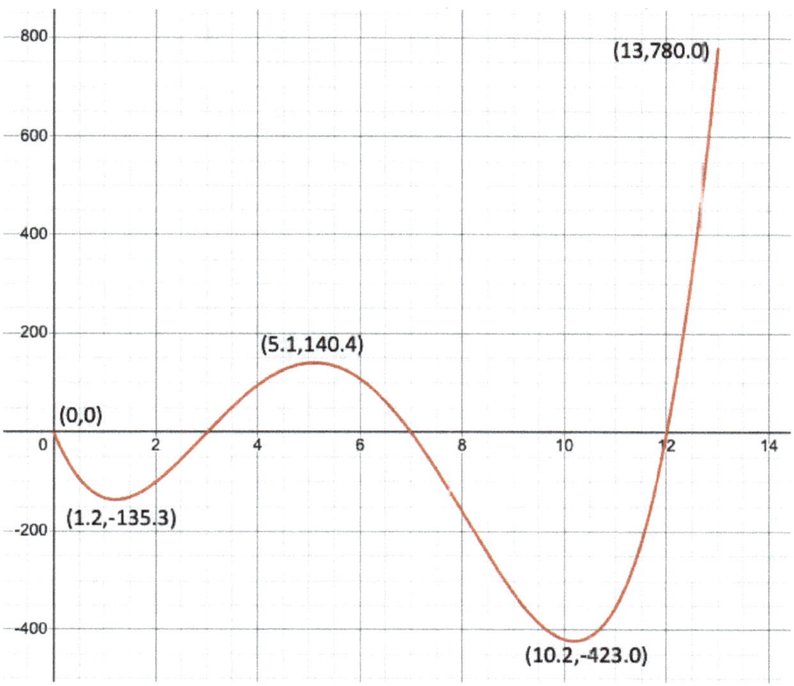

3

Linear Models and Equations

Section 3.1 Introduction to Linear Relationships

Consider the difference between running a marathon versus a sprint. With sprinters, it is all about acceleration. The sprinter relies on certain muscles to accelerate as fast as possible, and for as long as the duration of the sprint. If we compare the leg muscles of the sprinter versus the marathon runner we would notice some distinct differences.

Michal Sanca/Shutterstock.com

The marathon runner must maintain a constant speed for as long as possible, even for the duration of the race. The difference between winning and losing is more about endurance at that constant (required) speed, and less about how fast they can accelerate versus their opponent. Few marathon races come down to a sprint finish line race.

When shopping for a car, one of the features that buyers find attractive is the 0 to 60 rate of acceleration. How quickly a car can go from a complete standstill to 60 mph, generally is reported in seconds. Cars produced in countries using the metric system publish their 0 to 100 acceleration times because 100 kph is close to 60 mph and is basically a reference point for safe merging onto a highway.

Conversation Starter: What simple interest rate would yield the same balance as the compound interest situation in 10 years? Assume starting with $3000. How would we go about determining that? Hint: We need to get to $4886.68 or a little more, with 10 interest amounts that are all the same. Round up to $4900 as the final balance to make it a little easier.

What makes linear models so important is this: when we have dozens, sometimes hundreds, of variables anything more complex than a linear model would be impractical and unnecessary in most cases. Secondly, linear models can always be used to estimate any situation. If we were to search the New York Stock Exchange website for any publicly traded company stock price over a short period of time, it looks rather chaotic. But expand the graph to the largest possible time frame and all those fluctuations begin to smooth out and a pattern emerges. We can estimate that pattern with a ***linear function***.

Definition: A linear function, or model, has the equation $f(x) = mx + b$, where m is the common difference, or slope, of the line and b is the value of y when x = 0. The point (0,b) is called the y-intercept as a result. We can also write $y = mx + b$

Let us unpack this in the temperature conversion situation. If we recall, the temperature from Celsius to Fahrenheit is

$$y = \tfrac{9}{5}x + 32.$$

Instead of using °C and °F we are being consistent in the use of "x" as the input and "y" as the output. We can also write this same equation as

$$f(x) = \tfrac{9}{5}x + 32.$$

Until we become more comfortable around function notation, we will be writing equations both ways. As we learn about the connection between equations, graphs, and inputs/outputs we will continue to analyze a problem using all *four* tools. We will consider the equation, look at the graph, and we will use a table that gives us sample x-y pairs, all from a word description of the situation.

From the equation, we already know what the slope, or common difference, is. The slope, ***m*, is** 9⁄5. We also know what the y-intercept is: $b = +32$.

We can see very quickly how we arrived at b = 32. But the slope is not so easy to see right away. Just as we did with the simple interest, let us see the common difference in action here with temperature, using a table. The first column will be Celsius temperatures, the middle column will be the common difference, and the third column will be temperatures in Fahrenheit. Let us also use the decimal value for $9/5 = 1.8$. We will also choose starting and ending values that are labeled and closer together on the graph.

The common difference gets added to the previous Fahrenheit temperature and repeat this process all the way to the last row.

We added 1.8 a total of 12 times, which means to get from 77.0 to 98.6 directly, we could *save some time* and multiply 1.8 X 12.

$77.0 + 1.8 \cdot 12 = 77.0 + 21.6 = 98.6.$

The x column changes by 12 (total) 37 – 25 = 12 because there were 12 steps of +1.

Celsius Temperature (x)	Common Difference (Slope)	Fahrenheit Temperature (y)
25	-	77.0
26	1.8	78.8
27	1.8	80.6
28	1.8	82.4
29	1.8	84.2
30	1.8	86.0
31	1.8	87.8
32	1.8	89.6
33	1.8	91.4
34	1.8	93.2
35	1.8	95.0
36	1.8	96.8
37	1.8	98.6

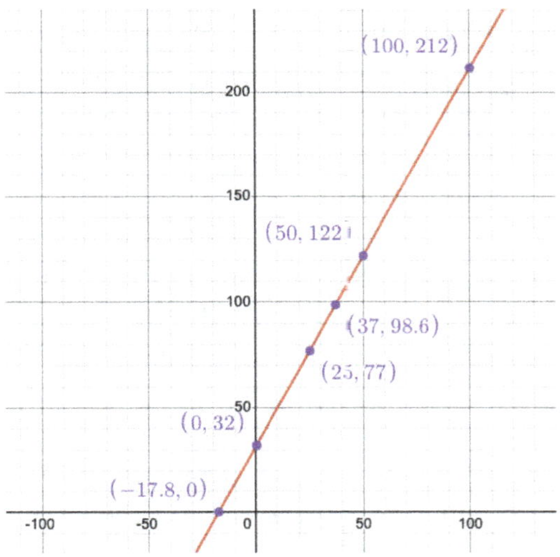

That is not an accident. From any known point, say, (0, 32) we can calculate an *unknown point* anywhere on the graph… literally anywhere… using the "change in x" as a multiplier of the common difference.

$$\Delta y = 1.8 \cdot \Delta x$$

Since x = 0 when y = 32,
$\Delta x = x - 0 = x$. Now that should look familiar…
$\Delta y = y - 32 = 1.8x$ which looks like $y = mx + b$

But what if we do not know the formula? How do we find the values of m and b? Well, we must start somewhere. We will either be given a graph, with at least two points (x, y) that are easy to figure out, OR we would be given two points on the line (x_0, y_0) and (x_1, y_1). The other possibility is that we are given a point (x_0, y_0) and the slope m. Our work is easier if we know the slope.

Recall the average rate of change formula. It turns out that the average rate of change on a linear function, *IS* the slope. We cannot tell the two concepts apart from each other.

Try this: Pick any two points on the Fahrenheit graph and calculate the average rate of change between the two points. No matter which two points you choose, you should always get 1.8 or $\frac{9}{5}$.

Example: A car is decelerating at a constant rate, meaning that the graph of speed over time is linear. The moment it began decelerating (x = 0), the car was traveling at a speed of 64 mph. Within 3 seconds the car slowed to 16 mph With time measured in seconds (x), write an equation for speed as a function of time in this situation. Then, figure out how long it will take for the car to come to a complete stop. Describe the domain and range.

Solution: First let us consider the units involved. Then we will develop the solution to this problem without units, using only x and y as representative of the two elements of the story. Namely, how fast the car is going each instant (which would be the speed displayed on the speedometer) and how many seconds have passed after starting to slow down.

So, the ***rate of change*** in this situation will be in "***miles per hour per second***". It answers the question of how many miles per hour are reduced every second of deceleration. We have been asked to provide several pieces to complete the picture. We will start with the equation.

Start with what we know. We have (x_0, y_0)= (0, 64) and we know another data point (x_1, y_1) = (3, 16). We also know that the deceleration is constant, so we know that $y = mx + b$ is the correct "model" for our equation/formula. We have been given $b = 64$ as a gift because it is the value of y when x = 0. Really the only thing we need to work out is the slope, m:

Vertical Calculation: Start with ***final point***, but instead of **x, y** write it as **y, x**. Underneath, place the ***initial point*** y , x

16 ,3
64 ,0

Subtract in each ***column***.

16 ,3
−64 ,−0

This is Δy ***and*** Δx −48   3 $-48 \div 3 = -16$

$\Delta y \div \Delta x$

The equation of the line is $y = -16x + 64$

Solution (continued): Next we answer the last part of the problem. We will figure out how long it will take for the car to come to a complete stop. Numerically what does "come to a complete stop" mean? Answer: Speed = 0. "How long will it take" means we are solving for x (number of seconds later). Answering this question will also show us what the domain and range are for the function, or better stated, the portion of the function, that is relevant to this problem. We will create a table that follows the car each second of the way, look at the graph, and consider the equation (how it is used to solve for x).

x	Rate of change	y
0		64
1	-16	48
2	-16	32
3	-16	16
4	-16	0

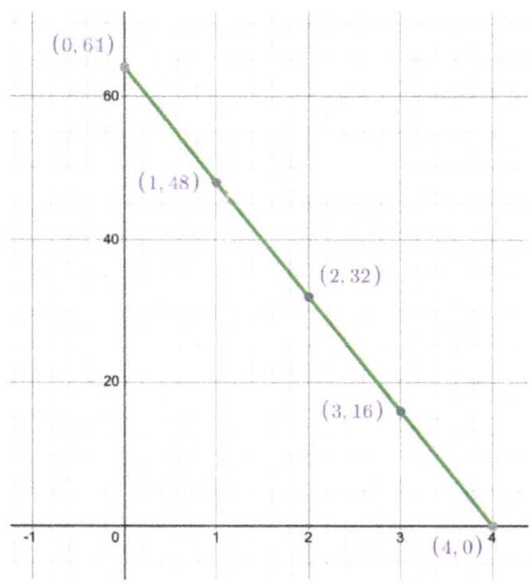

Important! Notice the common difference is the rate of change, which is also the slope. All mean the same thing.

The table and now the graph (made from the table) together allow us to visualize what is going on as the car slows down. Let us be clear. The graph is not the path of the car; it is important to keep in mind that we are seeing how the speed is decreasing from a peak, or high value of 64 mph to its lowest value of 0 mph. If we wanted to see the car's distance, we would need a different set of data, and a different graph.

Conclusion: The car will come to a complete stop in 4 seconds, which also means that the domain of this situation is [0, 4] seconds and the range is [0, 64] mph. We can use the equation $y = -16x + 64$ to verify this by calculating the value of y when x is 4.

Conversation Starter: We can state with certainty that the average speed during these 4 seconds was 32 mph, which is approximately 47 feet/sec. Using that information, how might we go about calculating the distance the car traveled before coming to a stop? (By the way, this number would be suggestive of a safe driving distance to the car ahead if a safe braking rate is −16 mph per second.)

We said it was a gift that the point (0, 64) was given in the previous example. This enabled us to identify the value of b without doing any additional work. What if we did not have data for y when x = 0? Before we look at our next example we need another definition.

Definition: For a linear function $y = mx + b$, where m and b are not known, but we have two points on the line (x_0, y_0) and (x_1, y_1), we first calculate $m = \frac{\Delta y}{\Delta x} = \Delta y \div \Delta x$, and then we can calculate b using our choice of the two points:

$$b = y_0 - m \cdot x_0$$

Example: A major retailer was tracking demand for a DVD set. The monthly quantity (x) in demand was 8 when the price (y) was \$44.00. The quantity in demand grew to 20 when the price was \$35. We are treating price as a function of quantity. Write an equation f(x) assuming that demand is a linear function.

Solution:

Calculate m: using our two data points (20, 35) and (8, 44)

$$\begin{array}{rr} 35 & ,20 \\ -44 & ,-8 \\ \hline -9 & 12 \end{array} \rightarrow\rightarrow -9 \div 12 = -0.75$$

$$\Delta y \div \Delta x$$

Now we calculate b using

$$b = y_0 - m \cdot x_0$$

$$(x_0, y_0) = (20{,}35) \text{ and } m = -0.75$$

$$b = 35 - (-0.75) \cdot 20 = 50$$

The equation of the line is $f(x) = y = -0.75x + 50$ §

Try this: A retailer was tracking demand for a video game console system. The monthly quantity (x) in demand was 5 when the price (y) was $475.00. The quantity in demand grew to 25 when the price was $425. We are treating price as a function of quantity. Write an equation f(x) assuming that demand is a linear function.

Solution: The equation is $y = 487.5 - 2.5x$ aka $f(x) = 487.5 - 2.5x$

SECTION 3.2 GRAPHS OF LINEAR FUNCTIONS

The graphs of functions alone, when labeled appropriately, can give us everything we need to know about a linear function. Since the two key ingredients are slope and y-intercept, we will now consider this process specifically. First, it might be helpful to see side-by-side what a line with negative slope, slope = 0, and positive slope, look like.

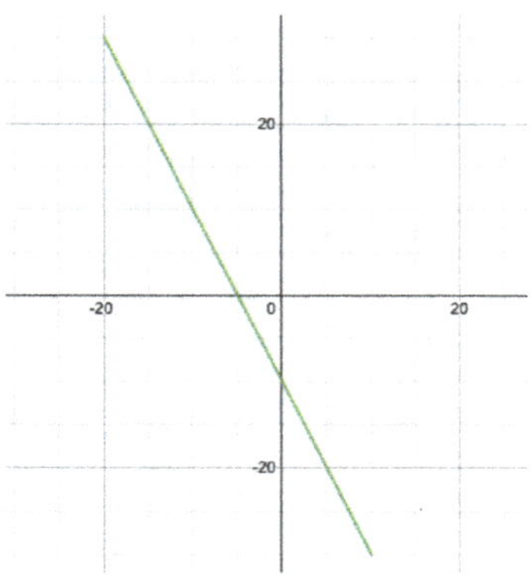

negative slope

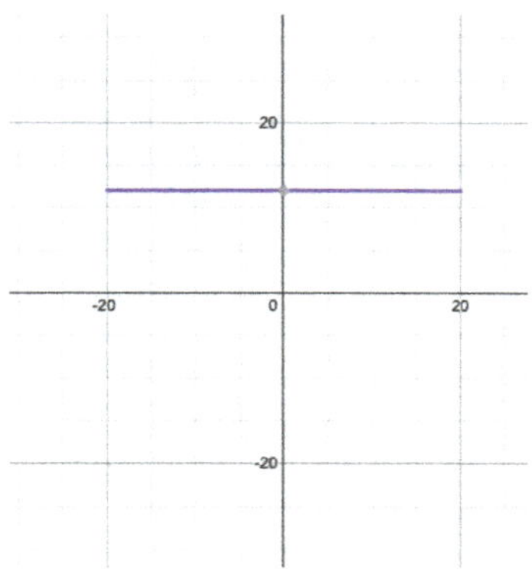

line with slope = 0

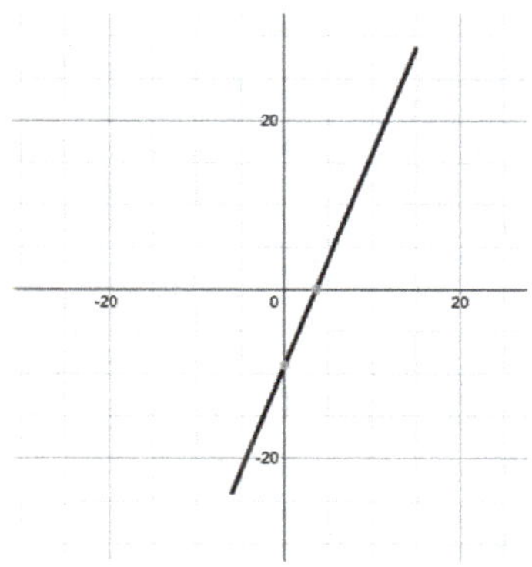

positive slope

Graphs can be observed at different scales. We can zoom in so that most of the points close to the origin (0, 0) are in view. We can zoom way out so that the origin is still at the center but numbers on both the x and y axis are well into the hundreds, thousands, even millions.

Here is the same line, viewed at *different zoom levels*:

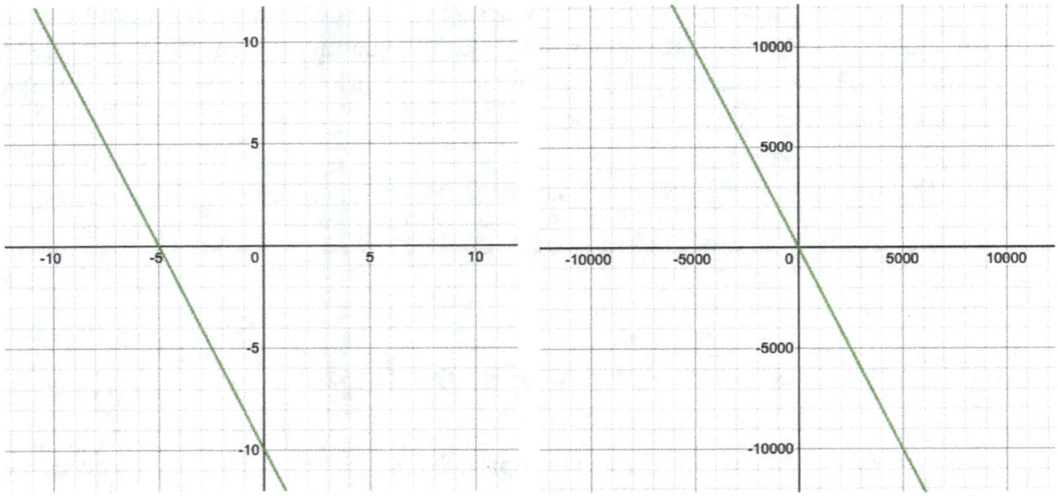

It is hard to imagine these two graphs are the same line, but they are. There is only so much detail we can see once zoomed out far enough.

Conversation Starter: Suppose we wanted to find the equation for the graph of the line shown on the previous page. Which of the two zoom levels makes that easier? Why?

When we concern ourselves with only *very large values of x and y*, and by that we are using the definition of ***large*** that means their absolute values are relatively large, the graph on the right is most useful. The farther from the origin we get, the more we are interested in what we call **end behavior** of a graph.

End Behavior of Linear Functions: If a linear function has *negative slope*, the x and y values will tend toward opposite in sign. Points on the line will look like (–, +) **or** (+, –) for large values of x and y.

On the other hand, if a linear function has *positive slope*, the x and y values will tend toward same in sign. Points on the line will look like (–, –) **or** (+, +) for large values of x and y.

There are more formal ways of stating end behavior. We are less interested in the formal definitions, and more interested in being able to *identify patterns*, and to use these observations to *anticipate* key features of the equation. Noticing some of the differences from one graph to another, based on certain features—namely, the ***sign*** of the number ***m*** in an equation $y = mx + b$ is sufficient for our purposes and study.

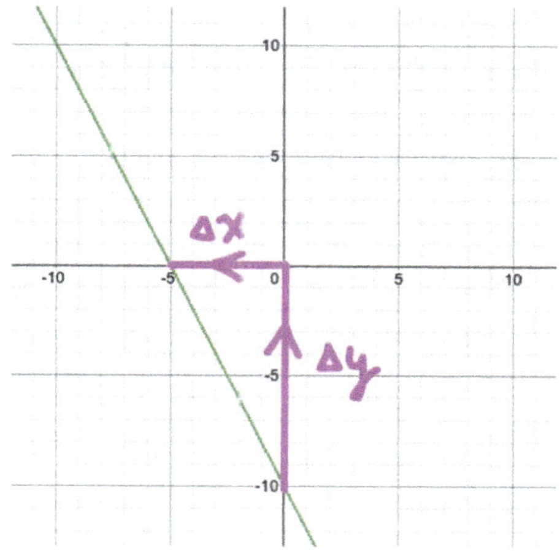

Example: Based on the graph alone, find the slope and equation of a line.

Solution: To find the slope between two points in a graph, we first choose a starting point. Here we will choose (0, −10) at the bottom as the start. Then we find a vertical and horizontal path from the start to another point on the graph. The second point is (−5, 0). Vertical direction and distance shown here is is $\Delta y = 10$. The 10 is positive because the vertical path went up, not down. Had it gone downward, then change in y would have been negative. Then the path continues to the left from (0, 0) to the second point that we chose.

Because Δx is going toward the left, $\Delta x = -5$.

$$slope\ m = \Delta y \div \Delta x = 10 \div (-5) = -2$$

This graph had end behavior in the 2nd and 4th quadrants, so *it makes sense that the slope would be negative.* Now we have sufficient information for the equation of the line. The graph shows that $b = -10$

$$y = -2x - 10$$

We can choose any two points that can easily be identified on the graph. Use them to calculate the slope. We only need the y-intercept for the value of "b". Here is one more example.

Example: Based solely on the graph, calculate the slope, and write the equation of the line.

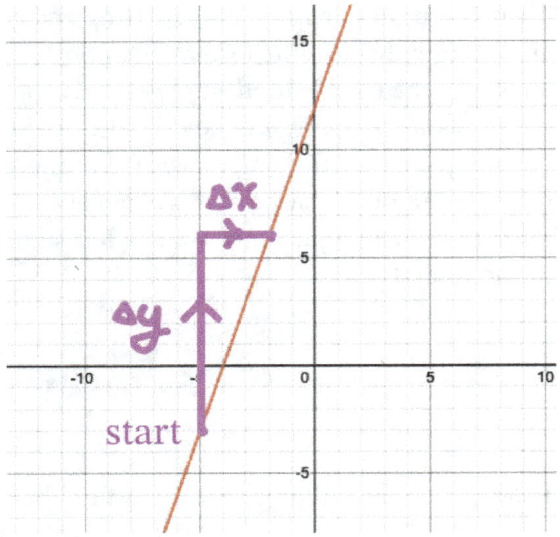

Solution: The two points used for slope calculation are the points (–5, –3) and (–2, 6). We are not even going to use their coordinates because all we need to do is count how many spaces up and how many spaces over (to the right) did we take for Δy and Δx. $\Delta y = 9$ and $\Delta x = 3$. $9 \div 3 = 3$. The steeper the line is, the larger the slope will be $m = 3$. Looking at the y axis, the value of b=12

This line has an equation of $y = 3x + 12$

Try this: Graph the line that passes through the points (0, 10), (12, 13), and (–40, 0). From the graph alone, write the equation of the line.

Solution: $y = 0.25x + 10$ or slope as a fraction $y = \frac{1}{4}x + 10$

When two or more functions are graphed together, we can observe points they have in common, ways the two functions may be the same, ways they are very different. We can infer facts about the two functions, especially if we know something about the quantities they represent. Consider this graph of supply and demand.

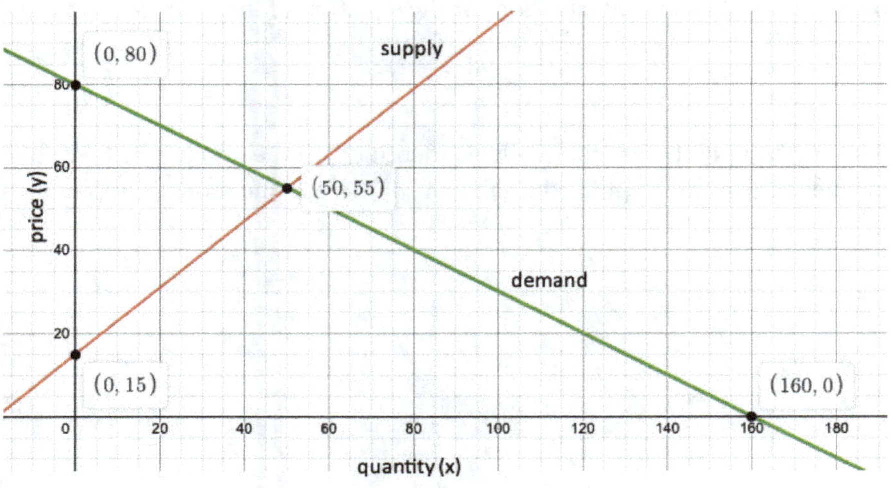

As is our custom, both supply and demand measure price over quantity. The demand function is easy to identify because its slope is negative. As the quantity demanded increases, the price must be decreasing. With supply, we have the opposite trend. As the quantity in supply (which accounts for over-production) increases, the price must be also increasing. When two lines have different slopes, there will always be a point in common. We call this the ***point of intersection*** between the two lines.

> **Definition:** Two lines that are distinct from one another, and with different slopes, have a single **point of intersection**. That point of intersection is called the **solution** to the system of two linear equations (which are represented by the graph).

> **Definition:** In the case of supply and demand, the point of intersection between the two lines is called the **equilibrium point**.

Example: Given the graph of supply and demand shown, what can be said about the equilibrium point?

Solution: The equilibrium point has coordinates (50, 55). This means that supply will meet demand when the quantity being produced/sold is 50, and the price is $55.

There are times when two lines do not intersect at all. When that happens, we say that the lines are **parallel**.

Shown here are 3 lines, all appearing to be slanted at the same way. What this means is that they all have the *same slope* but *different intercepts*. We have 3 **parallel** lines.

They will never intersect, so there are no points (x,y) that lie on any two of these lines.

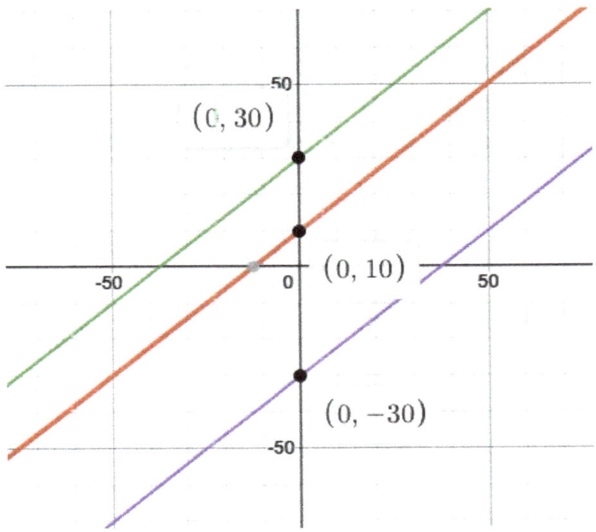

In a real business setting, not only would the variable costs likely increase but the fixed cost would likely increase as well. With the increased price for a jar of salsa, demand may fall. Then again, sometimes customers are very brand loyal. They will gladly pay a bit extra for something they value. Making good business decisions means knowing how to adjust when unexpected things happen.

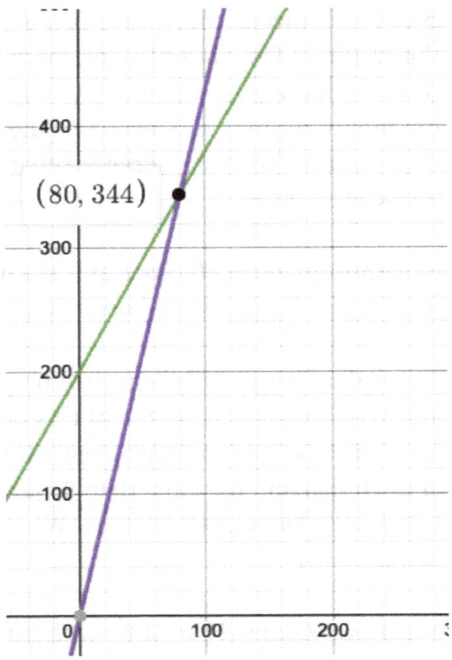

Example: Sauces-n-Salsas company owner decided to hire a consulting company to find out what the ideal retail price for a jar of corn salsa would be, and how many jars they should be producing to meet the demand at that price. The company provided a report that included this graph of supply and demand.

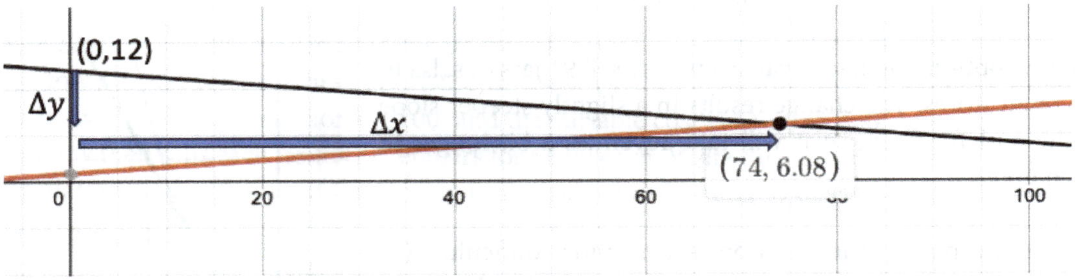

The demand for salsa would be x = 0 if the price was \$12. What is the demand equation *price* = $y = mx + b$?

Solution: From what we see on the graph, we have two points for the line: (0, 12) gives us b = 12 and (74, 6.08). The slope is $\Delta y \div \Delta x$ and if we start at the point (0, 12) we need to go *down* from 12 to 6.08 for a distance of 5.92, then to the *right* 74 to end up at (74, 6.08) which means $\Delta y \div \Delta x = -5.92 \div 74$

We can use the vertical (column) calculation for the slope as well.

Reverse (x,y) to (y,x)	6.08 ,	74
Remember to subtract!	−12.00 ,	− 0

$$-5.92 \div 74 = -0.08$$

$$m = -0.08$$

$$y = f(x) = -0.08x + 12$$ §

Conversation Starter: If the retail price of a jar of salsa is \$6.08, and the retailer is paying \$4.30 per jar to the manufacturer, what is the amount of markup? What is the % markup?

\$1.78 retailer makes on each jar, at 41.4% markup.

Section 3.4 Fitting a Linear Model From Data (Regression)

Can cricket chirps predict temperature? Or is this just a myth like woolly bear caterpillars or groundhogs seeing their shadows? The answer is yes, crickets rub their wings (not exactly chirping) faster or slower depending on how warm or cool it is outside.[1]

Joyce LCY/Shutterstock.com

1. _____. “Myth buster: Can a cricket really tell you the temperature?” *The Buzz*, Forest Preserve District of Will County, 1 September 2023, https://www.reconnectwithnature.org/news-events/the-buzz/myth-buster-can-a-cricket-really-tell-you-the-temperature/

In fact, scientist Amos Dolbear in 1897 published research in that he demonstrated that temperature in Fahrenheit was equal to the average number of chirps in 15 seconds plus 40. 15 seconds is ¼ minute, the formula becomes °F = $x/4$ + 40 where x = number of cricket chirps in a minute. Every species of cricket has a unique sound and pattern to their chirping, and there are other factors that can affect the rate. While not being entirely precise, the cricket is a reliable predictor of how warm it is outside. We will be using our own data to create another formula. We will then see how close it comes to Dolbear's equation $y = 0.25x + 40$.

Chirps (min)	Temp (F)
85	60
151	75
148	73
148	73
145	70
126	67
121	66
125	69
104	63
101	63
95	61
89	62
70	56
62	55
59	52
60	53
56	50
74	52
111	65
104	63
87	59
50	51
50	49
176	80
186	78
174	78
140	74
140	71

Crickets will generally chirp when temperatures are between 50°F and 100°F.

Conversation Starter: What is the temperature range in Celsius? What would be involved to create a model between cricket chirps and temperatures in degrees Celsius?

Using the data table, we will use a spreadsheet to create a scatter plot. Then we will ***add a trendline*** to the graph. Does the data support the equation? This process is what we call ***linear regression***. The table here is a sample of the data that was used to create the plot and calculate the line of best fit in a spreadsheet tool.

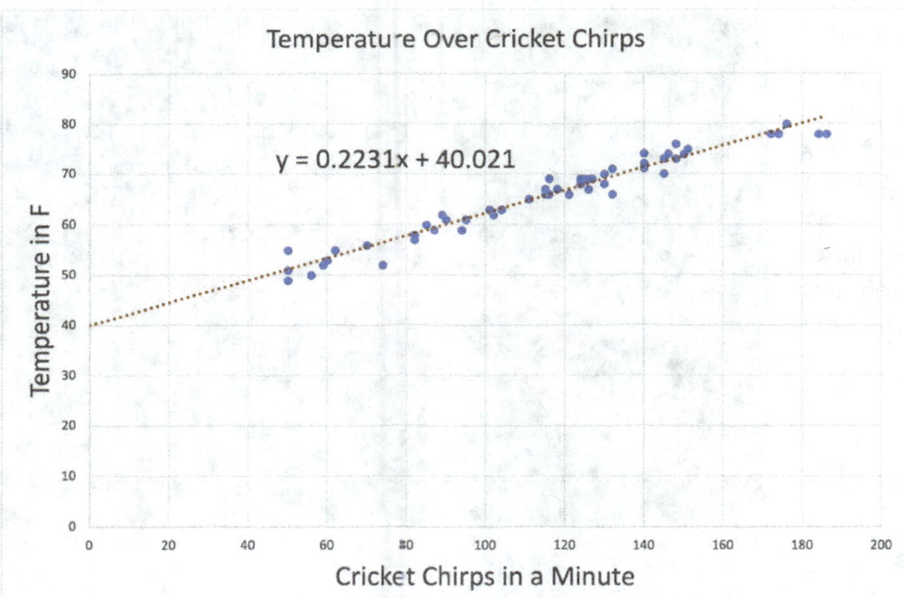

The dotted line is what we call the trendline. Our data is "fitted" to the equation that is displayed.

Definition: The **line of best fit**, or **trendline**, is found by using a method known as least-squares from a collection of ordered pairs of real-valued data. It minimizes the vertical distance from all the observed y values to the y values on the line. Using the equation, we can calculate the *predicted y values* for each x value in our dataset. The observed values are y, the predicted values are $\hat{y}$. We call this **y-hat**.

The scatter plot shows that there is a relationship between x and y for our data. But is it truly linear? Is it justified for the entire domain or just a portion of values? Is the error between our observed values and predicted values random, or does the error increase/decrease? To answer this, we need to plot something else about our data.

Definition: The set of **residuals** from a linear regression is paired with the predicted outcomes ($\hat{y}$) and is calculated by subtracting: observed – predicted y values: $y - \hat{y}$. We expect roughly half to be positive, and the other half to be negative, since some of our data sits above the line, while the rest sits below the line.

Here we see a scatter plot of the residuals over the predicted values ($\hat{y}$)

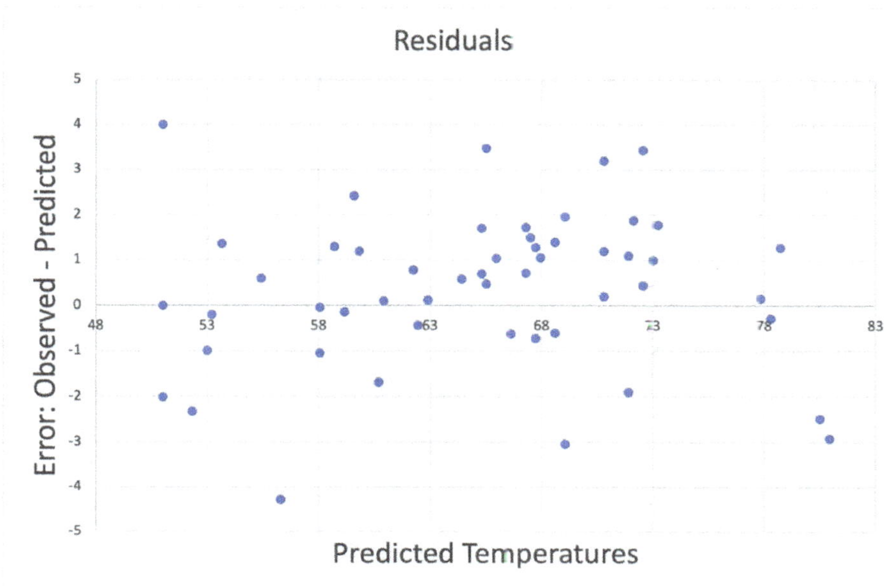

Our model does not need to be adjusted or corrected if there is *no discernible pattern* in the residual plot. The dots should appear to be randomly dispersed, with naturally more data points between 58 and 73 degrees because these temperatures occurred more than the ones at the lower and upper values.

Let us see some residual plots that would indicate there is a problem.

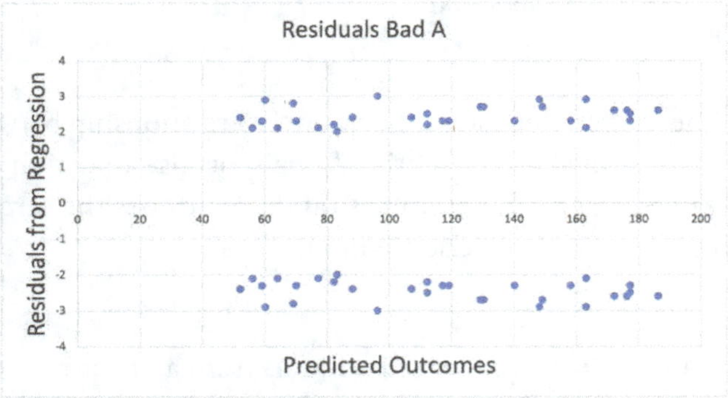

When residuals are randomly dispersed but are either large on the positive side, with nothing close to 0, and large on the negative side, we have a problem. We seem to have accidentally mixed two predictor variables, not just one. We may have recorded two different species of cricket. Assuming we have enough data, we should consider separating the data that created positive residuals from the data that created negative residuals. Perform regression on each subset of data.

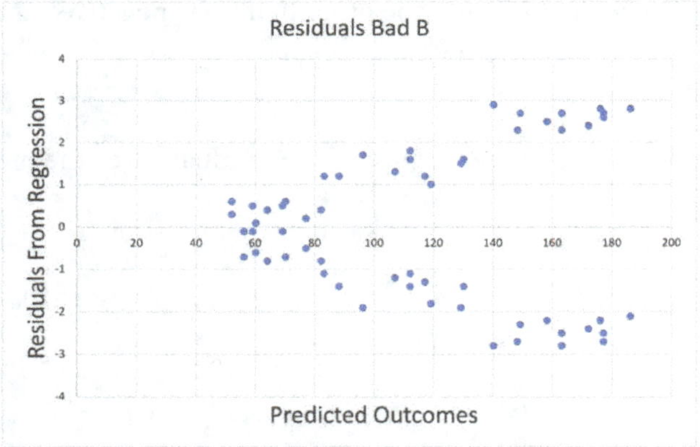

Another kind of problem that can occur is called *heteroscedasticity*. Now that is a million-dollar word! What this means is that the equation works better for some values than for others.

The evidence suggests that relying on only one predictor (x) may be insufficient. There may be a need to include another variable and perform regression using two predictor variables, not just one. Either that, or the x variable needs to be transformed. Both remedies are beyond the scope of this book. But we see from this plot how to recognize a problem.

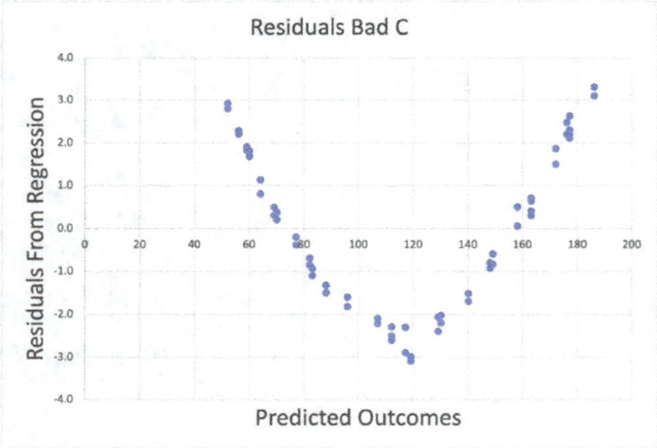

One more example of problems with the regression equation and the data that created it is that perhaps the model should not have been a linear one. Sometimes we have an x and y that are related, but the relationship is not linear.

Fortunately, our simple linear model predicting the temperature based on the one variable—cricket chirps, has none of these issues.

What is the point of all this? Why do we bother with trendlines, lines of best fit, in the first place? Usually, we do this so that we can perform interpolation or extrapolation with ***missing data***. Extrapolation is riskier, making predictions to extend outside of the range of the data. It is not to be done without justification. We need a definition and then we will see some examples.

Definition: **Interpolation** is the process by which we predict an outcome that is missing. The corresponding $(x, \hat{y})$ is in between two existing data points. In between, hence "in-ter"-polation.

Extrapolation is the process by which predictions are made that go outside the existing data points. The predicted outcome $(x, \hat{y})$ is beyond the range of our data.

Here we have the average price of a gallon of gasoline in the United States each year from 1994 until 2014. The variable (x) is tracking how many years after 1994, and the price is in \$. We have also arranged it so that 2006 (x = 12) and 2011 (x = 17) are missing.

Year (x)	Price (y)
0	1.078
1	1.158
2	1.245
3	1.244
4	1.072
5	1.176
6	1.523
7	1.460
8	1.386
9	1.603
10	1.895
11	2.314
13	2.843
14	3.299
15	2.406
16	2.835
18	3.680
19	3.575
20	3.437

There are two ways we can interpolate for the missing data.

Method 1: For 2006, we could take the two gasoline prices on either side and average them. $(2.314 + 2.843) \div 2 = 2.578$.

Then for 2011 do the same thing: $(2.835 + 3.680) \div 2 = 3.258$.

Method 2: Or we can find a line of best fit from the existing data and calculate the missing values from that. The prediction equation for this data is $\hat{y} = 0.1412x + 0.7199$

For x = 12 we get $0.1412 \cdot 12 + 0.7199 = 2.414$

For x = 17 we get $0.1412 \cdot 17 + 0.7199 = 3.120$

We happen to know that the price of gas in 2006 was \$2.618 and in 2011 it was \$3.576. Either of our methods of interpolating missing values would have been justified, though not very precise. The margin of error, due to wide variation in our data, allows a comfortable range for our estimation.

Gasoline prices fluctuate up and down dramatically, which makes it very hard to do extrapolation. If we start with the data from the years 1994 to 2014, we can use the regression equation (with the values for 2006 and 2011 filled in) which is altered slightly because of the two additional missing values:

$$\hat{y} = 0.1458 \cdot x + 0.7045$$

Year	x =	$\hat{y}$
2015	21	3.766
2016	22	3.912
2017	23	4.058
2018	24	4.204
2019	25	4.350
2020	26	4.495
2021	27	4.641
2022	28	4.787

The results of the extrapolation (to 2022)

We know that the price of a gallon of gas dropped to \$2.520 in 2015. It dropped again in 2016 to \$2.250. Then we saw it go up again until it dropped in 2019 and 2020. In 2022 the average price of a gallon of gasoline was \$4.059.

Gasoline prices are not well-suited to linear modeling, interpolation, and extrapolation from the year alone. The prices fluctuate too unpredictably. In truth, we need to find the right predictor variables. We see the danger of trying to use regression when it is not warranted.

We will close this chapter by doing some interpolation and extrapolation with our cricket data, which is warranted and appropriate. First, interpolation.

Example: Using the regression line from our data, predict the temperature in Fahrenheit if the number of cricket chirps is 160.

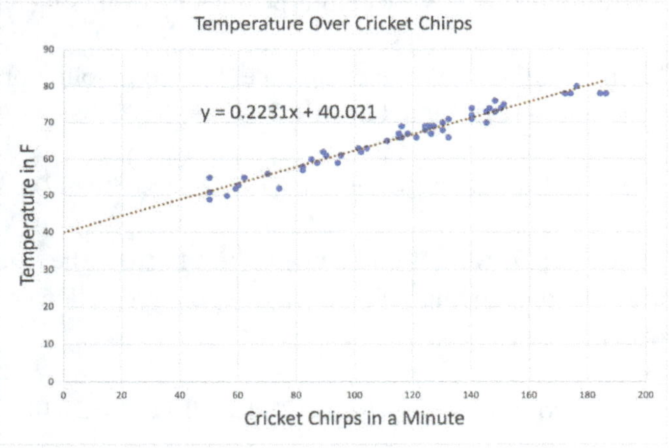

Solution: This is interpolation because we have data for chirps less than 160 as well as more than 160. The missing value is in between existing data. Let x = 160 in the equation: $\hat{y} = 0.22 \cdot 160 + 40 = 75.2$ which we will round to 75°F with a comfortable margin of error ±3°F.

Example: Use extrapolation to predict the temperature when the number of chirps is 48 in one minute.

Solution: We can use our model again, but with an asterisk* because the regression equation is most reliable for data between 50 chirps and 186 chirps. $\hat{y} = 0.22 \cdot 48 + 40 = 50.56$ which we will round to 51°F. We can ask if the prediction is reasonable given the science, and we can conclude that it is reasonable, given what is known about crickets and limits to their activity. Recall that we said crickets can be active in temperatures ranging from 50°F to about 100°F.

Try this: Use interpolation and extrapolation to predict what the temperature is each evening when the number of cricket chirps is counted at 82 the first night, 115 the second night, 190 on the third night, and 210 the fourth night.

PRACTICE EXERCISES

1. Find the equation (in terms of x) of the line through the points (–1,–5) and (4,10).

2. Last year, Pinwheel Industries introduced a new toy. It cost \$5600 to develop the toy and \$15 to manufacture each toy. Answer the following:
   A.) Give a linear equation in the form $C = mx + b$ that gives the total cost, C, to produce x of these toys.
   B.) The total cost to produce 1850 toys is what (in \$)?
   C.) With C = \$24350, how many toys can be produced?

3. Sketch a graph of $f(x)= \frac{3}{2}x - 1$

4. Find the point at which the line $f(x) = 2x - 6$ intersects the line $g(x) = -2x - 2$.

5. You decide to begin selling caramel apples at the local *booth park*. Your cost for each caramel apple is \$0.89 plus you must pay a fixed weekly fee of \$100 for the booth. Your plan is to sell each caramel apple for \$3.00.
   A.) Write a function, $C(x)$, to represent your total costs for the week if you sell x caramel apples.
   B.) Write a function, $R(x)$, to represent the revenue from the sale of x caramel apples during the week.
   C.) How many caramel apples must you sell to break even?

6. The table at right shows retail sales in drug stores in billions of dollars in the U.S. for years since 1995.

   Let $S(t)$ be the retails sales in billions of dollars in t years since 1995. A linear model for the data is $\hat{y} = 9.44t + 84.182$.

Year (t)	Retail Sales S(t)
0	85.851
3	108.426
6	141.781
9	169.256
12	202.297
15	222.266

Use the scatter plot to decide whether the linear model fits the data well. Select one:

A. The equation is not a good model for the data

B. The equation is a good model for the data.

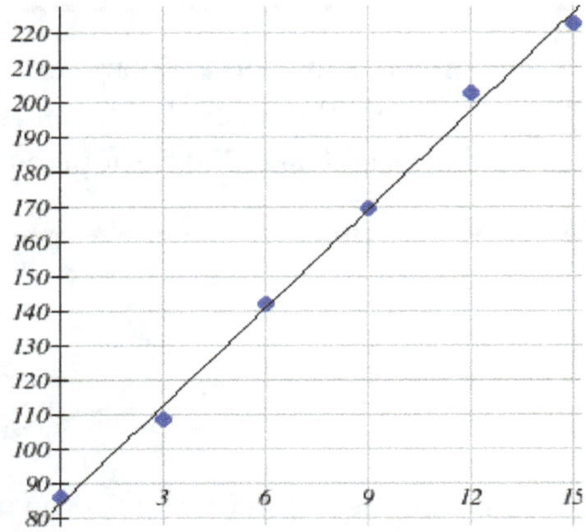

Interpolate: Use the model to estimate the retails sales in the U. S. in 2000.

Your answer will be in billions of dollars. Extrapolate: Use the model to estimate the retails sales in the U. S. in 2011. Your answer will be in billions of dollars.

Use the model to predict the year that corresponds to retails sales of $244 billion.

7. **Depreciation.** The depreciation of an asset can be calculated using a straight-line method. A company buys a printer at a cost of $7,500 and in 6 years it will have a salvage value of $1,500. Assume the printer depreciates in value by the *same amount every year*, and the book value is the value after depreciation is subtracted each year. Complete this depreciation table:

   Make a graph of book value (y) over year (x).

Year	Depreciation Amount	Book Value
0	(none)	$7,500
1		
2		
3		
4		
5		
6		$1,500

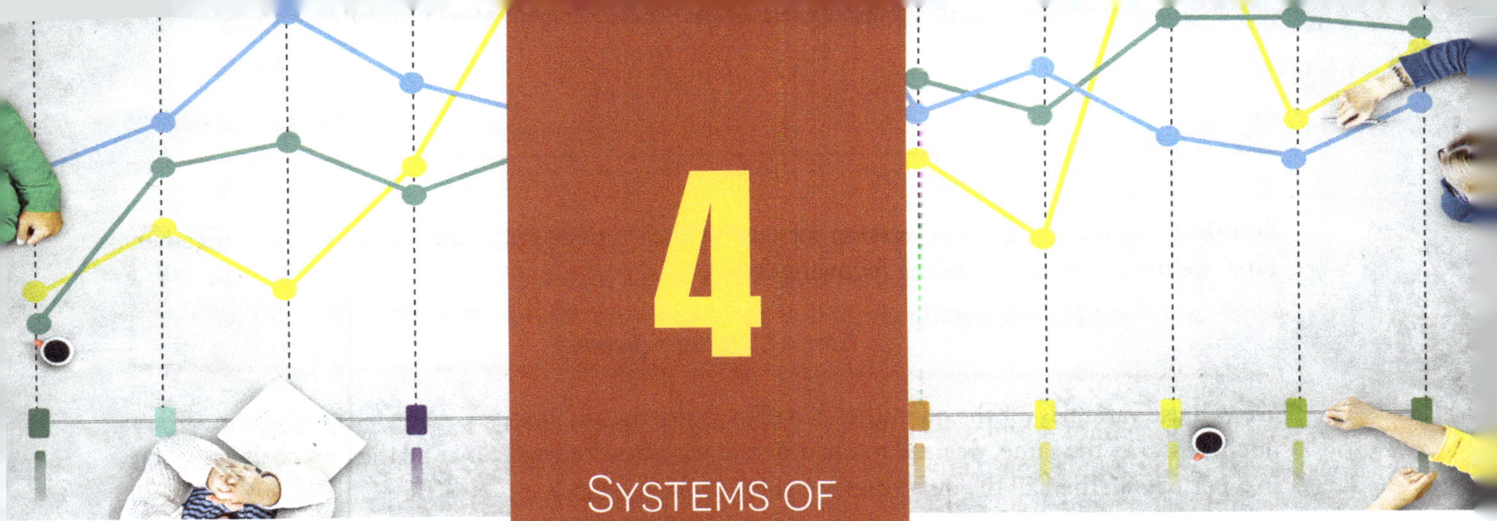

4

Systems of Linear Equations

Section 4.1 Introduction

When we were interested in the equilibrium between supply and demand, and the break-even point between cost and revenue, we were solving a system of linear equations. We say system when there is more than one equation, and two or more variables involved.

Definition: A **linear equation** in two variables can be written in the form $ax + by = C$, where a, b, and C are constants and either a or b is not zero. Letters near the beginning of the alphabet are treated as constants.
In three variables: $ax + by + cz = C$
In four variables: $ax + by + cz + dw = C$

When equations are written with all the variable terms together on one side of the = and only a constant on the other, we refer to this as ***standard form*** of the equation. In this chapter we will explore problem solving using linear combinations of unknown quantities, and what it means to find solutions.

Example: Suppose a shopper at the grocery store wants to buy some fruit in the produce section. They are interested in getting some apples (at \$2.40/lb), some bananas (at \$0.75/lb) and oranges (at \$1.90/lb). It is *not known* how many pounds of each will be purchased. Using a variable expression, what is the ***total cost*** of fruit?

Conclusion: We conclude, then, that the maximum amount of bananas is 16 pounds (and no apples). The maximum amount of apples is 5 pounds (and no bananas). This assumes that we are purchasing 1.58 pounds of oranges.

> **Try this:** Suppose the apples come in 3-lb bags. If one bag is selected, and a bunch of bananas is selected that weighs 3.2lb, how many pounds of oranges can be purchased so that the total comes to **$19?**
>
> (Round to 3 significant figures)
>
> **Solution:** 4.95lb oranges can be purchased. The solution as an ordered triple is (3, 3.2, 4.95)

So far, we have explored the concept of more than 2 dimensions using a specific situation. But we have not yet seen a system of equations, nor have we discussed how to obtain a solution if a unique solution even exists.

Without explicitly stating so, we *have* solved a system of linear equations. We just did not express the problem in system form. We will correct that oversight now. Here is what the "Try this" problem that we just solved looks like as a system of linear equations.

Try this (written as a system of linear equations):

$$2.4x + 0.75y + 1.9z = 19$$
$$x = 3$$
$$y = 3.2$$

Let us look at two more examples, this time express the problem as a system of linear equations, and then we will solve them by graphing.

> **Definition:** Given a system of linear equations, **S**, then a **unique solution** exists if and only if there is a single point of intersection among all the equations in the system. The point of intersection is the solution to the system.

Example: For x = quantity produced/sold (in thousands of pens), and y = sell price of a new rollerball pen, we know that the supply/demand system of equations is

$$3.2x + 7.5y = 60$$
$$0.3x - y = 0$$

Which is the supply, and which is the demand equation?
Where is the equilibrium between price and quantity?

Solution: The first equation is the demand equation, because it has negative slope. That makes the second equation the supply equation. We will find the solution by graphing the two equations on the same graph.

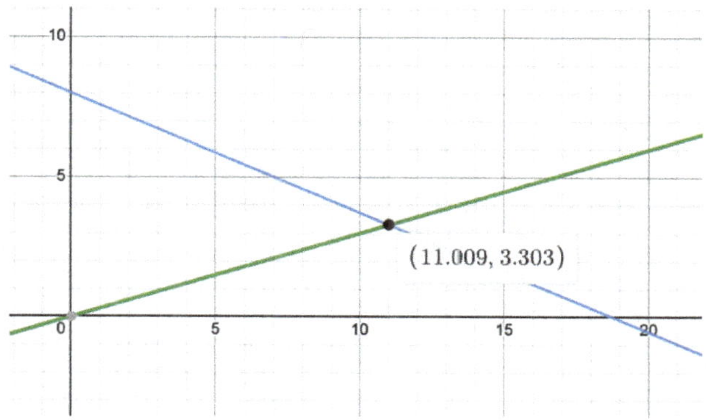

Equilibrium will occur when the price of the pen is \$3.30. The quantity is the first coordinate. Approximately 11,000 pens will be produced and sold at this price during an unspecified timeframe. Precisely 11,009 is the quantity on the graph.

When considering all possible outcomes there are three scenarios. A system of equations can have a unique solution, as we have already seen in two examples. When this occurs, the system is what we call **consistent** and **independent**.

> **Definition:** Given a system of linear equations that is both **consistent** and **independent**, the solution will be
> (x_1, y_1) if the system consists of two equations with two unknowns.
> (x_1, y_1, z_1) if the system consists of three equations with three unknowns.
> (x_1, y_1, z_1, w_1) if the system consists of four equations with four unknowns.

The number of equations and the number of variables can be a strong clue about the nature of the solution. Sometimes there are more equations than variables, and sometimes the opposite is true. These situations require more theory and practice than the scope of this book. In this chapter and the next, we will limit ourselves to systems that have the same number of equations as variables. In the case of two equations and two unknowns, let us look at the other two outcomes that can occur.

> **Definition:** Given a system of linear equations, when the solution is infinite we say that the system is **consistent and dependent**. When there is no solution we say that the system is **inconsistent**.

It may help to see what this looks like visually.

consistent and dependent	inconsistent
$\begin{cases} 3x - 5y = 2 \\ -6x + 10y = -4 \end{cases}$	$\begin{cases} 3x - 5y = 2 \\ 6x - 10y = 24 \end{cases}$
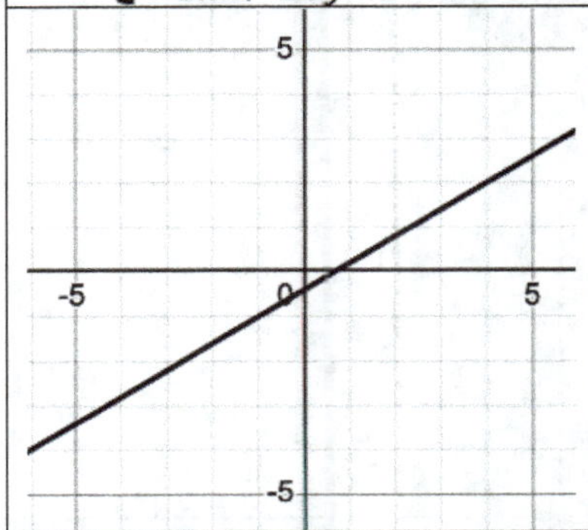	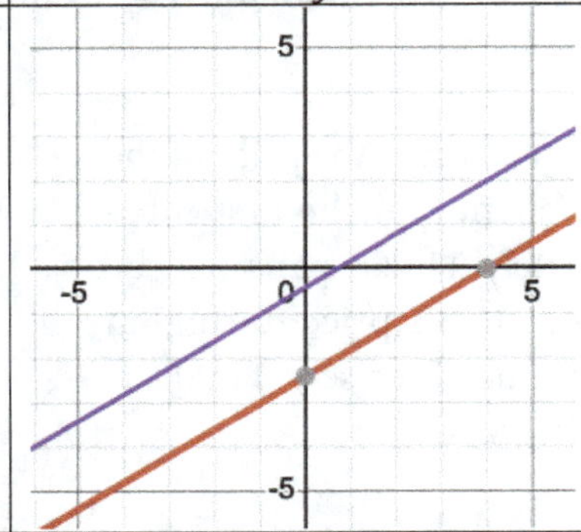
solution is infinite	no solution
Why? The two equations are the same line, so any ordered pair on one line is also on the other.	Why? The two equations are parallel, which means they will never intersect; no (x,y) pair will solve the system.

The reason we only see one line in the first picture is that both equations represent the same line. In the second image and graph we see two lines that are parallel. Parallel lines will never intersect.

Section 4.2 Matrix Representation and Technology

Solving systems of equations does not have to involve graphing, or algebraic manipulation. There is a way to solve that uses a spreadsheet as a calculator. For that, we do need equations to be in standard form.

Definition: The **coefficient matrix** M is made from the coefficients in a system of linear equations that are arranged into rows and columns in a square shape. Each column represents a variable. Each row represents an equation.

Examples:

Coefficient matrix M of a system of two equations	
$5x - 2y = 20$ $x + 10y = 25$	$M = \begin{bmatrix} 5 & -2 \\ 1 & 10 \end{bmatrix}$
Coefficient matrix M of a system of three equations	
$4x - 0.15y - 0.43z = -5$ $0.97y - 0.2z = 3$ $x + 8y = 200$	$M = \begin{bmatrix} 4 & -0.15 & -0.43 \\ 0 & 0.97 & -0.2 \\ 1 & 8 & 0 \end{bmatrix}$

Notice that we had to put 0 in the proper row and column when a variable is missing in the equation. If a matrix has 2 rows and 2 columns we say that the matrix is a "2 by 2" matrix. The first number is always the row count, the second number the column count.

> **Definition:** The **column matrix** C is made up of constants (numbers that are not variables) that are on the right-hand-side of the = in a system of equations. This matrix has one column and as many rows as there are equations.

Examples: Each column matrix from the two problems above are shown.

$$\textbf{2 } \boldsymbol{variables}: \mathbb{C} = \begin{bmatrix} 20 \\ 25 \end{bmatrix} \qquad \text{3 variables: } \mathbb{C} = \begin{bmatrix} -5 \\ 3 \\ 200 \end{bmatrix}$$

When solving a system of linear equations, it is necessary to perform an *inverse operation* with the coefficient matrix. Fortunately, spreadsheets have a built-in function for this process, which means we do not need to perform the sometimes-lengthy procedure ourselves. This function serves two purposes.

1. It will alert us to the possibility that a solution may not exist. Like what happens when we try to divide by 0, or take the square root of a negative number, the function will return an error code.
2. If a solution does exist, then the spreadsheet will produce the inverse of the matrix, which we then will use to calculate the solution automatically.

Spreadsheets are designed to handle ***matrix calculations***. Information will be entered into cells in the form of text (for labeling things), numbers (from the system of equations we are solving), and formulas. Once we are done, we can save the spreadsheet and use it to solve any system of two equations or three equations, although the process can be used to solve any system of equations of any size. First we will format the page to be used as often as we need. The use of explanatory words and filling cells with specific colors helps us to remember which cells belong to our inputs, and which cells we need to leave alone once the formulas are entered. Here is an example of a spreadsheet that is ready for numbers and formulas. The yellow shaded cells are for entering numbers from a system of equations we are solving. The uncolored cells are reserved for formulas, and the blue shaded cells will display the solution. These formatting details are not required, but it can make information easier to read and avoid accidentally erasing or altering cells that need to be left alone.

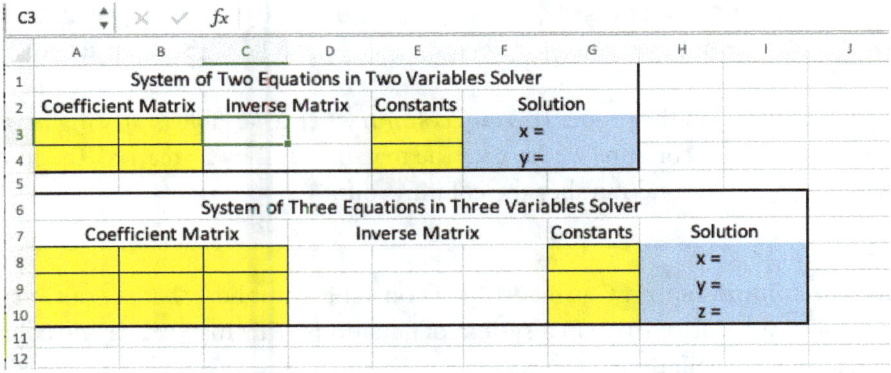

There are two functions we will use. One is the MINVERSE() function. The other is the MMULT() function. Assuming a spreadsheet setup just like the one shown here, the first coefficient matrix is in a block of cells that starts in A3 and ends in B4. We will start by solving a system of equations.

Example: Solve the system of equations. If a unique solution does not exist, then answer "does not exist".

$$2x + y = -9$$
$$-3x + 5y = 20$$

Solution: The coefficient matrix is $\begin{bmatrix} 2 & 1 \\ -3 & 5 \end{bmatrix}$ and the constant matrix is $\begin{bmatrix} -9 \\ 20 \end{bmatrix}$.

First we will enter these numbers into the spreadsheet in the corresponding cells.

Now we will use the spreadsheet as a calculator. Once these formulas are entered, we will not need to enter them again. Each time we solve a system of equations, we only need to input the numbers highlighted in yellow.

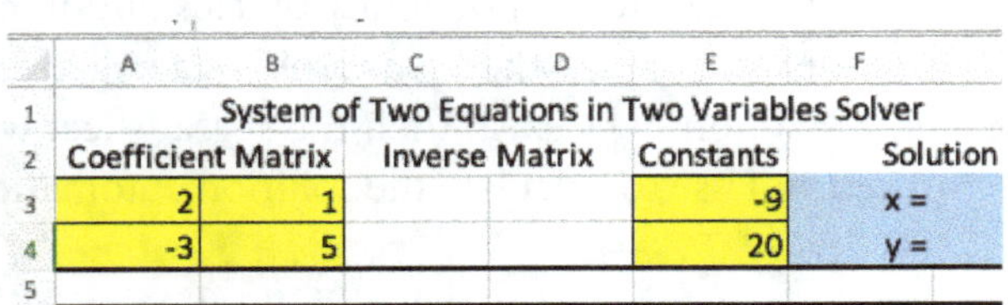

Cell C3 will be the upper left of the inverse. We will type the formula for the inverse in that cell ***using the "=" to activate the calculator***. With cell C3 selected, type **=MINVERSE(A3:B4)** and Enter. If the formula was entered correctly, we now see numbers in cells C3, D3, C4, and D4 that were not there before. They are most likely numbers with lots of decimal values.

Cells F3 and F4 have our variable names, so we will calculate the answers in column G. With cell G3 selected, type **=MMULT(C3#,E3:E4)**. The reason for the # symbol is that C3 contains a formula, and we want to ***use the result*** of that formula calculation.

The result is now displayed. The solution to the system of equations is

$$x = -5, y = 1 \text{ which is the ordered pair } (-5, 1)$$

Here is a system of equations that should not have a solution because it is inconsistent.

$$\begin{aligned} 3x - 4y &= 2 \\ 6x - 8y &= 18 \end{aligned}$$

When we enter the numbers into the spreadsheet calculator, cells C3 and G3 display **#NUM!** which is the error code that results when a calculation cannot be performed for one reason or another. What we do not know is if the calculation cannot be performed because the system is inconsistent or was the problem that the system was consistent and dependent. All we can do is report that there is not a unique solution.

Example: Solve this system of 3 variables using the spreadsheet. If a unique solution does not exist, then answer "does not exist".

$$\begin{aligned} -5x + 4y + 5z &= 4 \\ -x + 8z &= 11 \\ -2y + 12z &= 13 \end{aligned}$$

The coefficient matrix is $\begin{bmatrix} -5 & 4 & 5 \\ -1 & 0 & 8 \\ 0 & -2 & 12 \end{bmatrix}$ and the constant matrix is $\begin{bmatrix} 4 \\ 11 \\ 13 \end{bmatrix}$

These will now be entered into cells A8 through C10, and G8 to G10. With cell D8 selected, type **=MINVERSE(A8:C10)**. Numbers should appear in the previously blank cells D8 through F10. With cell I8 selected, type **=MMULT(D8#,G8:G10)**.

According to our calculations, the solution will need to be approximated. How many decimal values we include depends on the situation and the number of desired significant figures. Rounding to the nearest hundredth we have a unique solution.

$x = 7.18$, $y = 7.14$, $z = 2.27$ which is an ordered triple (7.18, 7.14, 2.27)

I8 f_x =MMULT(D8#,G8:G10)

	A	B	C	D	E	F	G	H	I	J
1	System of Two Equations in Two Variables Solver									
2	Coefficient Matrix		Inverse Matrix		Constants	Solution				
3	2	1	0.38462	-0.0769	-9	x = -5				
4	-3	5	0.23077	0.15385	20	y = 1				
5										
6	System of Three Equations in Three Variables Solver									
7	Coefficient Matrix			Inverse Matrix			Constants	Solution		
8	-5	4	5	-0.7273	2.636364	-1.4545	4	x =	7.18182	
9	-1	0	8	-0.5455	2.727273	-1.5909	11	y =	7.13636	
10	0	-2	12	-0.0909	0.454545	-0.1818	13	z =	2.27273	
11										
12										

If we increase to 4 variables and 4 equations, we will need an extra column for both the coefficient matrix and the inverse matrix. On the spreadsheet, this means the columns A through K, for example, will be needed. Columns A-D are for the coefficient matrix, columns E-H are for the inverse matrix, column I is for the constant matrix, and finally columns J-K will contain the solution(s). The number of rows will increase by 1. If row 11 is left blank, and there are 2 rows for headings, this means 6 rows, 12-17.

Important! The ***order*** we place the variables into columns for the coefficient matrix needs to be the ***same order*** in the solution column!

We will rely on this method for solving any system of linear equations, with one exception. We need a strategy for solving when the constant matrix is a column of zeros, ***AND*** the inverse of the coefficient matrix does not exist. Here are examples of what the constant (column) matrix would look like.

$\begin{bmatrix}0\\0\end{bmatrix}$ and $\begin{bmatrix}0\\0\\0\end{bmatrix}$ are what we call "zero vectors". When this occurs, the system of linear equations is called *homogeneous*. One of two things will be true.

- The first is that the solution to the system is what we call the ***trivial solution***. In two variables, this means (0,0) is the solution. $x = 0$ and $y = 0$. The unique solution exists, and all variables are zero. We have this if the coefficient matrix has an inverse. The spreadsheet will help in this regard.
- The second possibility is there are an infinite number of solutions. This occurs because one or more of the variables is dependent on the others. We identify the variable that is infinite, and then solve the reduced system. If the coefficient matrix does NOT have an inverse, then we are dealing with this situation.

Let us see how this is done. Consider the following problem.
Find a solution to the system.

$$x + 3y + 7z = 0$$
$$y + 3z = 0$$
$$2x + 4y + 8z = 0$$

When we try to solve using the previous method, we get an error. There likely is an infinite solution. We can explore what that means.

The coefficient matrix is $\begin{bmatrix} 1 & 3 & 7 \\ 0 & 1 & 3 \\ 2 & 4 & 8 \end{bmatrix}$ and the constant matrix is $\begin{bmatrix} 0 \\ 0 \\ 0 \end{bmatrix}$ making this a *homogeneous system* of linear equations. When we enter the matrix into our spreadsheet to see if the inverse matrix exists, we see that it does not. Here is where things get interesting. At least one of the three variables is what we call a ***free variable***. Our system of equations can now be visualized by combining the coefficient matrix with the constant matrix. We call the result an *augmented matrix* with one more column than there are rows:

$$\begin{bmatrix} 1 & 3 & 7 & 0 \\ 0 & 1 & 3 & 0 \\ 2 & 4 & 8 & 0 \end{bmatrix}$$

We may use an online calculator to perform ***row reduction*** operations with this matrix which will reveal to us that there *is* a free variable, and we can identify what that variable is with a close inspection of the result of the operation. This online calculator tool is called WolframAlpha.[1] Performing row reduction by hand is not a focus of this book and requires some experience with either a linear algebra or finite mathematics course.

The inline command we may use is "row reduce {{1, 3, 7, 0}, {0, 1, 3, 0}, {2, 4, 8, 0}}" without the " ". Each list of numbers inside { } represents a row of the augmented matrix. We use commas to separate entries in each row.

Here is the result from row reduction operations:

$$\begin{bmatrix} 1 & 0 & -2 & 0 \\ 0 & 1 & 3 & 0 \\ 0 & 0 & 0 & 0 \end{bmatrix}$$

If we change this matrix *back* into a system of equations, we get:

$$x - 2z = 0$$
$$y + 3z = 0$$
$$0 = 0$$

1. ____. *WolframAlpha*, Wolfram, 2024, https://www.wolframalpha.com/

The values of x and y both ***depend*** on z. The value of z is ***free to choose***. Suppose we are given additional information, that z = 10. Then, we can find a **particular solution** to the system. We will substitute z = 10 into the equations with x and y. Then solve each equation for the variable.

$$x - 2z = 0 \qquad y + 3z = 0$$
$$x - 2 \cdot 10 = 0 \qquad y + 3 \cdot 10 = 0$$
$$x - 20 = 0 \qquad y + 30 = 0$$
$$x = 20 \qquad y = -30$$

Our conclusion is that we have a ***particular solution*** of $x = 20$, $y = -30$, $z = 10$.

All this is to say that when solving a system of linear equations, we have two capable tools at our disposal. One is the spreadsheet operation. The other is row reduction, which may reduce a system of 3 variables to a system of 2 variables. We solve the reduced system, and we now have a solution to the original problem.

SECTION 4.3 A CLOSED ECONOMY INPUT-OUTPUT PROBLEM

Modern economies are very complex, with many sectors and subsectors. Each contributor to an economy also relies on portions of the others to function. Producers are also consumers. A producer will consume a portion of their own output, and the rest will be divided among the other sectors. Surplus may be needed to meet demand if there is external demand. Our first investigation will consist of a ***closed economy***. This means there is no demand outside the system. Let us take this step by step. First, we will be considering a local economy that is completely self-sustaining with zero waste. The business sectors are agriculture, housing (which includes lumber), and metalworking. Every economy functions best when there is balance, that is production equals consumption plus demand. Since demand is zero, it is removed from the equation. This is the foundation for each equation in our system. Please note that the units for x, y, and z are in whatever the local currency is used for trade.

production = consumption

We assign a variable to each sector in terms of how much it ***produces***.

x = amount ***produced*** *by agriculture*
y = amount ***produced*** *by housing*
z = amount ***produced*** *by metalworking*

Now we will describe what portions of each are consumed by producers.

1. Agriculture consumes 40% of its own production, 40% of housing's production, and 30% of metalworking's production.
2. Housing consumes 40% of agriculture's production, 30% of its own production, and 20% of metalworking's production.
3. Metalworking consumes 20% of agriculture's production, 30% of housing's production, and 50% of its own production.

We can provide the same information in tabular form. Each column sums to 100% because there is no waste. Everything that is produced is also consumed in production. The process is cyclical.

	Consumption		
Sector	***From Agriculture*** x	***From Housing*** y	***From Metalworking*** z
To Agriculture	40%	40%	30%
To Housing	40%	30%	20%
To Metalworking	20%	30%	50%

Before we write the system of equations, we need to convert each percentage to a decimal value. Remember that 40% = $^{40}\!/_{100}$ = 0.40. A percent is a portion out of 100. The table now looks like this.

	Consumption		
Sector	***From Agriculture*** x	***From Housing*** y	***From Metalworking*** z
To Agriculture	0.40	0.40	0.30
To Housing	0.40	0.30	0.20
To Metalworking	0.20	0.30	0.50

What this means in terms of x, y, and z?
Agriculture consumes $0.40x + 0.40y + 0.30z$ « The first row of the table.
Housing consumes $0.40x + 0.30y + 0.20z$ « The second row of the table.
Metalworking consumes $0.20x + 0.30y + 0.50z$ « The third row of the table.

Now we can write our production = consumption equations.

Agriculture: $x = 0.40x + 0.40y + 0.30z$
Housing: $y = 0.40x + 0.30y + 0.20z$
Metalworking: $z = 0.20x + 0.30y + 0.50z$

Try this: A village has 3 sectors. People choose between farming, baking, and crafting in which to work. Farming consumes 25% of its own production, 20% of baking's production, and 40% of crafting. Baking consumes 40% of farming's production, 30% of its own, and 20% of crafting. Crafting consumes 35% of farming's production, 50% of baking, and 40% of its own. Write a system of equations for this economy.

Solution: Let x = farming, y = baking, and z = crafting productions.

$$x = 0.25x + 0.20y + 0.40z$$
$$y = 0.40x + 0.30y + 0.20z$$
$$z = 0.35x + 0.50y + 0.40z$$

Now that we have a system of equations we will want to solve for x, y, and z. What production amounts by each sector will create a stable economy? Not every worker can be a farmer. When there are too many workers in one sector, the whole suffers because it puts a strain on the system.

An economist by the name of Wassily Leontief was largely credited with the development of a matrix method for solving problems like this. In math terms we call it "input-output" analysis.

Let us solve the problem that was introduced at the beginning of this section.

Agriculture: $x = 0.40x + 0.40y + 0.30z$
Housing: $y = 0.40x + 0.30y + 0.20z$
Metalworking: $z = 0.20x + 0.30y + 0.50z$

We see that our equations are not in standard form. That is, there are variables on both sides of the equation. Let us move all the variable terms to one side. Since there are no constants, the constant side will be zero. Also, the coefficients of x, y, and z are all 1. x is really $1.00x$ and so on…

$$0 = \mathbf{0.40x - 1.00x} + 0.40y + 0.30z$$
$$0 = 0.40x + \mathbf{0.30y - 1.00y} + 0.20z$$
$$0 = 0.20x + 0.30y + \mathbf{0.50z - 1.00z}$$

Now combine terms with the same variable by subtracting them.

$$0 = \mathbf{-0.60x} + 0.40y + 0.30z$$
$$0 = 0.40x - \mathbf{0.70y} + 0.20z$$
$$0 = 0.20x + 0.30y - \mathbf{0.50z}$$

The coefficient matrix is $\begin{bmatrix} -0.6 & 0.4 & 0.3 \\ 0.4 & -0.7 & 0.2 \\ 0.2 & 0.3 & -0.5 \end{bmatrix}$ and the constant matrix is $\begin{bmatrix} 0 \\ 0 \\ 0 \end{bmatrix}$.

It remains to be seen whether this system has an infinite number of solutions, or only one trivial solution. We will input the augmented system into a tool that will perform the reduction.

The augmented matrix is $\begin{bmatrix} -0.6 & 0.4 & 0.3 & 0 \\ 0.4 & -0.7 & 0.2 & 0 \\ 0.2 & 0.3 & -0.5 & 0 \end{bmatrix}$. Always put the coefficient matrix to the left of the constant column, which is all the way to the right.

Type "**row reduce {{-0.6, 0.4, 0.3, 0}, {0.4, -0.7, 0.2, 0}, {0.2, 0.3, -0.5, 0}}**" or perform row reduction operations on the matrix by hand if desired.

The resulting matrix consists of rational numbers that have been converted to repeating decimals. We will express each decimal rounded to the nearest thousandth (3 place values after the decimal point).

$$\begin{bmatrix} 1 & 0 & -1.115 & 0 \\ 0 & 1 & -0.923 & 0 \\ 0 & 0 & 0 & 0 \end{bmatrix}$$

Now we will write this "solved" system in equation form.

$$x - 1.115z = 0$$
$$y - 0.923z = 0$$
$$0 = 0$$

For a second time we see that x and y are both dependent on the value of z, whereas z is free to be whatever we need. Suppose, then, **z = 1200**.

$x - 1.115 \cdot 1200=0$ $\qquad x = 1338$

$y - 0.923 \cdot 1200=0$ $\qquad y \cong 1108$

In conclusion, when metalworking is producing 1200 currency units of output, housing needs to produce 1108 currency units and agriculture needs to produce 1338 currency units so that each sector can continue to function without changing its dependency on the other two.

Section 4.4 An Open Leontief Input-Output Problem

In an open model, the consumption side of the equation consists of everything in the closed system plus demand. In this topic we will consider the various business interests of a conglomerate, which can be viewed as its own miniature economy.

Example: A conglomerate has three divisions, which produce consumer electronics, IT & mobile communications, and device solutions. The consumer electronics division needs 2% of its own production, 4% of its IT & mobile communications, and 10% of its device solutions. The IT & mobile comm needs 18% of the consumer electronics, 5% of its own production, and 12% of device solutions. The device solutions division needs 1% of the consumer electronics, 2% of IT & mobile comm, and 5% of its own production. Demand has been estimated at 1 billion in consumer electronics, 3 billion in IT & mobile communications, and 2 billion in device solutions. How much should each division produce to meet demand?

Solution: Start with defining variables and what they represent. Let x be consumer electronics production, y is IT & mobile communications production, and z is device solutions.

$$\textit{production} = \textit{consumption}$$

On the consumption side of the equation, we will have all the terms as before, and the demand. Let us see what that looks like in a table.

	Consumption			
Division	***Consumer Electronics***	***IT & Mobile Communications***	***Device Solutions***	***Demand***
Consumer E.	0.02	0.04	0.10	1
IT & Mobile	0.18	0.05	0.12	3
Device Sol.	0.01	0.02	0.05	2

The columns here do not have to add up to 1.00 or 100% because there is external demand for most of what each division produces. Our task is to make sure that production meets demand with the least waste.

With the numbers in a table, we can more easily see where they appear in the equations.

$$x = 0.02x + 0.04y + 0.10z + 1$$
$$y = 0.18x + 0.05y + 0.12z + 3$$
$$z = 0.01x + 0.02y + 0.05z + 2$$

Notice that the demand quantities are numbers in billions of units. They are not multiplied by anything because they are constants. Next is to get the equations in standard form. This time we will move all the variable terms to the left side to keep the constants positive We will keep them in alphabet order as well.

$$\mathbf{1.00x - 0.02x} - 0.04y - 0.10z = 1$$
$$-0.18x + \mathbf{1.00y - 0.05y} - 0.12z = 3$$
$$-0.01x - 0.02y + \mathbf{1.00z - 0.05z} = 2$$

Combine the terms that have the same variable.

$$\mathbf{0.98x} - 0.04y - 0.10z = 1$$
$$-0.18x + \mathbf{0.95y} - 0.12z = 3$$
$$-0.01x - 0.02y + \mathbf{0.95z} = 2$$

Since this is not a homogeneous system of equations, we can use the spreadsheet to solve it. The coefficient matrix and constant matrix are

$$\begin{bmatrix} 0.98 & -0.04 & -0.10 \\ -0.18 & 0.95 & -0.12 \\ -0.01 & -0.02 & 0.95 \end{bmatrix} \text{ and } \begin{bmatrix} 1 \\ 3 \\ 2 \end{bmatrix}$$

The solution is an ordered triple $(x, y, z) = (1.395697, 3.699966, 2.197849)$ with each of those numbers in billions of units of currency.

PRACTICE EXERCISES

1. Find the market equilibrium point for the following demand and supply equations, where x is the quantity both in supply and in demand.

   Demand: $p = -3x + 227$ Supply: $p = 8x - 466$

2. Graph the following system of equations and find the solution. Graph each line and plot the solution as a point on the graph. Write the solution as an ordered pair.

$$x - 2y = 1 \quad \text{and} \quad 3x + 2y = -8$$

3. Solve the given system of linear equations.

$$\begin{aligned} x - 2y - z &= 7 \\ 5x + 2y + 2z &= -13 \\ 3x - y + z &= 1 \end{aligned}$$

4. A simplified version of input-output analysis of a national economy has the following input-output matrix:

	Agriculture	Manufacturing	Households
Agriculture	0.245	0.102	0.051
Manufacturing	0.099	0.291	0.279
Households	0.433	0.372	0.011

   A. Interpret the matrix: How many units of Manufacturing are needed to produce one unit of Agriculture?

   B. Given Demand (in billions of dollars) for the three sectors are as follows
   34.4 = Manufacturing, 3.4=Agriculture 30=Households
   Find the amount of each commodity that should be produced (nearest 0.1 billion)

5. The input-output (consumption) matrix for a closed economy is given below. Solve the associated input-output model. Use if you need a variable in your answer. (free variables use r)

$$\begin{bmatrix} 0.41 & 0.05 & 0.3 \\ 0.33 & 0.27 & 0.31 \\ 0.26 & 0.68 & 0.39 \end{bmatrix}$$

5 Quadratic and Polynomial Functions

Section 5.1: Quadratic Functions

We now continue our study of functions and will start with a definition.

> **Definition:** A function is called **quadratic** if it can be written in standard form $f(x) = ax^2 + bx + c$
>
> where a is a constant not 0; b, c can be any constant, including 0.

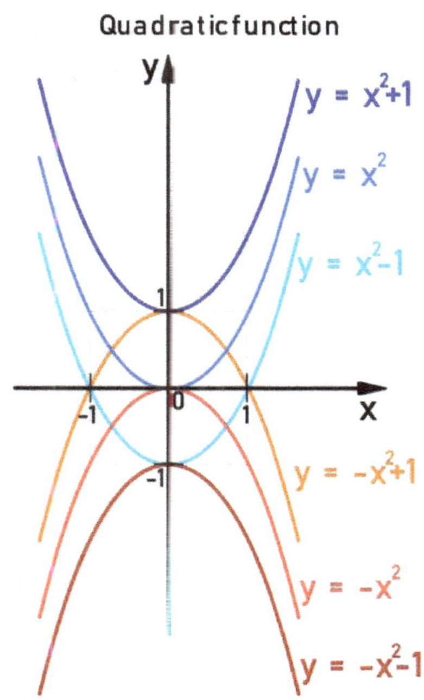

The graph of a quadratic function is basically u-shaped, with an arc that widens as it grows longer. It is also symmetric, meaning that half can be folded over onto the other half. Here we see some quadratic function graphs where $a = 1$ or $a = -1$ and $b = 0$.

A striking feature of the graph is the *orientation* of the curve. We say that the graph of quadratic function ***curves upward*** when a is a positive number $a > 0$. The graph ***curves downward*** when a is a negative number $a < 0$.

The constant c is a shifting constant. If c is positive the entire graph retains its shape but shifts upward. If c is negative the graph shifts downward. The **y-intercept** occurs at $y = c$, or the point $(0, c)$.

We can see the symmetry for each of these equations. The graph is identical on either side of the y axis. In the case where $b = 0$ we say that the *axis of symmetry* is the y axis.

Notice also that not every quadratic graph will cross or touch the x axis. Some have only one point on the x axis. Others have two points on the x axis. Linear functions have exactly one y-intercept and one x-intercept. This is one way that quadratic functions are different from linear functions. There are other differences as well. Some important features of quadratic functions need to be identified.

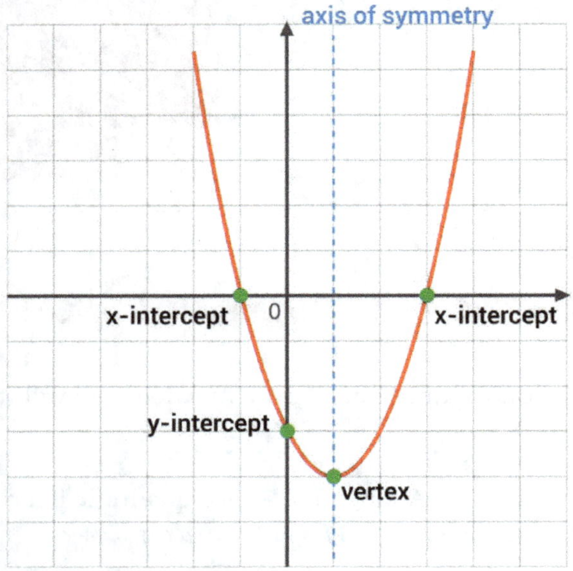

We see the axis of symmetry on this graph. Every quadratic function has a y-intercept. Not every quadratic function has x intercepts. This one has two x intercepts. Note that they are the same distance away from the axis of symmetry. Every quadratic function has a *vertex*. A vertex is also called a *turning point*. Saying "turning point" is a bit more descriptive, since the y values go from decreasing to increasing or vice-versa.

Definition: For any quadratic function $f(x) = ax^2 + bx + c$, the **vertex** or turning point has coordinates (h, k) where

$$h = -\frac{b}{2a}, k = -\frac{b^2}{4a} + c$$

Any quadratic function can be written in vertex form. Given (h, k) the quadratic function can be written as

$$f(x) = a(x - h)^2 + k$$

The **axis of symmetry** is the vertical line that passes through the vertex and is given by the equation $x = -\frac{b}{2a}$

We can see how the vertex form of the quadratic function can be transformed (rewritten) into standard form by expanding it. For that we need another definition.

Definition: For any binomial $(x - h)$ or $(x + h)$ the **square of a binomial** is $(x - h)^2 = x^2 - 2hx + h^2$ when the sign is negative and when the sign is positive we have $(x + h)^2 = x^2 + 2hx + h^2$.

Example: Identify the vertex of the function, and then rewrite the function $f(x) = 5(x - 3)^2 - 20$ in standard form. Identify *a, b, and c.*

Solution: The vertex is (h, k) with $\mathbf{h = 3, k = -20}$ because we need to take the *opposite sign* of the constant that is inside ( ) with x.

$$f(x) = \underset{a}{5}(x - \underset{h}{3})^2 - \underset{k}{20}$$

With each step of the process transforming f(x) from vertex form to standard form, watch what happens to *a, h, and k* as we go.

Start here.	$5 \cdot [x - 3]^2 - 20$
1. Square the binomial and keep inside [ ].	$5[x^2 - 2 \cdot 3 \cdot x + 3^2] - 20$
The middle term always gets multiplied by 2.	
2. Perform the operations.	$5[x^2 - 6x + 9] - 20$
3. Distribute to eliminate [ ].	$5x^2 - 5 \cdot 6x + 5 \cdot 9 - 20$
4. Perform the operations.	$5x^2 - 30x + 45 - 20$
5. Combine the last two constants.	$5x^2 - 30x + 25$
6. Write the solution	

$$Solution: a = 5, b = -30, c = 25 \ \ and\ (h, k) = (3, -1)$$

It is left up to the reader to verify that the values of *a, b, and c* in the previous example can be calculated using the next formulas showing how to convert from vertex form to standard form.

Definition: Any function $f(x) = a(x - h)^2 + k$ can be rewritten in standard form $f(x) = ax^2 + bx + c$ because $a = a$,
$b = -2ah$ and $c = \frac{b^2}{4a} + k$

Symmetry is perhaps the most important feature of quadratic functions. This leads to another important piece of information, and that is the nature and quantity of x-intercepts. We can graph the function, or we can obtain the information directly from the equation in standard form.

> **Definition:** Given a quadratic function in standard form, $f(x) = ax^2 + bx + c$, then the **discriminant** is $D = b^2 - 4ac$.

One way to remember the word discriminant is that it helps to *discriminate* between quadratic functions that have no x-intercepts, one x-intercept or two distinct x-intercepts (and whether the x-intercepts are two rational numbers or irrational). Here are all the possibilities.

<table>
<tr><th>$D = b^2 - 4ac$ is:</th><th>Then we conclude:</th><th>x-intercept calculation:</th></tr>
<tr><td>a negative number</td><td>there are no x-intercepts</td><td>N/A</td></tr>
<tr><td>zero</td><td>there is one x-intercept, and it is the vertex</td><td>$x = \frac{-b}{2a}$</td></tr>
<tr><td>a positive number that is a perfect square</td><td>there are two distinct x-intercepts; they are rational numbers</td><td rowspan="2">$x = \frac{-b + \sqrt{D}}{2a}, \frac{-b - \sqrt{D}}{2a}$</td></tr>
<tr><td>a positive number that is not a perfect square</td><td>there are two distinct x-intercepts; they are irrational numbers</td></tr>
</table>

Quadratic Function $y = ax^2 + bx + c$

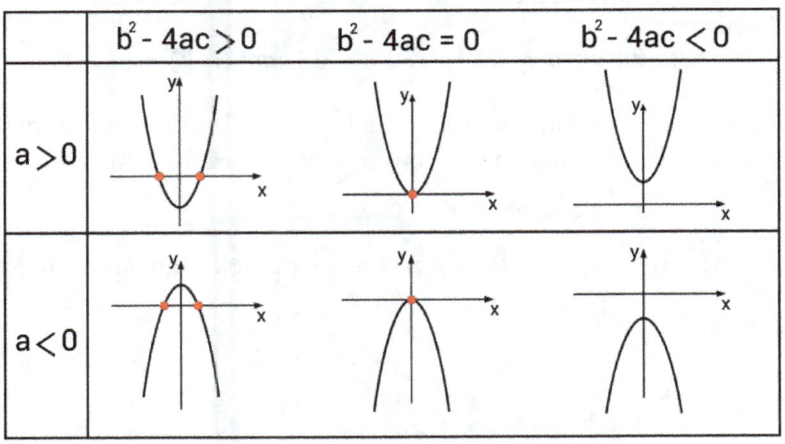

Now we are ready to list all the important features of a quadratic function and show the function in standard form as well as vertex form. What are the important features? They are the vertex, the axis of symmetry, the y-intercept, orientation, and x-intercept(s) (if any).

Examples: For each function, list all the important features and write the function in vertex form as well as standard form.

$$a.\ f(x) = x^2 - 6x + 5$$
$$b.\ f(x) = -2x^2 + 18$$

Solution a): Start with $f(x) = x^2 - 6x + 5$. Note that the equation is in standard form. Important features will be in **boldface**.

The coordinates of the vertex (h, k) are $h = -\frac{b}{2a}$, $k = -\frac{b^2}{4a} + c$

For that we need to know *a, b, and c*. First, $a = 1$ because the coefficient of x^2 is 1. $b = -6$, and $c = 5$. Now we will use these numbers to calculate h and k. Negative signs can be tricky. Please take care! $-b^2 = (-1) \cdot b^2 = (-1) \cdot (-6)^2 = (-1) \cdot 36$ and will always be negative because the square portion is positive.

$$h = -\frac{(-6)}{2 \cdot 1} = \frac{6}{2} = 3 \text{ and } k = \frac{-36}{4 \cdot 1} + 5 = \frac{-36}{4} + 5 = -9 + 5 = -4$$

The **vertex** is at (3, −4). The **axis of symmetry** is the vertical line $x = 3$. The **y-intercept** is at $(0, c) = (0, 5)$. Because $a = 1$ (*positive*) the orientation is **curves upward**. The vertex form of the function is $f(x) = 1(x - 3)^2 - 4$ and does not require writing the "1" in front. So, we can write $f(x) = (x - 3)^2 - 4$.

What about **x-intercepts**? First calculate

$$D = b^2 - 4ac = 36 - 4 \cdot 1 \cdot 5 = 36 - 20 = 16$$

D is both positive and a perfect square, so there are two rational x-intercepts.

$$x = \frac{6 + \sqrt{16}}{2}, \quad \frac{6 - \sqrt{16}}{2}$$

which simplifies to: $x = 5$ *and* $x = 1$. The points are (5, 0) and (1, 0).

Solution b): $f(x) = -2x^2 + 18$. The equation is in standard form.

Start with $a = -2$, $b = 0$, and $c = 18$. The **vertex** is at $(h, k) = (0, 18)$. Since $b = 0$ we have the vertex is also the **y-intercept**. The **axis of symmetry** is the y axis. The orientation is **curves downward**, because $a = -2$ (*negative*)

Vertex form is technically $f(x) = -2(x - 0)^2 + 18$ but we never see expressions written like that when $h = 0$.

Important! When $b = 0$, **standard form** is also **vertex form.** $f(x) = -2x^2 + 18$ is an equation in both standard form and vertex form.

All that remains are the x-intercepts. We have a clue concerning this because the vertex is on the y axis (at (0, 18)) and the orientation curves downward. So, we do expect to have two x-intercepts, and we expect them to be on the left and right of the y axis, equal and opposite each other.

$$D = 0^2 - 4 \cdot (-2) \cdot 18 = 144$$

D is both positive and a perfect square! Because b = 0 the formula simplifies to

$$x = \frac{\sqrt{144}}{2 \cdot (-2)}, \quad \frac{-\sqrt{144}}{2 \cdot (-2)}$$

which simplifies to

$$x = \frac{12}{-4} = -3, \quad x = \frac{-12}{-4} = 3$$

Because of symmetry and the vertex on the y axis it makes sense that the two x-intercepts would be equal and opposite in value. The **x-intercepts** are at (−3, 0) and at (3, 0).

What if the value of D is not a perfect square? In that case, we have two options. We can leave the square root term written in ***radical form***. Or we can use a calculator and approximate the solution to a specified number of decimal places.

Example: Find the x-intercepts for $f(x) = x^2 + 6x - 5$

Solution: First we need to calculate D and make sure we have a solution.

$$D = 6^2 - 4 \cdot 1 \cdot (-5) = 36 + 20 = 56$$

D is positive and it is not a perfect square.

$$The\ two\ x's\ are: \ \frac{-6 + \sqrt{56}}{2} \ and \ \frac{-6 - \sqrt{56}}{2}$$

Written this way, the solution is in ***radical form***. This is not very practical, but from a mathematics point of view we call these two values conjugates of each other. What does "conjugate" mean? Though these two values are irrational (the decimal is nonrepeating and infinite), when we multiply them we get a rational number. For illustration purposes, we will simplify the two radical expressions, then multiply them to see how the product of two irrationals can be rational. To simplify, we need to use a property of radicals.

Definition: Product/Quotient Property of Radicals is

$\sqrt{a} \cdot \sqrt{b} = \sqrt{a \cdot b}$ also $\frac{\sqrt{a}}{\sqrt{b}} = \sqrt{\frac{a}{b}}$ so long as *a* and *b* are both positive.

Simplify $\frac{-6+\sqrt{56}}{2}$, $\frac{-6-\sqrt{56}}{2}$ using the quotient property of radicals.

We will be using a convenient fact: $2 = \sqrt{4}$

$$\frac{-6}{2} + \frac{\sqrt{56}}{2} = -3 + \frac{\sqrt{56}}{\sqrt{4}} = -3 + \sqrt{\frac{56}{4}} = -3 + \sqrt{14}$$

$$\frac{-6 - \sqrt{56}}{2} = -3 - \frac{\sqrt{56}}{\sqrt{4}} = -3 - \sqrt{14}$$

Conversation starter: Using a calculator, show that

$$\frac{-6 + \sqrt{56}}{2} \cong 0.742 \ , and \ \frac{-6 - \sqrt{56}}{2} \cong -6.742$$

then show that

$$-3 + \sqrt{14} \cong 0.742 \ , and \ -3 - \sqrt{14} \cong -6.742$$

What does this prove/verify when simplifying this radical expression? Also, what does this tell us about the location of the vertex?

Now we will see what happens when we multiply two radical conjugates.

Multiply: $(-3 + \sqrt{14}) \cdot (-3 - \sqrt{14})$

$$-3 \cdot (-3 - \sqrt{14}) + \sqrt{14} \cdot (-3 - \sqrt{14}$$

$$9 + 3 \cdot (\sqrt{14}) + \sqrt{14} \cdot (-3) - \sqrt{14} \cdot \sqrt{14}$$

$$9 \qquad + 0 \qquad - \sqrt{196}$$

$9 - 14$ which is equal to -5

Definition: $(a + \sqrt{b}) \cdot (a - \sqrt{b}) = a^2 - b$ is the product of two radical conjugate expressions.

As an aside, it turns out that any whole number can be expressed as the product of two radical conjugates. Take the number 17, for example.

We need to be able to find a^2 and b so that $17 = a^2 - b$. Start with a^2 (which is any squared number). The nearest square number that is ***larger than*** 17 is 25.
$17 = 25 - 8$.

$$17 = a^2 - b$$

which means $a^2 = 25$ and $b = 8$... so $a = 5$
Plug those numbers in for $(a + \sqrt{b}) \cdot (a - \sqrt{b})$
$(5 + \sqrt{8}) \cdot (5 - \sqrt{8})$

We will leave it up to the reader to verify that the number we get when multiplying those two expressions is indeed 17 using the definition of the product of two radical expressions.

Section 5.2: Graphs of Quadratic Functions

We can also identify important features of a quadratic function from its graph. The graph can help us to identify the equation, but unlike a straight line we need at least 3 points. Then we can write the equation. We will start with two basic examples, with only the knowledge that the curve is a quadratic curve. Then we will create a graph from data that represents a situation known to be quadratic in nature. In all three examples we will use information that is given to come up with the equation. Let us start with the graph of a quadratic function.

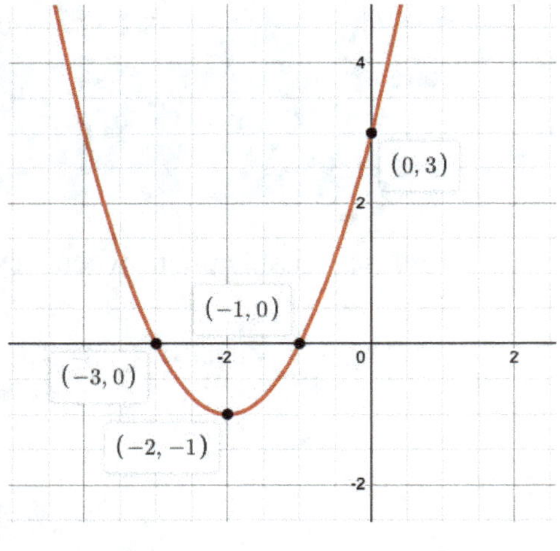

In the graph shown, we have labeled the vertex, the two x-intercepts and the y-intercept. The graph curves upward, which means that the leading coefficient must be positive. This is the simplest possible scenario. The symmetry occurs across the vertical axis $x = -2$ and there is a minimum value at the point $(-2, -1)$.

To write the equation, we could choose either standard form or vertex form. Since the vertex is known, it may be timesaving to use vertex form of the equation $f(x) = a(x - h)^2 + k$.

Step 1: $(h, k) = (-2, -1)$, so $h = -2$ and $k = -1$

Step 2: Put these numbers in place of *h and k*. Write out what we have. Important: Remember to change the sign of *h*

$$f(x) = a(x + 2)^2 - 1$$

Notice we also must remember to keep the power of 2 with the x!

Step 3: Solve for using any of the other labeled points on the graph. Remember that $y = f(x)$. The point $(-1, 0)$ for example is actually $(-1, f(-1))$!
Here is what that looks like using our formula/equation:

$$f(-1) = 0 = a(-1 + 2)^2 - 1$$

Clean that equation up:

$$0 = a \cdot 1^2 - 1 = a - 1$$
$$0 = a - 1 \ \textit{becomes}\ a = 1$$

The vertex form of the equation is:

$$y = f(x) = 1(x + 2)^2 - 1$$

Politeness requires us to hide the awkward looking 1 in front of the ( ).

Our answer is $f(x) = (x + 2)^2 - 1$

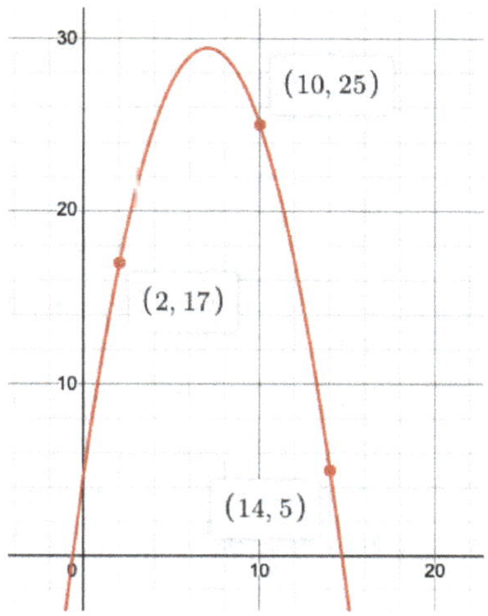

Here is another example, however this time we have three random points. Our task is to write the equation in standard form using only the 3 known points.

We need to solve for the values of *a*, *b*, and *c* in our equation $y = f(x) = ax^2 + bx + c$

Start with the point (2, 17) where $x = 2$ and $y = 17$.

$$y = ax^2 + bx + c$$
$$17 = a \cdot 2^2 + b \cdot 2 + c$$

which cleans up to

$$17 = 4a + 2b + c$$

Notice the "x" and "y" are gone and all that remains are are *a*, *b*, and *c*. In the previous chapter we learned that when we have 3 unknowns we need a system of 3 equations and then we can solve the system using our spreadsheet solver.

> **Try this:** Use the point (10, 25) to get the equation
> $25 = 100a + 10b + c$ and then use the point (14, 5) to get the equation $5 = 196a + 14b + c$.

Now we have a system of 3 equations in 3 unknowns. Let us solve it.

$$17 = 4a + 2b + c$$
$$25 = 100a + 10b + c$$
$$5 = 196a + 14b + c$$

Matrix A is $\begin{bmatrix} 4 & 2 & 1 \\ 100 & 10 & 1 \\ 196 & 14 & 1 \end{bmatrix}$ and the Constant column is $\begin{bmatrix} 17 \\ 25 \\ 5 \end{bmatrix}$. In our spreadsheet, the only mental adjustment we need to make is in how to use the solution. Instead of variables ***x, y, and z*** we have ***a, b, and c.***

Here is what the system looks like in the spreadsheet, along with the solution in column J.

	A	B	C	D	E	F	G	H	I	J	K
1			Matrix A			Inverse of A		Constants		Solution	
2		4	2	1	0.01	####	0.02	17	x =	-0.5	
3		100	10	1	###	0.50	####	25	y =	7	
4		196	14	1	1.46	####	0.42	5	z =	5	
5		x	y	z							

$$a = -0.5,\ b = 7, \text{ and } c = 5$$

Conclusion: The equation of the function is $f(x) = -0.5x^2 + 7x + 5$

In our second example, suppose all we have is a table of data values. Suppose we also know that this data represents the height of an object in freefall. We know from Physics that the height of an object in freefall is represented by a quadratic equation. The variable x represents time, in seconds, and the variable y represents height in meters.

We can enter this data into a spreadsheet and create a scatter plot with "smooth lines and markers." Along the way, we will "Add a Chart Element" Trendline just as we did in a previous chapter when

x	y
1	113
2	116.5
3	110
4	93.5
5	67.5
6	31.5

finding a linear trendline. But instead, we will identify the trendline as a "polynomial of order (degree) 2." That is what a quadratic equation is—a polynomial of degree 2. For aesthetics, we will also include data labels on each of the marked points on the graph.

There are different spreadsheet applications available. They all seem to have certain common terminology. When using data, or graphing (x,y) table of values, the chart type is a "smooth line." The user can customize the chart or graph by adding data labels, and a ***trendline equation***. This was the result when using a common spreadsheet application.

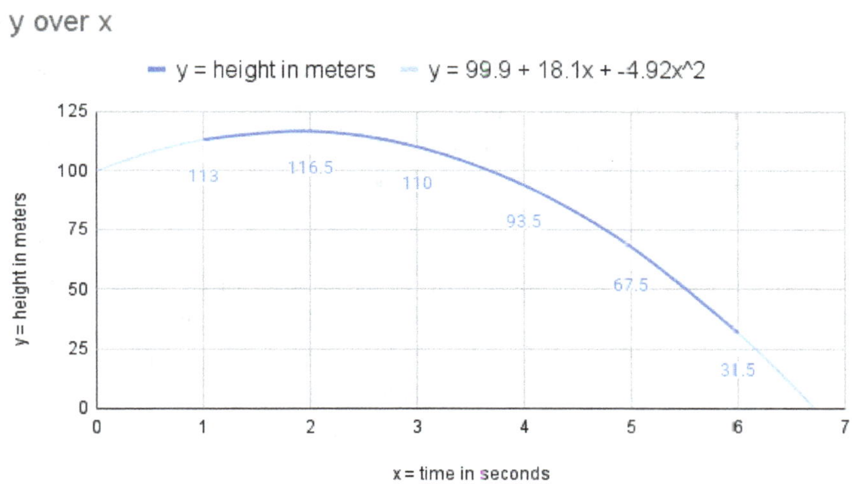

The horizontal axis was adjusted to start at 0 and end at 7, again for aesthetics purposes. The equation displayed is $f(x) = -4.9x^2 + 18x + 100$ when rounding to two significant digits.

SECTION 5.3: POLYNOMIAL MODELS

The word polynomial comes from Latin "poly" meaning many and "nom" meaning name, in this case a single name for a quantity – x. In Latin, the suffix "ial" is used to change a noun to an adjective so that the word polynomial is not a thing, but it is describing something else. We have seen the simplest versions of polynomial functions, i.e. linear and quadratic type functions. We know that when two linear functions are combined we get another linear function. When two quadratic functions are combined the result is in the same family. But when two or more of these functions are multiplied the new function will have higher degree, or order, than its component parts.

Example: Multiply $f(x) = x + 7$ with $g(x) = x^2 - 2x + 9$ to create a new function $h(x) = f(x) \cdot g(x)$

Solution: We will multiply these two quantities using the distributive property. Then combine like terms

$$(x + 7)(x^2 - 2x + 9)$$
$$x(x^2 - 2x + 9) + 7(x^2 - 2x + 9)$$
$$x^3 - 2x^2 + 9x + 7x^2 - 14x + 63$$
$$x^3 + 5x^2 - 5x + 63 = h(x)$$

The result of multiplying a quadratic expression with a linear expression was a polynomial expression of with an x^3 which means the degree = 3.

Definition: A **polynomial** of a single variable consists of a sum of whole number powers of that variable with integer or rational coefficients and constants.
The **degree** of a polynomial of a single variable is the largest power of the independent variable. (Note that the independent variable throughout this book is x or t.)

In the example above, we say that the quantity $(x + 7)$ is a **factor** of the new polynomial $h(x) = x^3 + 5x^2 - 5x + 63$ because $(x + 7)$ could be multiplied by another polynomial expression to create the new one. We multiplied an expression of degree = 1 by an expression of degree = 2 and obtained an expression of degree = 3. This was not coincidence, that 1 + 2 = 3.

Definition: The degree of the product of two or more polynomials is the sum of the degrees of each factor.

The above is not so much a definition as it is a fact. The reason we care about the degree of a polynomial is in the distinctiveness from one polynomial to another, and what the degree can tell us. We will compare four polynomial functions and make some observations about their prominent features. Before we do that we need another definition.

Definition: The **leading term** of a polynomial is the term with the highest order. If the polynomial has only one independent variable, the highest power term of that variable, along with its coefficient, is the **leading term**.

In general, polynomials belong in one of two primary categories with two distinct subtypes in each. In common terms, these categories track when something is increasing and when it is decreasing. We are interested in monitoring the value of an asset over time, principally. Also, we are interested in describing other behaviors, in that sometimes they are increasing, sometimes they are decreasing. It is this up/down/up pattern that is prominent with polynomials. Here are the ***four types*** for our observations.

Odd Degree with Domain: $(-\infty, \infty)$	**Even Degree with Domain:** $(-\infty, \infty)$
Leading Coefficient is **Positive** Graph is "Up/Down/Up" Increasing End Behaviors Range (of y values): $(-\infty, \infty)$	Leading Coefficient is **Positive** Graph is "Down/Up/Down/Up" Decreasing then Increasing End Behaviors Range: $[Minimum, \infty)$
Leading Coefficient is **Negative** Graph is "Down/Up/Down" Decreasing End Behaviors Range: $(\infty, -\infty)$	Leading Coefficient is **Negative** Graph is "Up/Down/Up/Down" Increasing then Decreasing End Behaviors Range: $(-\infty, Maximum]$

We will see a graph for each of these categories.

Conversation starter: Match the function with the graph below and decide which of the four types (odd/even degree, positive/negative leading term). Discuss end behaviors and other features worth noting.

1) $f(x) = -0.005x^4 - 0.03x^3 + 0.42x^2 + 1.72x - 4.8$
2) $f(x) = 0.2x^3 - 0.8x^2 - 4.2x$
3) $f(x) = -0.15x^3 - 0.15x^2 + 4.95x - 9.45$
4) $f(x) = 0.1x^4 + 0.2x^3 - 1.5x^2$

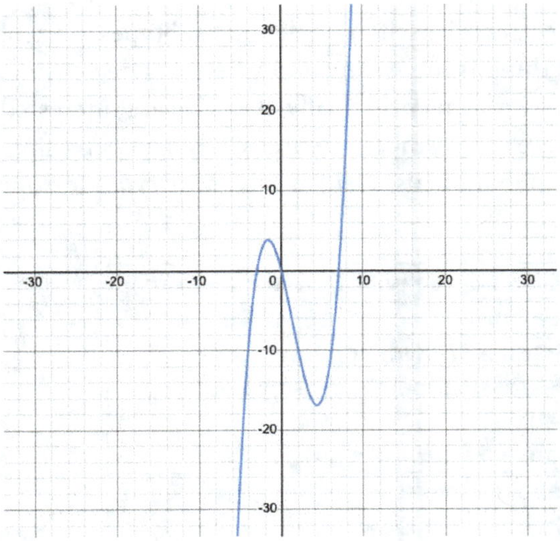

Graph A

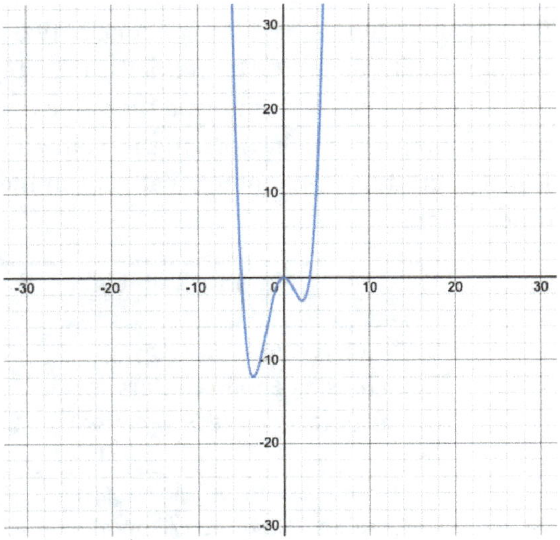

Graph B

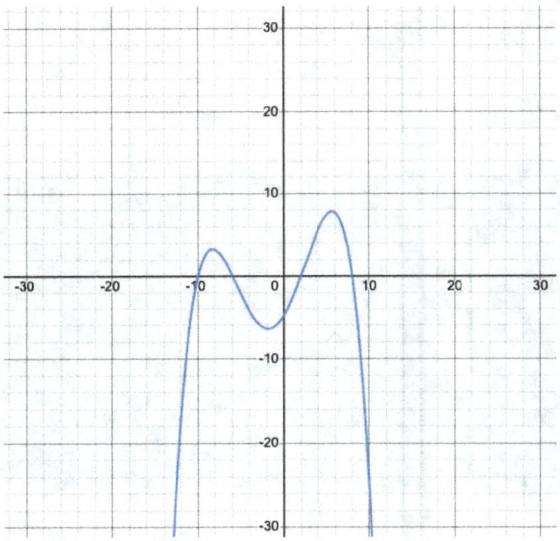

Graph C

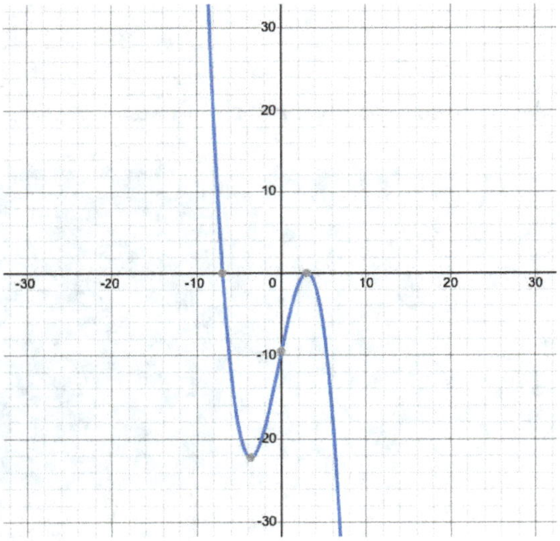

Graph D

In real world applications, the equations that represent a quantity of study will be limited to values of x that make sense. We are not so much interested in the outer parts of the function but focus on what occurs to the y values over a specific interval. The equation can be a distraction in these situations.

Here we see the graph of a polynomial which we are told is *valid for x in [0, 15]*. The points where something interesting occurs are all labeled. We will start by identifying intervals on which the function is increasing and decreasing.

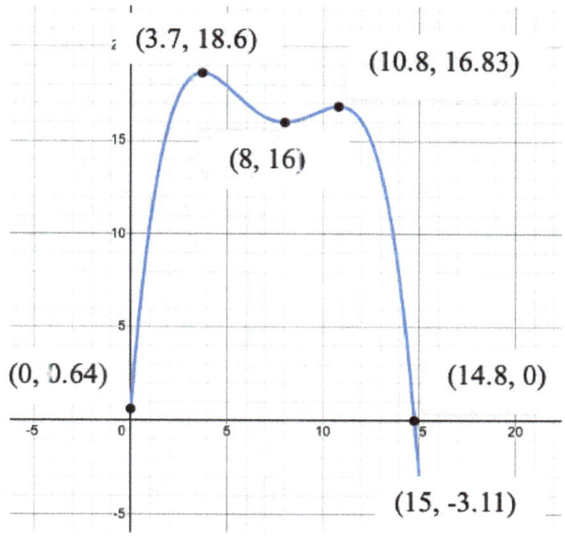

To do this, we will *ignore the y values* and focus only on the x coordinates for each point of interest. We see that the *graph is rising* for x between **0 and 3.7**, then *again* for x between **8 and 10.8**. The intervals on which the function is increasing are: *x in* {(0, 3.7) ∪ (8, 10.8)}

Similarly, we see the *graph is falling* for x between **3.7 and 8**, then *again* for x between **10.8 and 15**. The intervals on which the function is decreasing are: *x in* {(3.7, 8) ∪ (10.8, 15)}

The use of the ∪ symbol is like a conjunction. We can think of it as the word "and." What does this accomplish? Without having to rely on the graph, we can now pick a value of x at random: say, $x = 5$. The question is... is the function increasing or decreasing at x = 5? Answer: 5 is inside the interval (3.7, 8) which we identified as decreasing. Conclusion: The function is decreasing at $x = 5$.

When we were studying quadratic functions, we learned about the vertex. It was pointed out that the vertex of a quadratic is either a **minimum** or a **maximum** value on the function. These are what we call **extrema**. On a polynomial the word "vertex" does not apply, but we do have extrema. They occur at **endpoints** or **turning points** on the graph. In order from left to right on the graph, our first extreme value is the point (0, 0.64). It is a minimum because it is an endpoint, and the graph rises upward (increases) as x values go away from 0 toward 3.7. Not only is it a minimum, this point is also the y-intercept.

Here we see a description of the points of interest, identifying them as extrema where appropriate. If extrema, we often need to state if they are a maximum or minimum. Other points of interest are the y-intercept and any x-intercepts (of which there can be more than one).

Point of Interest	Reasons Why it is a Point of Interest
$(0, 0.64)$	Endpoint which means Extreme Value Minimum y-intercept which in some contexts represents a **fixed** starting value (cost/revenue/profit)
$(3.7, 18.6)$	Turning Point which means Extreme Value Maximum: 18.6 is at the upper end of the range, so this maximum is **absolute** (nothing else goes higher)
$(8, 16)$	Turning Point which means Extreme Value Minimum
$(10.8, 16.83)$	Turning Point which means Extreme Value Maximum
$(14.8, 0)$	x-intercept which means a so-called zero of the function; in some contexts, this is a "**break even**" point
$(15, -3.11)$	Endpoint which means Extreme Value Minimum: -3.11 is at the lowest end of the range, so this minimum is **absolute** (nothing else goes lower)

Try This: For the function $f(x) = 0.005x^3 - 0.275x^2 + 4.25x - 15$ and x in $[0, 32]$ use the tool of your choice to make a graph. Identify the seven (7) points of interest and state what it is that makes them points of interest (POI for brevity.)

Solution: The point (0, —15) is an endpoint, a minimum, an absolute minimum, and it is the y-intercept; (5, 0) is an x-intercept and potential break-even point; (11.069, 5.131) is a turning point, a maximum, an absolute maximum; (20, 0) is an x-intercept; (25.598, —2.538) is a turning point and a minimum; (30, 0) is an x-intercept; (32, 3.24) is an endpoint, and a maximum.

Section 5.4: Applications With Quadratic or Polynomial Models

In the context of revenue, cost, and profit in a business setting, it is helpful to understand what certain coefficients and constants mean, as well as interpreting points of interest and other mathematical features. We will explore meaning in quadratic and polynomial equations when seen in problems involving price, cost of doing business, revenue from sales, and profit.

Example: Suppose unit price for a product is (based on demand) $D(x) = -1.75x + 250$ where x is the number of units produced and sold. The business cost function is $C(x) = 750 + 0.8x^2$
A. What is the company's fixed cost?
B. Write the revenue equation where revenue, $R(x) = price \cdot x$
C. Write the profit equation, $P(x) = R(x) - C(x)$
D. What are the cost, revenue, and profit when 14 units are being made and sold?

Solution:

A. The fixed cost can be determined from either $C(x)$ or $P(x)$. It is the part of the function that is *constant*. Fixed cost is also the y-intercept. Here, that would be \$750.

B. No need to multiply through ( ). However, it is important to include ( ) around the expression for unit price. We will complete the multiplication because of what we are about to do in part C.

$$R(x) = x \cdot (-1.75x + 250)$$
$$-1.75x^2 + 250x$$

C. Profit equation is going to be a quadratic function. We may want to identify the "three values" *a, b, c* of the quadratic, so we will simplify the expression:

$$P(x) = x \cdot (-1.75x + 250) - (750 + 0.8x^2)$$
$$-1.75x^2 + 250x - 750 - 0.8x^2$$
$$-2.55x^2 + 250x - 750$$

D. For this we set x = 14. $C(14) = 750 + 0.8 \cdot 14^2 = \$906.80$ (cost)
$R(14) = -1.75 \cdot 14^2 + 250 \cdot 14 = \$3157.00$ (revenue)
$P(14) = \$3157.00 - \$906.80 = \$2250.20$ (profit)

Example: A company's profit from producing/selling x (in thousands) of a product is given by $P(x) = 0.2x^3 - 22x^2 + 720x - 6450$
A. What are the company's startup costs?
B. How many items does the company need to sell to break even?
C. How many items should the company sell to maximize profit?
D. At what point does the company start to lose money again, as production increases beyond 30,000?

Solution:
A. What are the company's startup costs? Startup cost and fixed cost are generally accepted to be the constant part of the function. We see it as a negative value because startup and fixed costs work against profit. Here we see the constant is \$6450.00.

B. How many items does the company need to sell to break even? As a point of interest on the graph of $P(x)$ this would be the first positive value of x where the graph goes from negative to positive (ie an x-intercept).

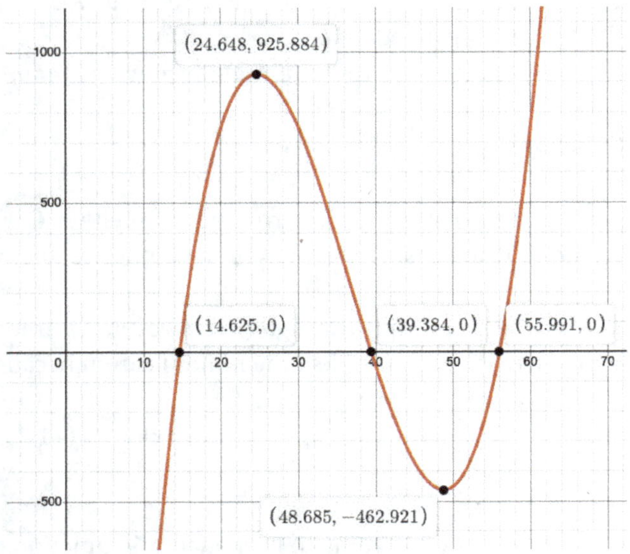

Profit is negative (meaning the company loses money) until x = 14.625. We are told x is in "thousands" so 14.625 is really 14,625 items.

That is what we call the *break-even point.*

C. From the graph we can also get the number of items produced and sold to *maximize profit.* That is another *point of interest* and is the first *turning point* (extremum). This occurs at x = 24.648 or 24,648 items.

D. Assuming this profit formula holds, we see profits beginning to go down again as x goes from the peak in part C. down to 48.685. The place where the company starts to lose money again is at the second x-intercept at x = 39.384 or 39,384 items.

This example combines concepts we have learned about linear and quadratic equations/models.

Example: A minor league baseball team stadium holds 30,000 spectators. With the ticket price at $8 the average attendance has been 14,000 fans. Once the ticket price dropped to $5, attendance rose to 19,000. Assume demand is linear. What ticket price would maximize revenue?

Solution:
Start by deciding what x and y will be. Then we will be entering the data in a spreadsheet application. Since demand is linear, both the x and y number patterns will be linear. We have said that multiplying two linear things results in a quadratic thing. We can see that play out in the spreadsheet with the data. Since the problem is asking to solve for "ticket price" we can make that "x." The numbers given to us in the problem are shaded in a gold color. It is ***vitally important*** that 5 and 19,000 are in the same row. Also, 8 and 14,000 are in the same row. Use a spreadsheet formula to calculate revenue. Headings are shaded blue. Shown here is exactly what is entered into each cell. In column C the result of the multiplication will display.

There is a potential disadvantage in answering the question this way. In the data we are missing values in between. Mathematically, we may not be as precise in our answer. But in practice sometimes precision is not as important as accuracy.

On the table, we can see that the $8 ticket price results in the highest revenue among those prices listed. We can feel better about the answer if we see a graph.

		A		B	C
1	To fill down more x values, continue to add 3. Subtract in the reverse direction.	x	To fill down more y values, subtract 5,000. Add in the reverse direction.	y	Revenue = $x \cdot y$
2		2		24,000	$= A2 * B2$
3		5		19,000	$= A3 * B3$
4		8		14,000	and so on...
5		11		9,000	
6		14		4,000	
7		17		-1,000	

Using the scatter plot with smooth lines and markers option, we can see that any whole dollar ticket price in either direction such as $7 or $9 would result in a decrease in revenue. If we wanted to get a more precise ticket price down to the nearest 10 cents, we would need the equation for revenue.

The equation for demand (y) is linear. We can use the two points (5, 19000) and (8, 14000) and the demand equation is $y = -1667x + 27333$

This means revenue is calculated by $R(x)=-1667x^2 + 27333x$

Use any preferred method to find the vertex and we see that precisely $8.20 ticket price will result in the highest revenue. By charging 20c more per ticket revenue can increase by $41.52, because at $8 we had a revenue of $112,000.

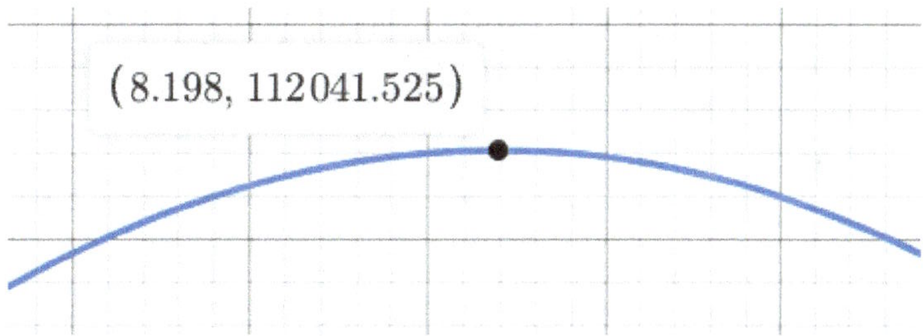

Conclusion: We could argue for the $8 ticket price or the $8.20 ticket price. Either answer would be correct from a certain point of view. $8 is accurate but not precise. It is accurate if rounding to the nearest whole $. $8.20 is both accurate and precise.

Practice Exercises

1. This infographic displays the difference between accuracy and precision. Write a few sentences about the difference between accuracy and precision, based on this and the conclusion at the end of Section 5.4, and what is more important?

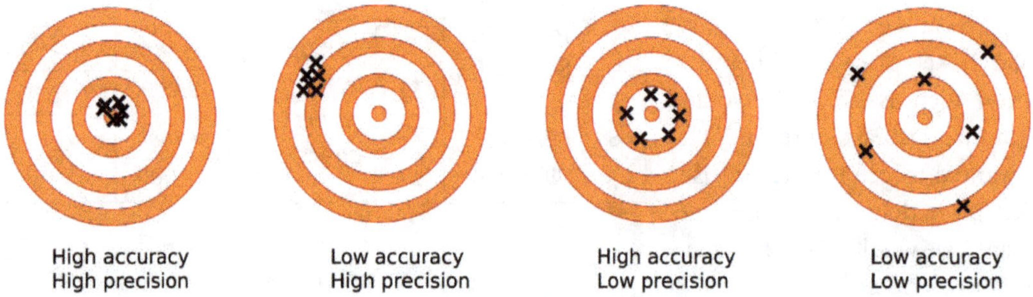

2. For each quadratic function, list the following points as ordered pairs: the vertex, the vertical intercept, and x-intercept(s) if any. Identify important features. (You may use any appropriate method.)
   a) $f(x) = x^2 - 4x - 21$
   b) $f(x) = -4x^2 + 14x - 7$

3. An oven temperature graph is shown over a certain thirteen-minute time interval and y is degrees over room temperature. So, if y = 0 the oven is at room temperature. It is valid only for x in [0,13]. There are five points of interest. Name them (estimate based on the graph) and describe what was going on with the oven temperature and when. What was the maximum temperature if room temperature is 70°F? On what intervals was the temperature increasing? decreasing?

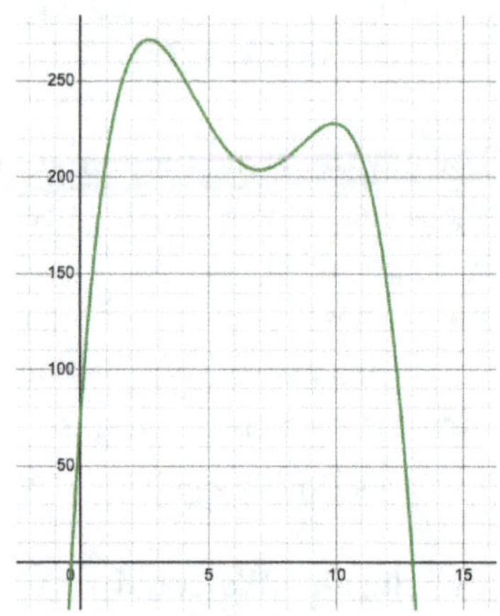

4. A company's profit when it sells x thousand items is predicted to be $P(x) = -2x^2 + 884x - 10000$. What is the company's startup cost? How many items does the company need to sell to break even? (round to the nearest whole number of x) How many items should the company sell to maximize profit?

5. A baseball team plays in a stadium that holds 54000 spectators. With the ticket price at \$9 the average attendance has been 21000. When the price dropped to \$6, the average attendance rose to 27000. Assume that attendance is linearly related to ticket price. What ticket price would maximize revenue? Choose a ticket price to the nearest 25c (or \$0.25).

   Suggestion: If using a spreadsheet to plot revenue over ticket price, once you have the trend-line equation and decide the maximum occurs between two whole number values of x, use the equation on 25c increments in between. Or graph the equation using a tool that will identify the appropriate spot that we need to answer the question.

6. In one of the spreadsheet labs for this course, you will create depreciation tables using different methods for depreciating an asset. Here we have data for depreciating an asset using a method called "Sum-of-digits."
   Use any three (3) of the (x,y) ordered pairs or all six (!) and find an equation $y = ax^2 + bx + c$ that fits the data with y = book value (in \$thousands) and x = year.

Depreciation of an Asset: Sum-of-Digits Method			
Original Cost	Salvage Value	Depreciable Base	Years (N)
6500	1000	5500	5
Current Year (x)	Book Value (in $thousands) (y)	Years Remaining	Depreciation Amount
0	6.5	5	
1	4.667	4	$1,833.33
2	3.2	3	$1,466.67
3	2.1	2	$1,100.00
4	1.367	1	$733.33
5	1	0	$366.67

6

Exponential and Logarithm Functions

Section 6.1: Exponential Functions and Models

In this chapter we will explore another type of relationship between two quantities that is important in business applications, and that is the exponential function. This function is required in financial operations that involve compound interest. When we studied the quadratic expression x^2, we discovered that it is nearly impossible to study the square of something without also studying its inverse operation, the square root. We made use of the square root when solving for x in $f(x) = ax^2 + bx + c$.

For that reason, it will be necessary for us to define and use the inverse of the exponential which is the logarithm. Let us take it one step at a time. We will start with a definition.

Definition: An exponential function $y = f(x)$ is a relationship between x and y that can be written as

$$f(x) = a \cdot b^x$$

where both a and b are constants. Notice that the variable x is now the power of the base b.

Let us see the difference between a linear pattern of numbers, a quadratic pattern, and an exponential pattern. We will start with a list of x from 1 to 10. Next to it will be a linear pattern on x, then a quadratic pattern, then an exponential one.

x	y = 2x	$y = x^2$	$y = 2^x$
0	0	0	1
1	2	1	2
2	4	4	4
3	6	9	8
4	8	16	16
5	10	25	32
6	12	36	64
7	14	49	128
8	16	64	256
9	18	81	512
10	20	100	1024

This comparison shows us that simply adding the same number repeatedly, while it does result in an increase, the increase is a bit like climbing stairs. Each step is just as high as the previous one.

In the next column if the increase Δy is the height of the next step, each step is getting higher in a linear pattern.

In the last column we see something curious. For x = 3 it looks as though x^2 is going to win. Then x = 4, and something a bit unexpected occurs: $4^2 = 2^4 = 16$! But if we look at $4 \cdot 4$ and rewrite each 4 as $2 \cdot 2$ the mystery is solved. But, then we get to x = 5, 6, and so on. By the time we get to x = 10 the y value on the 2^x column is 10 times that of the x^2 value, and 50 times that of the $2x$ value. If human population worked this way, our planet would have been overrun with people a long time ago. Let us see what this looks like on a graph.

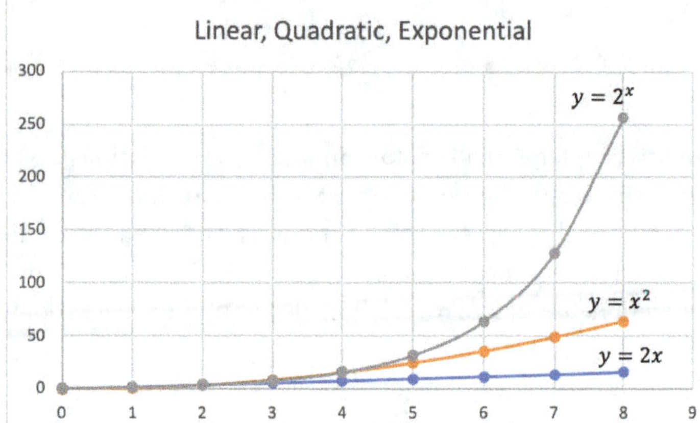

When we put these three functions on the same graph, the exponential growth makes the quadratic look like a straight line and the line looks basically flat. In fact, what if we change the base of the exponent… instead of 2, what if the base is 3, or 5, or 10?

Try This: Using your favorite graphing tool, make a graph of $y = 3^x$, $y = 5^x$, and $y = 10^x$. Let x be in [0, 8]. Put the (x, y) pairs in a table as well. Make a statement about the size of the base b and its effect on $y = b^x$.

Unlike quadratic patterns, we do not have symmetry with exponential functions. Also, the base b can be any real-valued number. There is no requirement that it be a whole number or integer. The base b can also be a decimal value smaller than 1. But it *does have to be positive.*

The important features of exponential functions involve whether the graph is increasing or decreasing and what is the *rate of increase/decrease.* We have an increasing pattern when the base b is larger than 1. We have a decreasing pattern when the base b is strictly between 0 and 1. When an exponential pattern is increasing, we say that we have "exponential growth". When an exponential pattern is decreasing, we say that we have "exponential decay" such as half-life of radioactive material, evaporation of a liquid, or the decomposition of organic matter. In business we often see exponential decay in the depreciation of an asset. The rate at which something is growing or decaying is at the heart of what it means to be exponential as a function. Let us unpack this. First let us establish some facts about exponential functions.

$y = a \cdot b^x$			
In all situations, a is the value of y when x = 0. In word problems we see it described as the "initial value" of a quantity that is growing/decaying. b can't be a negative number, though the exponent (x) can. The y-intercept of a function in this form is the point $(0, a)$			
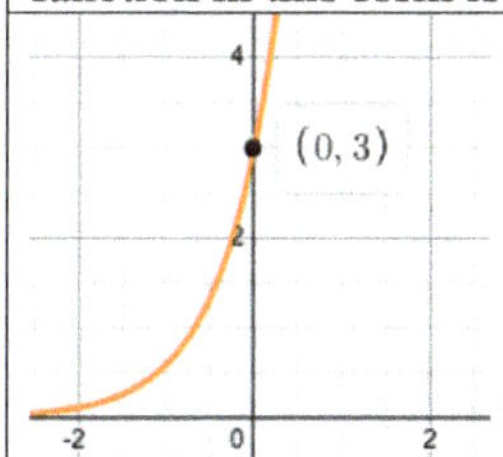	$a = 3$ $b > 1$	Exponential growth (appreciation)	Calculate the rate r of growth: $b = 1 + r$ $r = b - 1$
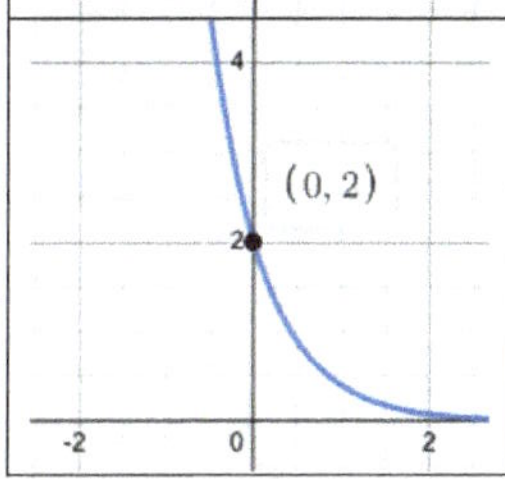	$a = 2$ $b < 1$	Exponential decay (depreciation)	Calculate the rate r of decay: $b = 1 - r$ $r = 1 - b$

Before we look at a few examples we need to talk about a special number of the base b. Everyone, or most everyone, knows about π. It measures half the circumference of a circle that has a radius of 1 unit. There is another number that we all should be familiar with, because it is associated with interest calculations of a certain type which we will explore later. The number is famously known as Euler's number, ***e***. When saying the name Euler aloud, it is pronounced ***oy'-ler***.

Definition: The natural number, ***e*** **≈ 2.718**, is a nonrepeating decimal that is the base for computing ***natural logarithms***. If $y = e^x$, its inverse relationship is $x = \ln y$. "ln" is referred to as the natural log of a number. ***e*** is known as Euler's number.

There is one other formula we need before we proceed. Since the growth or decay rate is tied to the base b, sometimes we are given an expression in terms of Euler's number, ***e***, which we then must convert to a number to the x power. Let us see what that looks like.

Definition: When there is a number in front of x in the exponent of an expression we can rewrite it as follows: Let e, m, b be given with $e \approx 2.718$ and b any positive number.

$e^{mx} = b^x$ if and only if $e^m = b$.

Example: Suppose $y = 35.4 \cdot e^{0.8x}$ is given. What is the rate of growth of y with respect to x? Use this to estimate the first 4 values of y for x = 0, 1, 2, 3.

Solution: When $y = a \cdot b^x$ we know that the *rate of growth* is $r = b - 1$. So, we need to find, or solve for, b. We will use the change of base formula.

$e^{0.8x} = b^x$ is the same as saying

$$e^{0.8} = b$$

We can use a calculator. Remember that e is special with its own key on a calculator. $e^{0.8} \approx 2.2255$ but we will round to 2.23.

$$b = 2.23$$
$$r = 2.23 - 1 = 1.23$$

To express that as a % we multiply r by 100%:

Conclusion: The rate of growth of y with respect to x is 123%.

To get the first four values of y, start with $a = 35.4$. Then multiply by $b = 1 + r = 2.23$ over and over until we have our first four values.

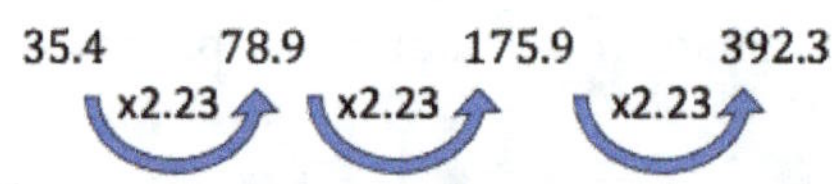

What does it mean that the rate of growth is 123%? And why is it not the same as b = 2.23? or 223%?

Let us suppose that y is measuring a rabbit population in thousands. So, y = 35.4 is really 35,400. Also, x is really time, in years. This gives our problem a bit more meaning. We estimate that the population went from 35.4 to about 78.9 in the first year. That is more than double. *Doubling* would mean that our base b would be 2. ***More than double*** means our base is a bit *larger than 2*. In this example, it was 2.23. The rate of growth, on the other hand, tells us by how much the population ***increased***.

If we ***subtract*** 78.9 – 35.4 = 43.5 we get the ***amount of increase***.

$$\text{rate of growth (\%)} = \frac{\text{amount of increase}}{\text{what we started with}} \cdot 100\%$$

and yes, the *numerator can be larger than the denominator*! Placement of the numbers is about what they represent, not their size.

$$\text{rate of growth (\%)} = (43.5 \div 35.4) \cdot 100\% \approx 123\%$$

Let us write a concluding statement about rabbit population in the first year.

Conclusion: We estimated that the rabbit population grew from 35,400 to 78,900 which was an *increase of* 123% over the first year. Each year we estimate that the population is *multiplied by* 2.23.

Try this: A bacteria is growing by the equation $y = 10 \cdot e^{0.35x}$ with x in minutes. What is the rate of growth of the bacteria? Use this to *estimate* how many bacteria cells will be present in 30 minutes.

Solution: The rate of growth, r, is given by $r = b - 1 - e^{0,35} \quad 1$

$$r = 0.419$$

$$0.419 \cdot 100\% = 41.9\%$$

In 30 minutes (x = 30) we have $y \approx 10 \cdot 1.419^{30} \approx 360{,}000$

Or, using the equation, $y = 10 \cdot e^{0.35*30} = 10 \cdot e^{10.5} \approx 360{,}000$

Estimation requires us to round our answer to two significant digits.

Example: We know that we had 400mL of liquid before evaporation began. After a day there was 380mL. If the amount of liquid is exponential, what is the evaporation rate? How much liquid will be left in two weeks? Write the equation for liquid as a function of time in days. In two weeks, have we lost more than half the liquid?

Solution: The rate of decay is given by $r = \frac{\textit{amount of decrease}}{\textit{what we started with}}$. No need for %.

$$r = \frac{400 - 380}{400} = \frac{20}{400} = 0.05$$

This answers the first question: Evaporation rate is 0.05.

To answer the two-week question, we can either first write an equation or we can use a table. The variable x is in days, so we need to continue the pattern of evaporation from x = 0 to x = 14. For this we need the multiplication factor, ***b***.

We are dealing with *decay* so $\mathbf{b = 1 - r = 0.95}$

x	y (amount)	How y was calculated:
0	400	<- given in the problem
1	380	<- given in the problem
2	361	= 0.95 · 380
3	342.95	= 0.95 · 361
4	325.80	= 0.95 · 342.95
5	309.51	
6	294.03	
7	279.33	
8	265.36	
9	252.09	
10	239.49	
11	227.52	
12	216.14	
13	205.33	
14	195.06	

The downside of using a table is that we rounded each time a new value of y was calculated. This will inevitably lead to a slight rounding error. Just how bad is the rounding error in this case?

Let us calculate y for x = 14 using the ***equation***... which in this situation is
(This is the answer to the 3rd question)

$$y = 400 \cdot 0.95^x$$

$$y(14) = 195.07 \approx 195$$

Using the table method our calculations were off by 0.01. We can only justify giving an answer of whole mL units anyway. This is why we included decimal values in our calculations until the end. Answer to second question: In two weeks, we will have 195 mL of liquid left.

Have we lost more than half the liquid?

Yes, since half the liquid was 200 mL and we lost 205 mL.

SECTION 6.2: LOGARITHM FUNCTIONS AND MODELS

Suppose we have a savings account in which we deposited \$500, and we know the *balance in the account* each year is given by the equation $y = 500 \cdot 1.03^x$ where x is in years. We want to know how long it would take for the balance to double. How would we go about doing that? Double \$500 is \$1000.

Solve $1000 = 500 \cdot 1.03^x$
Divide by 500:

$$2 = 1.03^x$$

Now what? How do we solve for x? For that we need to understand what the inverse operation of the exponent is. Not just understand it, but someone needs to name it. As it happens, we have many options not just one because just as there are many bases of exponential expressions, there is a logarithm for every base. Fortunately, we will not be exploring all of these. We can solve any problem using one of the more common bases. One is base-10, which is what our number system is based on. The base-10 logarithm is written $log\,x$ *or* $Log\,x$. On some calculators we see it displayed $log_{10}x$. The other is base-*e*. When Euler's number is the base, the associated logarithm function is called the *natural log*. We will use base-*e* since that is what spreadsheet software uses.

Definition: Given two numbers, x and y, and y is a positive number (this is necessary), and base b also positive, the following statements are *equivalent*:

$$y = b^x \text{ and } x = lny \div lnb$$

Secondly, $y = e^{ax}$ is equivalent to $x = lny \div a$

The only difference between the two equations seen in this definition is that one is in what we call exponential form, and the other is in logarithmic form. It all comes down to which quantity we are interested in finding.

Now we can answer the question of when will the savings double:

$2 = 1.03^x$ becomes $x = ln2 \div ln1.03 = 0.69315 \div 0.02956 = 23.45$

We can expect to double our initial deposit in about 23 ½ years, using the equation given at the start of this topic.

We will see that formula for x again in applications of compound interest.

In a previous chapter, we saw that inverse operations can be used to create new functions out of existing ones. Let us recall one of the more common pairs of inverse functions, that is $f(x) = x^2$ and $g(x) = \sqrt{x}$. In this case, x must be 0 or a positive number. For every (x,y) ordered pair that belongs to $f(x)$ we reverse the order for $g(x)$. To be specific, (2, 4) belongs to $f(x)$ but (4, 2) belongs to $g(x)$. In a similar way, we now have another pair of inverse functions with the exponential and the logarithmic types. We see how the ordered pairs reverse themselves on the graph of $f(x) = e^x$ and $g(x) = ln\ x$.

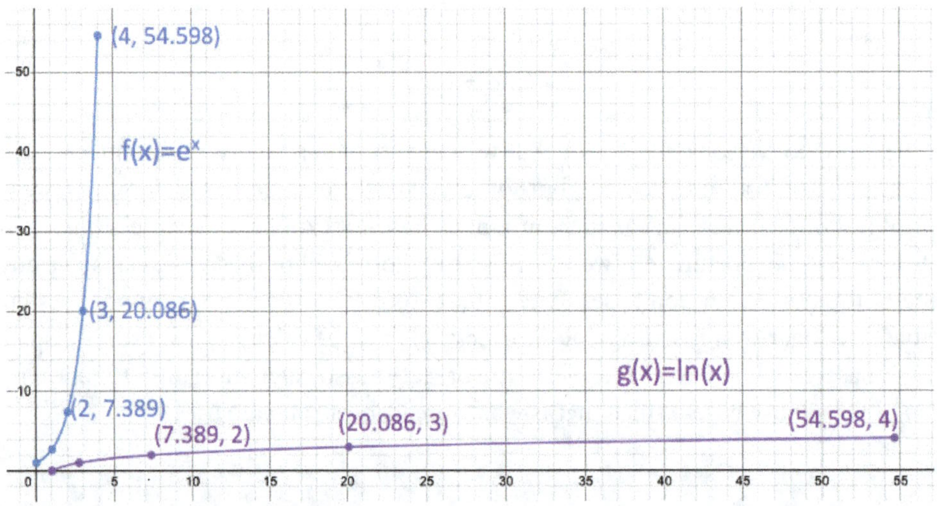

Try This: Using a graphing tool of your choice, make a graph of $y = e^x$ using integer values of x in [−3, 3] and x = e.
Graph $y = ln\ (x)$ using values of x in [0.2, 20]. For the natural log, let x = 0.2, 0.4, 0.6, 0.8, 1, e, 5, 10, e^e, 20.
What is e^e? [Hint: It is a bit more than 15 but less than 15.2]
Locate the point (e, e^e) on the graph of $y = e^x$. Now locate the point (e^e, e) on the graph of $y = ln\ (x)$

Solution: Both functions are shown on the same graph. A few points are labeled, including the *decimal approximations* for (e, e^e) and (e^e, e). This means we have $e^e \approx 15.154$. Note how (x, y) on one graph becomes (y, x) on the other.

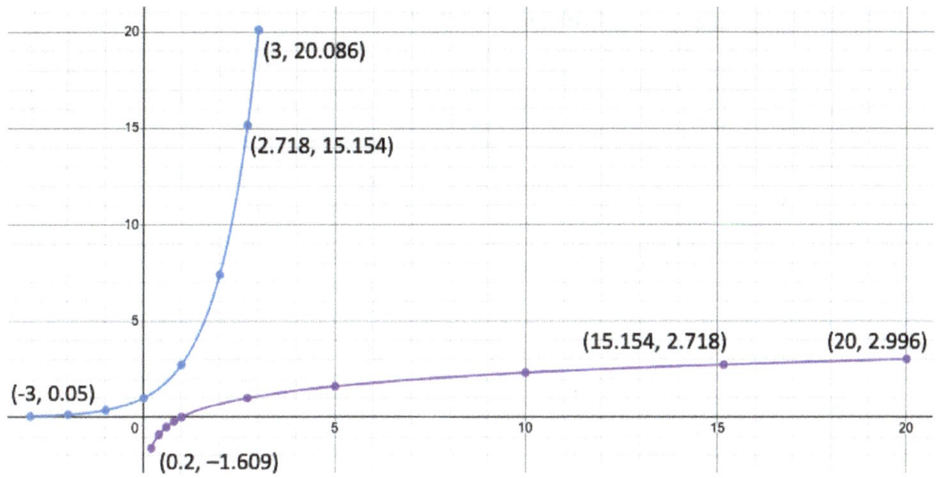

Now that we have a basic understanding of exponents and logarithms as inverses of exponents, we can begin to use them to solve problems.

Example: For x in years after a certain disease was discovered, the number of patients testing positive for a certain STD has the following data: (8, 50), (20, 300), (35, 2860), and (52, 36600). Assume an exponential pattern. Use a spreadsheet to make a scatterplot of the data and write the equation that best fits. Then make a prediction for when the number of patients reached 2100.

Solution: Entering the data into a spreadsheet in tabular format, we have two columns of numbers which we will type the headings "x" and "y" over the appropriate lists.

A scatter plot is made and trendline is given by the equation

$$y = 15 \cdot e^{0.15x}$$

	A	B
1	x	y
2	8	50
3	20	300
4	35	2860
5	52	36600

Note that the numbers are rounded because the data does not support more than 2 significant figures.

The graph of the data with trendline is this:

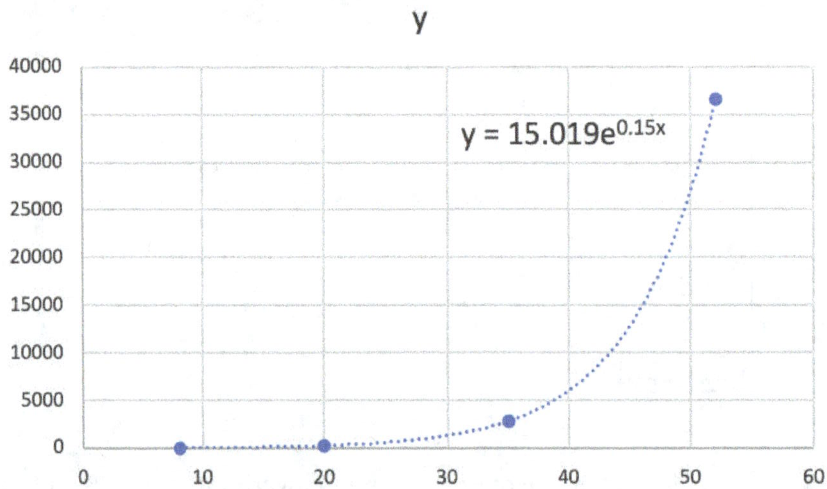

The data does in fact support the exponential model assumption.

This means at the time of discovery, there were approximately 15 patients with the disease.

The question asks when the number of patients reached 2100. In terms of our model, this means we solve for x and put 2100 in for y.

$$2100 = 15 \cdot e^{0.15x}$$

First divide by 15:

$$2100 \div 15 = 140$$

$$140 = e^{0.15x}$$

Now restate for x:

$$x = ln140 \div 0.15 \approx 33$$

We wait until the end to do any rounding. It took about 33 years after discovery for the disease to reach a confirmed 2100 patients.

SECTION 6.3: ASSET DEPRECIATION

Now that we have learned about the most essential functions in business and personal finance we can explore a topic that is critical to business finance. That is the topic of physical asset depreciation. A physical asset is something that has a use or function as part of the day-to-day business operations. These are not consumable goods like paper and pencils. Anything the business has purchased or built for business use and not for resale is potentially a physical asset.[1]

In this topic we will see three of the function types that we have studied. Let us see an overview of each type here.

Linear	Quadratic	Exponential Decay
$y = x$ 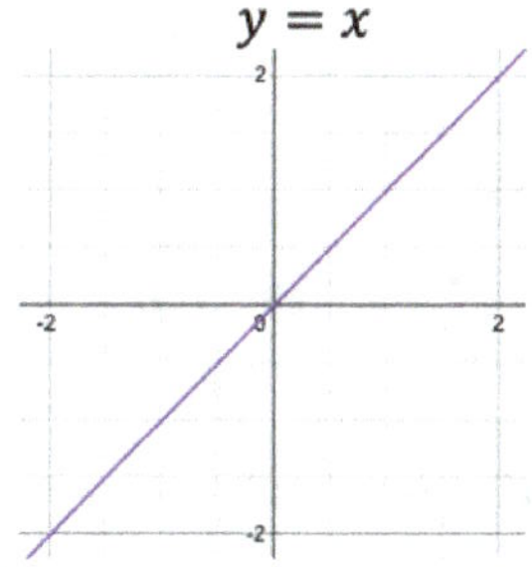	$y = x^2$ 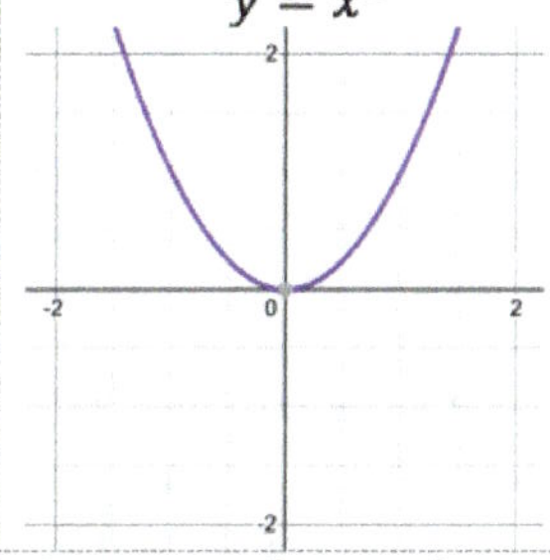	$y = 0.5^x$ 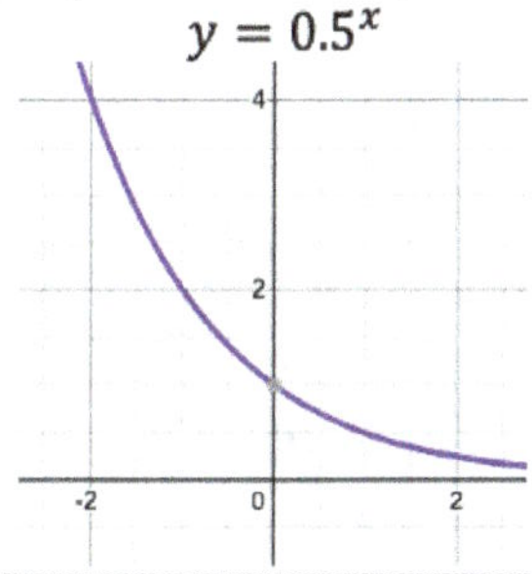
domain x: $(-\infty, \infty)$ range y: $(-\infty, \infty)$	domain x: $(-\infty, \infty)$ range y: $[0, \infty)$	domain x: $(-\infty, \infty)$ range y: $(0, \infty)$

What does it mean for something to depreciate? Physical assets tend to decline in value over time (exceptions might be works of art or a vintage car). These assets have a limited useful life and eventually need to be replaced, repaired, or restored. Depreciation is a way to measure how much of an asset's value has been lost—or spent—each year or part of a year.

Conversation starter: What are some reasons businesses use depreciation to record the cost of an asset? Hint: Corporate taxes may have something to do with it. Research balance sheets and income statements for some more clues.

1. Tuovila, Alicia. "Depreciation: Definition and Types, With Calculation Examples." *Corporate Finance: Accounting*, Investopedia, 31 October 2023, https://www.investopedia.com/terms/d/depreciation.asp

There is some shorthand, abbreviations of special terms we will be using when introducing formulas for calculating depreciation. Let us list the terms and definitions.

OC = original cost (what the asset cost as "new")
SV = salvage value (what the asset will be worth at the end of its useful lifespan)
OC–SV = depreciable base (the total cost of the asset over its lifespan)
BV = book value, or "carrying value" (previous ***BV*** – depreciation amount)
N = life span in years
X = how much useful life (in years) ***remains*** (including the current year)
Σ = the sum (by adding) all useful years $\Sigma = N \cdot (N + 1) \div 2$
(for example, if ***N*** = 10 then $\Sigma = 1 + 2 + 3 + \ldots + 10 = {}^{10\times11}/_2$)

WAYS TO CALCULATE DEPRECIATION

Straight-line method	***Sum-of-Digits method***	***Declining method***	***Double Declining method***
To ***calculate the amount of depreciation***, use these formulas			
$(OC - SV) \div N$	$(OC - SV) \times X \div \Sigma$	$BV \div N$	$2 \times BV \div N$
A graph of **Book Value (y)** over **time (x in years)** reveals what function/pattern?			
Linear	*Quadratic*	*Exponential (decay)*	*Exponential (decay)*
$y = mx + b$ $m = \frac{\Delta y}{\Delta x}$ $= \frac{OC - SV}{N}$ $b = OC$	$y = ax^2 + bx + c$ $a = (OC - SV) \div (2 \cdot \Sigma)$ $b = -\frac{(OC - SV) \cdot (2 \cdot \Sigma + N^2)}{2 \cdot N \cdot \Sigma}$ $c = OC$	$y = a \cdot b^x$ $a = OC$ $b = 1 - \frac{1}{N}$	$y = a \cdot b^x$ $a = OC$ $b = 1 - \frac{2}{N}$

Writing the model, or equation, for the book value for a specified value of x is not our primary goal. The fact that book value can be linear, quadratic, or exponential over time is meant for comparison and for understanding how depreciation changes from one method to another. We want to create a depreciation schedule that shows what the depreciation amount is each year and the book value at the end of each year that carries forward for the next year's calculations.

Example: Assume CMYK Interior Painters buys a \$23,000 truck to assist in the performing of residential interior painting work, and the business owner creates a new truck asset on the books with a value of \$23,000. Due to factors such as the total mileage and service history, the truck is assigned a *useful life of five years*. Salvage value is the remaining value of the asset at the end of its useful life. CMYK decides to depreciate the asset using the straight-line method with a $3,000 salvage value. The ***depreciable base*** is the $23,000 original cost minus the $3,000 salvage value, or $OC - SV = \$20,000$.

Using the formula: annual depreciation = $20,000 divided by 5, or $4,000 (per year). The **end-of-year book value** of the truck changes each year because of the additional depreciation in value that is posted annually. The truck's ***book value (BV)*** is seen in this table:

Year	Depreciation Amount (Expense)	Accumulated Depreciation	End-of-Year Book Value
0	$(OC - SV) \div N$		Cost = $23,000
1	4,000	4,000	19,000
2	4,000	8,000	15,000
3	4,000	12,000	11,000
4	4,000	16,000	7,000
5 = N	4,000	20,000	3,000 = SV

This is what we mean by a depreciation schedule. We have a spreadsheet activity associated with this topic that gives us more practice. For now, let us create a depreciation schedule using all four methods given this example.

Example: You decide to start a 3D-printing business to make custom PVC fittings. The printer costs $29,000 brand new. The manufacturer claims that it has an 8-year life span if it is being used 11 hours/day every day, with regular recommended service. The salvage value of the printer is listed as $2,900. Create an 8-year depreciation schedule using all four methods presented.

Note: Both the declining method and double declining method are used if the salvage value is not used to calculate depreciation, and the remaining value of the printer is based on an ***exponential decay*** model.

Under these two depreciation models the BV will never get to zero. But the asset loses more of its value in the first year than in the second, and so on. If the salvage value is known and we are using one of the declining methods, we need to be careful not to let the book value fall below the salvage value. Also, N = 8.

	Declining Method		**Double Declining Method**	
Year	Depreciation Amount	Book Value (BV)	Depreciation Amount	Book Value (BV)
0	$BV \div N$	Cost = 29,000.00	$2 \times BV \div N$	Cost = 29,000.00
1	3,625.00	25,375.00	7,250.00	21,750.00
2	3,171.88		5,437.50	
3				
4				
5				
6				
7				
8				

It is left up to the reader to complete the rest of the table. Now we will compare these results with the schedule created when using the straight-line and sum-of-digits methods. For these we will need to know the salvage value and use it in the calculations. We will have four depreciation schedules for comparison when done.

	Straight-line Method			**Sum-of-Digits Method**	
	$OC - SV = 29,000 - 2,900 = 26,100$			$\Sigma = 8 \times 9 \div 2 = 36$	
Year	Depreciation Amount	Book Value (BV)	X	Depreciation Amount	Book Value (BV)
0	$(OC - SV) \div N$	Cost = 29,000.00		$(OC - SV) \times X \div \Sigma$	Cost = 29,000.00
1	3,262.50	25,737.50	8	5,800.00	23,200.00
2	3,262.50	22,475.00	7	5,075.00	18,125.00
3			6	4,350.00	
4			5	3,625.00	
5			4		
6			3		
7			2		
8			1		

Again, the first few rows are shown. It is left to the reader to complete the rest of the table. Be ready to talk about the differences between these approaches.

Conversation starters:

What assumptions do you think are made? If the printer becomes less productive as time goes on, resulting in 5% less operating time each year from one year to the next, and as a result income also decreases by 5% of the previous year's income which model makes the most sense from a cost-income perspective?

Which method depreciates the most in the first year?

Do any of the methods end with a book value greater than the salvage value?

The book value can never get lower than the salvage value. Did that happen with any of these methods?

Try This: Using a spreadsheet application, enter two columns of numbers. Let x be the year after purchase and let y be the book value. Make a scatter plot with smooth lines and add a trendline for each of the four methods. One will be a linear equation, another will be quadratic, and the other two will be exponential (decay). What are the equations for each?

PRACTICE EXERCISES

1. A vehicle purchased for $22,400 depreciates at a rate of 8%. Determine the approximate value of the vehicle 14 years after purchase. Round to the nearest whole dollar. [Hint: 8% is the rate of decay.]

2. Which equation is a match for which graph? Graphs are labeled O, K, G, R, B.

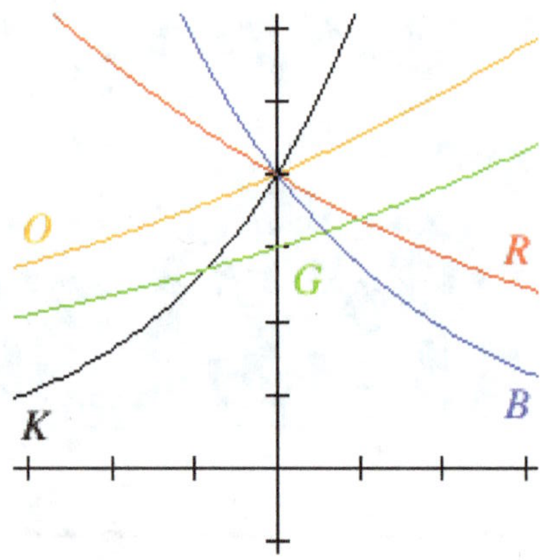

   a. $y = 4 \cdot 0.85^x$
   b. $y = 4 \cdot 1.09^x$
   c. $y = 4 \cdot 0.70^x$
   d. $y = 4 \cdot 1.80^x$
   e. $y = 3 \cdot 1.09^x$

3. The balance at any time in a savings account is given by the equation $A = 5000 \cdot 1.007^{12x}$ with x measuring time in years. How much will be in the account in 15 years? How long will it take for the amount to double?

4. Solve for t: $400(1.24)^t = 22{,}160$

5. A loan accrues interest with an annual growth rate of 5% and the amount borrowed (initial value) is $12,000. Write an exponential equation that describes the value as it grows. The borrower will pay back the balance in full at the end of 4 years. How much will the borrower need to pay back? How much of that is in addition to what was borrowed?

6. A certain radioactive material decays by 2.2% each year. Find the half-life of the substance (time it takes for the substance to go from a to ½ a. Round to two decimal places.

7. A camera with a value of $20,000 has a life expectancy of 20 years. Its salvage value will be $4,000. What % of the depreciable base will be lost each year under the straight-line method? [Convert from fraction to %]

8. A photocopier has a value of $8,000 and a life of 10 years. What is the percentage depreciation of the book value each year using the double declining method? If we use the sum-of-digits method instead (with a salvage value of $900) compare the book values at year 3.

7 The Mathematics of Finance – Interest

Section 7.1: Simple and Compound Interest

Money can be borrowed when needed to pay for something, or it can be invested when saving for the future. Both situations involve a transaction between a borrower and a lender, or an investor and an investment manager (like a bank or credit union). Both situations involve a promise of a return on the investment. In time value of money scenarios, $1.00 is worth more now than it will be in the future. The reason for this is the buying power of $1. It buys more goods/services now than it will in several years' time. In any society that uses currency for a means of exchange, there will be people who are lenders and people who are borrowers. Some people do both. As a borrower, an individual may be interested in a loan. The lender is willing to loan money but *charges a fee* which *translates as interest* on the amount of the loan. What is interest and how does it work?

VectorMine/Shutterstock.com

Here is a simple example to illustrate this concept. Sam needs \$30 now. Pendo has \$30 to loan to Sam, but Pendo was going to buy some shoes. Not needing the shoes right now, she knows that one month from now the shoes will cost somewhere between \$28 and \$33.

There is a certain amount of uncertainty so Pendo assumes the price will be at the upper end of the estimate. She agrees to loan money to Sam with the understanding that Sam will pay back \$33 one month from now. The concept here is this. Sam is not just borrowing \$30. They are borrowing the future purchase power of \$30, which is a pair of shoes to Pendo.

The difference between the amount of the loan, \$30, and the amount to be paid back, \$33, is called interest \$33 –\$30 = \$3. The interest portion of what is paid back divided by the loan amount × 100% is called the **interest rate.** $(3 \div 30) \times 100\% = 10\%$. This was a short-term interest rate, so we call it **simple one-time interest rate**, and $I = P \cdot r = 30 \cdot 0.10 = \$3.00$.

Sam will pay back the full amount, so the **term** or length of the loan is one month. This is the agreed-upon length of time Sam has, after which they will owe Pendo \$33.

The amount borrowed or deposited is called a lump sum. The terms of the loan or investment include how much time until it ***matures*** (in years) and a fixed interest rate is applied to the lump sum, which can be calculated in advance. Certificates of deposit (CDs) are examples of an investment that matures. In a fixed amount of time, the bank that sold the certificate returns money to the investor and the CD is completed.

Definition: A lump sum amount that is borrowed or invested is called the **present value**, or **principal**, which will be designated **P**. The **future value**, or **accrued value** is designated **A**. The difference between A and P is the amount of interest, **I**.

$$I = A - P$$

$$\text{or } A = P + I$$

There are basically two ways interest is calculated. If the interest is calculated on the principal alone without being recalculated every time the balance changes, we call this simple interest. When interest gets recalculated at regular intervals on the new balance, we call this compound interest.

Definition: Simple interest is the fee on a cash-valued asset calculated in advance and paid in full at maturity or in equal payments until maturity. $I = P \cdot r \cdot t$ and $A = P + I$ can be rewritten as $A = P(1 + rt)$

If we were solving for P, we have $P = A \div (1 + rt) = \frac{A}{(1 + rt)}$

For consistency, we will assume ***r*** is an *annual interest rate* in situations that involve a period of at least one year.
I is the amount of interest.
A is the end amount (future value).
P is the lump sum amount (principal).
t is time in years.

Anyone who votes in local and state elections in the United States is familiar with ballot questions in which cities and states ask voters permission to issue a bond for the purposes of construction projects or other community project. These types of bonds are referred to as municipal bonds.

Example: Suppose your town/city is going to build a new high school, and issues bonds to raise the money. The amount they need to raise is \$43.2 million after a grant provides them with half the building cost. Bonds sell for \$5000 with a promise to pay 5% interest annually that matures in 8 years. The purchaser will get the interest in equal payments twice a year for 8 years. How much interest will be earned, and what will the purchaser receive every 6 months?

Solution: This is a simple interest situation because the interest is calculated up front and the purchaser is going to receive the interest in equal payments until the bond matures. We calculate the total amount of interest, and then divide it by because 2 payments per year for 8 years is 16 payments.

$$I = 5000 \cdot 0.05 \cdot 8 = 2000$$

This answers the question of how much interest will be earned.

Every 6 months the purchaser will receive $2000 \div 16 = \$125$

At the end of 8 years the purchaser also receives the original \$5000.

Definition: The **simple interest formula** can be rewritten depending on what quantity we are solving for. $I = P \cdot r \cdot t = Prt$ is what we use when solving for interest amount. Make sure to use ( ) when dividing by a quantity! Order of operations matters. If the amount of interest is known, we can solve for *P*, *r*, or *t* using *I*.

Solving for P: $P = I \div (r \cdot t) = \frac{I}{rt}$

Solving for r: $r = I \div (P \cdot t) = \frac{I}{Pt}$

Solving for t: $t = I \div (P \cdot r) = \frac{I}{Pr}$

Short term loans can seem like a good deal, and they can be. But they can end up costing more than consumer credit cards. It is always a good idea to shop for ways to borrow cash when needed and to pay balances off as soon as possible. Keeping a credit card balance longer than a year can start a financial spiral that can be difficult to escape.

Example: Jorge needs $750 to finance some extra equipment for his lawn care business. He has two options:

Option 1: A local credit union has offered Jorge a 3-month loan of $750. He must pay $12/month for the first 2 months, then $760 the 3rd month.

Option 2: A major bank has offered Jorge a business revolving credit account with no fee. The APR is 19% and he is approved for $750 credit.

Which has the better interest rate? Is that necessarily the better option? Why or why not?

Solution: Figure out which has the better interest rate first. For Option 1, the amount borrowed is P = $750. The amount of interest is the extra he pays. Since the total of his payments is A = 12 + 12 + 760 = 784, then I = A – P = $34. Also, we need the annual interest rate. Time (t) is **3 months = 3/12 year = 0.25 year**.

Option 1 interest rate (r) is $\frac{I}{P \cdot t} = 34 \div (750 \cdot 0.25) \times 100\% = 18.133\%$

Option 2 interest rate (r) is APR = 19%

Option 1 has the better interest rate. But it is not necessarily the better option.

Here are some factors to consider:

1) With a revolving credit account, Jorge has flexibility in paying off the balance as quickly or slowly as needed without harming his credit rating, if he can make regular minimum payments. If flexibility is most important, then Option 2 may be the better choice.
2) Maybe Jorge already has a revolving credit account and does not need/want another one.
3) Perhaps Jorge wants to establish himself with the local credit union and there is a potential for future business opportunities. Good local business relationships can help Jorge's own business to grow by reputation.
4) There may be tax benefits from choosing the type of loan in Option 1 over the type of credit situation in Option 2. It is a good idea to check with a tax accountant about borrowing and corporate taxes.

Try This: A loan company charges $11 for a loan of $500 for one month. What is the APR for this loan?

Solution: The APR is $(11 \times 12 \div 500) \times 100\% = 26.4\%$

Most long-term loans and savings accounts involve **compound interest**. There can still be a lump sum amount that is borrowed or deposited, but the interest is compounded over time. Before we see the formulas for this, let us see what happens to $1 invested with r % interest compounded annually. It may suggest a formula.

Time Past	Balance Carried Forward From Previous Row	Calculate Interest (Multiply by r)	New Balance (Add Columns 2 and 3)
1	Start with: $1	$1 \cdot r = r$	$1 + r = (1 + r) \cdot 1$
2	$(1 + r) \cdot 1$	$(1 + r) \cdot r$	$(1 + r) \cdot 1 + (1 + r) \cdot r = (1 + r) \cdot (1 + r) = (1 + r)^2$
3	$(1 + r)^2 \cdot 1$	$(1 + r)^2 \cdot r$	$(1 + r)^2 \cdot 1 + (1 + r)^2 \cdot r = (1 + r)^2 \cdot (1 + r) = (1 + r)^3$
4	$(1 + r)^3 \cdot 1$	$(1 + r)^3 \cdot r$	$(1 + r)^3 \cdot 1 + (1 + r)^3 \cdot r = (1 + r)^3 \cdot (1 + r) = (1 + r)^4$

The pattern we see emerging is that each year the new balance is found by taking the previous balance and multiplying it by (1 + r). This is curious because it should remind us of exponential functions. We had said that in an exponential pattern, the base b is equal to 1 + r when there is exponential growth. The number r represented the rate of growth. And that is exactly what we have.

Definition: The future value of a monetary asset in which interest is compounded annually is given by

$$A = P \cdot (1 + r)^t$$

If the interest rate, r, is an annual interest rate but the number of compounding periods is more than once per year, then we need to adjust the formula. Let k = the number of compounding periods in a year. Then our formula becomes

$$A = P \cdot (1 + r \div k)^{kt}$$

kt is how many times interest is accrued in t years
r/k is the adjusted (periodic) interest rate when the annual rate is cut into k-sized portions.

We should also become familiar with words used to describe the most common compounding rates. Biannually, semiannually, quarterly, monthly, and daily all refer to the frequency interest is calculated. The words biannual and semiannual have come to mean the same thing (twice a year) but biannual can also mean "every two years" just like bicentennial was the 200th year of an event. We will summarize them and their respective k values.

Definition: Here are the frequencies of compounding interest and the corresponding value of k

Annually means $k = 1$
Semiannually/Biannually means $k = 2$
Quarterly means $k = 4$
Bimonthly means k = 6
Monthly means $k = 12$
Biweekly means $k = 26$
Weekly means $k = 52$
Daily means $k = 365$

It may be helpful to solve a couple of concrete examples, and solutions will be given as if using a scientific or graphing calculator as well as using spreadsheet as a calculator for problems involving compound interest. We will start with annual compound interest and move from there to an example that involves k.

Example: A high-yield savings account offers 5.25% interest compounded annually on a minimum balance of $2500. If a person deposits $3000 and lets the account earn interest for 20 years, how much will be in the account? How much interest was earned?

Solution: In reality, no high-yield savings account or other investment can offer a guarantee on the interest. But let us assume that we have had this account for 20 years with the interest rate going up and down. So, we will assume that the balance in 20 years would be consistent with a 5.25% fixed interest rate.

Method 1: On a calculator with an exponent key

Look for a key or button on the calculator like one of these:

[^] [y^x] [$x^{\blacksquare}$] or [x^y]

Each of these buttons does the same thing to a number.

The rate is 5.25% which gets converted to the decimal value 0.0525. Time is 20, P is 3000. To calculate $P \cdot (1 + r)^t$ we will not assume a calculator with a window that displays actual mathematical expressions. This problem can be done on any calculator with an exponent key, one operation at a time without the need to round as we go. *Not rounding is important*, because rounding anything before the end will lead to errors. [y^x] can be any of the exponent keys going forward.

Key the following in this exact order:

1 [+] 0.0525 [=], then [y^x] 20 [=], then [×] 3000 [=].

At each step of the process, you see the result of the operation that was entered. On the display at the end should be 8347.632954366...
Our answer should be given to the nearest cent. $8347.63

To solve for A using compound interest (with k = 1) our formula looks like this in calculator terms. Input the appropriate numbers for r, t, and P.

1 [+] r [=], then [y^x] t [=], then [×] P

Method 2: Spreadsheet Calculation (Repeatable)

This is the preferred method if proficiency with spreadsheet software is one of the goals. The suggestion is to include a banner at the top of the sheet explaining what the sheet does. Then set up columns for each variable or each component that will be needed to input into the formula, as well as columns for answers/outputs. Anyone familiar with compound interest would see this and understand both what it is for, and what each column shaded in blue will answer.

	A	B	C	D	E	F	G	H	I
1	Time Value of Money - Simple and Compound Interest - Using the spreadsheet like a calculator, find the future value of an account when a lump sum deposit is made and interest is calculated over time with different compounding options.								
2				Simple	Compound 1x per year	Compound 2x per year	Compound 4x per year	Compound 12x per year	Compound 365x per year
3	*r*	*P*	*t*	*A1*	*A2*	*A3*	*A4*	*A5*	*A6*
4				$0.00	$0.00	$0.00	$0.00	$0.00	$0.00

The cells highlighted in gold represent the parameters of the problem. A parameter is a necessary piece of information required to be input by hand. Those cells are currently blank. In columns D through I we will input the appropriate formulas. It may be interesting to see the difference in outcomes when interest is compounded more frequently versus less frequently.

The built-in formula for calculating the future value of a financial asset with compounding interest is called the FV() formula. This formula has space for up to 5 inputs, which we will relate to this problem we are solving.

The FV function as seen when we search for it shows up as this:

FV(rate,nper,pmt,[pv],[type]) <-- leave blank

This will give us A, the future value of the account. Inside the brackets ( ) we will input the appropriate cell references along with either multiplying or dividing by k. Assume cell locations as seen in the image given above. pmt and [type] are left blank intentionally because they do not apply.

$$rate = r \div k = {}^{A4}/_{k}$$
$$nper = t \times k = C4 * k$$
$$[pv] = -P = -B4$$

It is up to the individual to use values for k that are appropriate in each column. Here we can see exactly what was entered in column H, cell H4, for interest **compounded monthly, k = 12**. Note the placement of commas with a double ,, between the number of periods and the present value. We simply enter the values from our problem into cells A4, B4, and C4.

In cell A4, we type 5.25%. in cell B4 we type 3000. In cell C4 we type 20.
Now enter this into cell H4:

=FV(A4/12,C4*12,,-B4,)

For this problem we are solving, k = 1. We enter this into column E, in cell E4.

```
=FV(A4,C4,,-B4,)
```

We see that in 20 years there will be $8347.63 in the account.

Adjust the value of k in the other columns and we now have a spreadsheet calculator for future value of a financial asset when there is a single lump sum payment. Lastly, the future value for simple interest does not use a built-in function. We calculate as seen here.

$$A = P + P \times r \times t$$

```
=B4+A4*B4*C4
```

We have notably different results for different compounding types, and a stark difference over simple interest, because of the length of time.

			Simple	Compound 1x per year	Compound 2x per year	Compound 4x per year	Compound 12x per year	Compound 365x per year
r	*P*	*t*	*A1*	*A2*	*A3*	*A4*	*A5*	*A6*
5.25%	3000	20	$6,150.00	$8,347.63	$8,457.62	$8,514.59	$8,553.34	$8,572.31

Let us take a closer look at the difference compounding makes.

Example: Assume an annual interest rate of 5% and initial deposit of $1000. Make a table and graph of simple interest versus monthly compound interest for 35 years. Approximately when did each account double in value? What type of model best describes each pattern?

Solution: For an interest rate of 5% and a starting balance of $1000, we can use a spreadsheet to calculate the balance over 35 years. We will start by incrementing time by about 3 years, then after 20 we will increment by 5 years. This will allow us to see a general pattern. We will then tweak values of t to answer the doubling question, as needed.

Years	Simple	Compound 12x per year
t	*A1*	*A3*
0	$1,000.00	$1,000.00
3	$1,150.00	$1,161.47
6	$1,300.00	$1,349.02
9	$1,450.00	$1,566.85
12	$1,600.00	$1,819.85
14	$1,700.00	$2,010.83
17	$1,850.00	$2,335.52
20	$2,000.00	$2,712.64
25	$2,250.00	$3,481.29
30	$2,500.00	$4,467.74
35	$2,750.00	$5,733.72

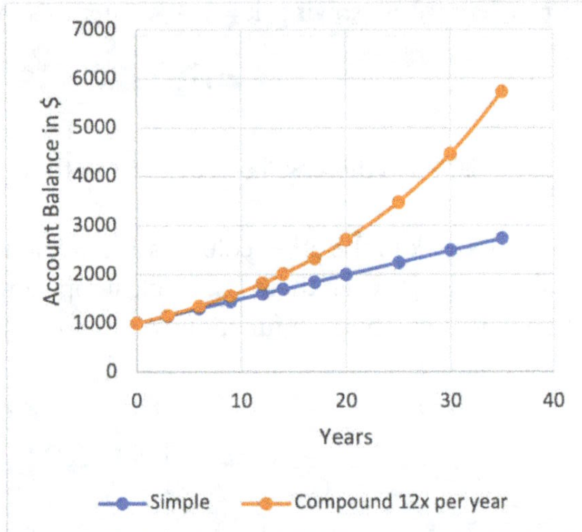

This reminds us of another graph in a previous topic when we were comparing a linear pattern, quadratic pattern, and exponential pattern. Though the exponential growth is not as intense, the compounding pattern is exponential. The account growth under simple interest is a linear pattern. We can also answer the doubling question.

Double $1000 is $2000. Under simple interest the balance reaches $2000 after 20 years. Under compound interest the balance reaches $2000 around year 14. (When we try t = 13, we get $1912.96.) Under compound interest, it took 14 years versus 20 years to double in value.

Try this: Anya wishes to open a savings account and has two options. #1 is offered with 4% interest compounded monthly. #2 is offered with 4.5% interest compounded annually. She has $500 to deposit. Which offer is better in 1 year? Which is better in 10 years?

SECTION 7.2: LUMP SUM DEPOSIT APPLICATIONS

There are other questions we may like to answer, that involve solving for something other than the future value.

What do I need to deposit now to reach a desired amount in the future?

How long would it take to reach a financial goal?

What interest rate would let me start here and end there in 20 years?

Any of these involves some algebra, so we will only show how one formula is derived with the hope of demonstrating the math thinking that is involved.

Definition: When solving for the present value or principal we use:

$$P = A \cdot (1+r)^{-t} \quad when \quad A = P \cdot (1+r)^{t}$$

and

$$P = A \cdot (1 + r \div k)^{-kt} \quad when \quad A = P \cdot (1 + r \div k)^{kt}$$

This is not so absurd when we consider that the exponent is moving us forward or backward in time. It makes perfect sense that time would be negative when we are looking back from a future value to the initial principal. We can even think of P as the past value. The algebra says we need to divide by $(1 + r)$ but dividing by $(1 + r)$ is the same as multiplying by $(1 + r)^{-1}$.

Example: At 8% interest compounded quarterly, what would need to be deposited now to reach $10,000 in 15 years?

Solution: What is known? r = 8% = 0.08, k = 4, A = 10,000, and t = 15. We need to solve for P. We will be using the formula $P = A \cdot (1 + r \div k)^{-kt}$.

Let us address the negative exponent first. Calculators differ in how to make a number negative. First, let us be clear. On handheld calculators, making a number negative does not use the subtraction key! We must look for one of these.

(–), +⇄– or +/–. If we want the number we either put the number in first, then change the sign or we put the sign then the number. The symbol on the key tells us which is which.

–30 will be (–) *then* "30", or it will be "30" *then* +/– or +⇄–.

Here is another timesaving and error-saving tip for exponents kt or $-kt$. Before calculating for P, we will first figure out the exponent in our calculation. $k \cdot t = 4 \cdot 15 = 60$. This means our exponent will be –60.

On the calculator, we will follow order of operations:

$r \div k + 1$ comes first, then do the exponent, then multiply by A.

On one calculator, it will be entered this way:

0.08 ÷ 4 + 1 =, then $x^{\blacksquare}$ (–) 60 =, then × 10000 =

On another calculator pay attention to the key order for –60:

0.08 ÷ 4 + 1 =, then y^x 60 +⇄– =, then × 10000 =

We arrive at the answer of $3047.82

To solve this and other similar problems in a spreadsheet application, create a new sheet like the one we used for future value except this will be solving for present value.

	A	B	C	D	E	F	G	H	I
1	Time Value of Money - Simple and Compound Interest - Using the spreadsheet like a calculator, find the present value of an account when a lump sum deposit is made and interest is calculated over time with different compounding options.								
2				Simple	Compound 1x per year	Compound 2x per year	Compound 4x per year	Compound 12x per year	Compound 365x per year
3	*r*	*A*	*t*	*P1*	*P2*	*P3*	*P4*	*P5*	*P6*
4	8%	10,000	15	$4,545.45	$3,152.42	$3,083.19	$3,047.82	$3,023.96	$3,012.34

In each of the blue cells in row four we will enter our calculations. This time we use the PV() built-in function instead of FV(). We see our answer in column G, which is compounding 4x per year.

PV(rate,nper,pmt,[fv],[type]) <-- leave blank
=PV(A4/k,C4*k,,-B4,)
simple interest, type = B4/(A4*C4+1)

Try this: At an interest rate of 6.3% compounded daily, what would need to be deposited now to be valued at $30,000 in 18 years?

Now we will answer a question of the type *how long it will take to reach a financial goal.* For this we need to solve for t in the formula for compound interest. That means solving for the exponent, which in turn means using the natural log. Logarithms are necessary when solving for the exponent.

Start with	$A = P \cdot (1+r)^t$
Divide by P	$A \div P = (1+r)^t$ Let $b = 1 + r$
Taking a logarithm makes use of these two facts: $\ln b^t = t \cdot \ln b$ and $\ln(A \div P) = \ln A - \ln P$	
Apply ln to both sides:	$\ln A - \ln P = t \cdot \ln b$
Divide by $\ln b$:	$t = (\ln A - \ln P) \div \ln b$
Put $b = 1 + r$ back in:	$t = (\ln A - \ln P) \div \ln(1+r)$

Definition: To solve for time in an interest-bearing account we use

$$t = (\ln A - \ln P) \div \ln(1+r) \quad when \quad A = P \cdot (1+r)^t$$

and

$$t = (\ln A - \ln P) \div [k \cdot \ln\left(1+\frac{r}{k}\right)] \quad when \quad A = P \cdot \left(1+\frac{r}{k}\right)^{kt}$$

Let us look at an example. We will review order of operations on the calculator. In future, suggestions may be given but detailed calculator keys will not be shown. We will also solve the problem using a spreadsheet function.

Example: A money market fund is expected to grow at a rate of 6.2% compounded monthly. How long would it take for $5,000 to grow to $20,000? Give your answer in years and months to the nearest month.

Solution: What we know... r = 6.2% = 0.062, k = 12, P = $5000, and A = $20,000. We are solving for t (time) in years.

On calculators with the (–) key, calculate in this order of operations only use numbers in place of the letters they represent:

ln (r ÷ k + 1) = , $x^{■}$ (−) 1 = ,
× (ln A − ln P) = , ÷ k =

On calculators with the +/− or +⇄− key, and the screen only displays one number at a time, key in the following. (Be aware y^x = x^y and +/− = +⇄−). Again, use the numbers we have in place of letters.

r ÷ k + 1 = ln , y^x 1 +/− = ,
× (A ln − P ln) = , ÷ k =

We arrive at t = 22.4173 which is in years. To get years and months, we take the decimal portion and multiply by 12. $0.4173 \times 12 = 5.0076 \approx 5$

Our answer is 22 years and 5 months.

Calculations like these are much easier in a spreadsheet application using one of the built-in formulas. When solving for time, we are interested in the number of periods, which is called NPER(). We divide that by k to get time in years.

How many years to reach a financial goal?

r/k , , P , −A,
NPER(rate/k,pmt,pv,fv,type)/ k gold leave blank
=NPER(0.062/12,,5000,-20000,)/12

No fancy sheet is required. On a blank cell, just type in the above calculation starting with the "=" and the spreadsheet returns 22.4173.

> **Try this:** A parent wants to start a savings account for a newborn's future by depositing $10000. If the account earns interest at 3.75% compounded daily, how long would it take for the amount to become $50,000?

The final kind of question we might have about lump sum accounts concerns shopping for interest rates that will allow the investment to grow to a desired amount in a desired time. This is difficult because there are no guarantees with interest rates. However, it is possible to make a reasonable guess given a range of acceptable outcomes. It may be that after calculating the needed interest rate, a person may decide that the desired goal is not achievable. Then there are other ways to raise money beyond this topic.

Definition: When solving for the interest rate, r, we use

$$r = \left(\frac{A}{P}\right)^{1/t} - 1 \text{ when } A = P \cdot (1 + r)^t$$

and when k is involved, let $n = k \cdot t$

$$r = \left[\left(\frac{A}{P}\right)^{1/n} - 1\right] \cdot k \text{ when } A = P \cdot \left(1 + \frac{r}{k}\right)^{kt}$$

For this formula, the tricky part on the calculator is again the exponent. When raising a number to a power that is a fraction, it is wise to use ( ) around the exponent. For example,

$2^{1/3}$ *is* 2 [y^x] [( ] 1 [÷] 3 [ )]

Example: Steve is considering different kinds of savings accounts but is curious about what interest rates are needed if he wants \$500 to grow to \$700 in 5 years. Assume interest is compounded quarterly.

Solution: We will solve this problem in our spreadsheet application. The built-in function for this is called RATE() and instead of the usual 5 arguments, this function uses 6 arguments. However, only 3 of them are required. Just make sure to insert commas , , in the proper places.

What is the interest rate needed to reach a financial goal?

```
k*t,     , P , -A ,    ,
RATE(nper,pmt,pv,fv,type,guess)* k   gold can leave blank
=RATE(4*5,,500,-700,,1.75%)*4
```

The guess is what we expect $r \div k$ to be (optional)

This function returns the periodic rate, which is $r \div k$, and is why we multiply by 4 at the end. The cell that we enter this function into will return a decimal value for the interest rate unless we configure the cell for a percent % style number. The decimal is 0.067864 or about 6.8% annually. Since interest rates fluctuate, Steve should consider current interest rates – do they tend to be higher or lower than average? Use that when we shop around for a way to invest the \$500.

Conversation starter: Given what we have learned about differences between interest rates, compounding frequencies, and how much a person must commit to something up front, discuss ways a person can achieve the most favorable outcome with a deposit of $1000. Should they deposit it and let it sit for 8 years? Or should they choose short-term CDs and just reinvest every 6 months for 8 years? What are the pros and cons for different types of cash investments?

SECTION 7.3: SAVINGS ANNUITIES

An annuity can be interpreted as any financial product that has these basic structures in place:

1) There is a fixed, regular payment that is applied to the balance (either it is withdrawn, or it is deposited)
2) There is a fixed or average interest rate that is compounded at the same time as payments are made
3) Payments are made at the end of each interest period, though there are some situations where payments are made at the beginning.

focal point/Shutterstock.com

We will start with a savings type annuity. 401K plans, IRA accounts, some college 529 plans, some insurance policies, and sinking funds are all examples of savings annuities. A sinking fund is generally shorter term than a retirement savings account. People set up annuities to save for a vacation as well. Interest is typically tax-deferred until the account matures and the investor begins to make regular withdrawals from it. Most of these types of savings do not allow the investor to have access to any of the money until it matures. For that reason, federal income tax does not apply until the individual receives the funds.

This is the vehicle people use to build cash when they have little to no assets to invest at first. A portion of their earnings gets put aside into something that will accumulate and eventually provide a substantial lump sum that can then be reinvested into something that creates wealth, a tangible asset that can be bought and sold for gain.

Start with \$0.00. Now deposit \$2.00 at the end of each month for an entire year. Suppose the interest rate is 3%. That translates into $r/k = 0.03 \div 12 = 0.0025$ monthly rate. What is in the account at the end of a year? Let us apply interest to each payment and see what that looks like in a table.

Deposit amount	Month Count	Time in account	Future Value (column 4)	Multiply by 1.0025 (column 5)
\$2.00	1	11 m	$2 \cdot (1+0.0025)^{11}$	$2 \cdot (1+0.0025)^{12}$
\$2.00	2	10 m	$2 \cdot (1+0.0025)^{10}$	$2 \cdot (1+0.0025)^{11}$
\$2.00	3	9 m	$2 \cdot (1+0.0025)^{9}$	$2 \cdot (1+0.0025)^{10}$
\$2.00	4	8 m	$2 \cdot (1+0.0025)^{8}$	$2 \cdot (1+0.0025)^{9}$
\$2.00	5	7 m	$2 \cdot (1+0.0025)^{7}$	$2 \cdot (1+0.0025)^{8}$
\$2.00	6	6 m	$2 \cdot (1+0.0025)^{6}$	$2 \cdot (1+0.0025)^{7}$
\$2.00	7	5 m	$2 \cdot (1+0.0025)^{5}$	$2 \cdot (1+0.0025)^{6}$
\$2.00	8	4 m	$2 \cdot (1+0.0025)^{4}$	$2 \cdot (1+0.0025)^{5}$
\$2.00	9	3 m	$2 \cdot (1+0.0025)^{3}$	$2 \cdot (1+0.0025)^{4}$
\$2.00	10	2 m	$2 \cdot (1+0.0025)^{2}$	$2 \cdot (1+0.0025)^{3}$
\$2.00	11	1 m	$2 \cdot (1+0.0025)^{1}$	$2 \cdot (1+0.0025)^{2}$
\$2.00	12	0 m	2.00	$2 \cdot (1+0.0025)^{1}$
Column adds up to:			A	$1.0025 \cdot A$

Subtract column 5 – column 4. Everything connected with an arrow will subtract and become zero (0). Anything not connected remains. We end up with the equation

$$1.0025A - A = 2 \cdot (1 + 0.0025)^{12} - 2.00$$

$$0.0025A = 2 \cdot (1 + 0.0025)^{12} - 2.00$$

And we have $A = [2 \cdot (1 + 0.0025)^{12} - 2.00] \div 0.0025$

which simplifies to $A = [2 \cdot (1 + 0.0025)^{12} - 2.00] \times 400 = \$24.33$

We can generalize the formula. Instead of a lump sum deposit, which we have called $\boldsymbol{P}$, we have regular payments, which we will call $\boldsymbol{p}$.

Definition: The future value of a savings annuity with regular payments, $\boldsymbol{p}$ and A, r, t, k as in compound interest formulas is

$$A = \left[\boldsymbol{p} \cdot \left(1 + \frac{r}{k}\right)^{kt} - \boldsymbol{p}\right] \cdot \frac{k}{r}$$

Note that k represents the pattern of payments and compounding periods in a year. They must be the same.

The best calculator advice for formulas like this one is to start with the most complex part, start on the inside and work your way outward. Also, it is common for r/k to be a repeating decimal. When that happens, it is best to keep the decimal as it is and continue with the calculations. The calculation also is made simpler by figuring out what $k \cdot t$ is in advance. Putting one number in the exponent is easier than having to perform a calculation. It is easy to forget to use brackets ( ) when doing exponents or using function keys on the calculator.

The best way to get comfortable with your calculator is to use it. Practice a lot. When you get something wrong, take notes on what you did and go back through the process, jotting down each step of the way. Carefully tracking steps is a good way to find out where you went wrong.

Example: Anika works for a small company that does not offer pension benefits. She wishes to start her own retirement account. If Anika deposits \$100 every two weeks in an account that earns 5% interest, how much will be in the account in 22 years?

Solution: If using a calculator, we will make use of what is given in the problem knowing that we need four things: *p, r, k, and t.* Anika is depositing money in the account ***every 2 weeks***. There are 52 weeks in a year, so biweekly would be $k = 52 \div 2 = 26$. $r = 5\%$ or 0.05, $p = \$100$, and $t = 22$
We will pre-calculate $n = k \cdot t = 26 \times 22 = 572$.

It is tempting to round when we get $3.00099428399 \approx (1 + 0.05 \div 26)^{572}$
Let us see what happens to our calculations:

Next step:	Rounding to 3. Result of the next calculation:	Keeping all decimal values results in:
× 100	300	300.099428399
−100	200	200.099428399
× 26	5200	5202.585138379
÷ 0.05	\$104,000	\$104,051.70

An error of \$51.70 was made. This is about half of one of Anika's payments. These errors would start to matter much more if the regular contribution had been a four-digit amount. We should not round until the end.

To solve this in a spreadsheet application, we make use of the FV() function but this time we put in the regular payment. We need to use $pmt = -100$!

```
FV(rate,nper,pmt,[pv],[type]) <-- leave blank
=FV(0.05/26,22*26,-100,0,)
```

We get the same result... $104,051.70.

Try this: In the preceding example, suppose Anika has another offer from a different bank with 5.2% interest under the same payments but she will be charged a $90/year administration fee. Which is the better deal?

If we want to solve for the payment needed to reach a financial goal, we will use an alternate form of the future value equation.

Definition: The future value of a savings annuity with regular payments, $\boldsymbol{p}$ and A, r, t, k as in compound interest formulas can be written as

$$A = p \times \left[\left(1 + \frac{r}{k}\right)^{kt} - 1\right] \times \frac{k}{r}$$

To solve for p: Calculate the $[\dots] \times \frac{k}{r}$ expression first, divide by A, then raise to the (−1) power.

This is the same formula for future value of an annuity, but we factored out p from the inside part. Let us see an example of this type of problem.

Example: Levi wants to save for a cruise in 5 years. He/they will want to have $7000. If interest on a sinking fund is 8% and it compounds semiannually, what amount needs to be deposited regularly and how often?

Accounts like this do not give added benefit if the account holder makes more frequent payments, hoping to get a higher return. Levi is better off sticking with the scheduled interest. This means making a payment twice a year, on time for interest calculation. What we know/what we need to know:

$$t = 5, p = ??, A = 7000, r = 8\% = 0.08, k = 2, \text{ so } n = kt = 10$$

On the calculator, we will do $(1 + 0.08 \div 2)^{10}$ first. Then proceed as seen in the table. With more practice, these calculator exercises begin to get a bit less stressful. Hit the Enter key after each step and write down the result. Always remember in the first step that division comes before adding 1.

Order of Operations	On the calculator display:
$(1 + 0.08 \div 2)^{10} - 1$	0.480244284918344...
$\times 2 \div 0.08$	12.006107122958598...
$\div 7000$	0.001715158160423...
x^y 1 +/− or $x^{■}$ (−) 1	$583.04

Using the PMT() function in a spreadsheet application will also do the trick. As usual, we need to make the future value negative.

The PMT() function looks like this for this example:

PMT(rate,nper,pv,fv,type)<-- leave blank
=PMT(0.08/2, 2*5, 0, -7000,)

Both methods give us $583.04 as the twice-a-year payment.

Try This: A person might want to have $200,000 when they retire (in addition to other assets). If we assume interest rates average about 3% find the difference in annual payments between the following:

A) make regular payments monthly for 30 years (k = 12)
B) make regular payments quarterly for 30 years (k = 4)

Answer the same question if the average rate was 4%.

PRACTICE EXERCISES

1. Use the *Banker's Rule* in which a year is adjusted to 360 days instead of 365 to calculate the interest and balance due on a loan of $36,000 with 9.2% interest rate for 40 days. [*t in days*, $I = P \cdot r \cdot t/360$]

2. $500 is deposited in an account earning 3.4% interest compounded annually. How much will be in the account in 11 years? What would the interest rate need to be to have $800 in the account in 11 years?

3. How much money needs to be deposited now to have $2000 in the account in 5 years if the interest rate is 2% compounded monthly?

4. Give the time needed, in years and months (rounded to the nearest month), for an investment of $9000 to grow to $16,000 if interest is 7.5% per year, compounded quarterly. Decimal needs to be converted to months.

5. A business sets up a sinking fund so they will have $72,000 in 7 years to replace equipment that will reach its end-of-life. If the business makes a regular deposit every quarter for 7 years and the investment pays 6.8% interest, what amount needs to be deposited?

6. An individual can deposit $400 every month into a retirement fund, IRA, in which the account earns 4.7% interest. How much will be in the account in 35 years?

7. A person only has 15 years until retirement, when they want to have $300,000 cash available for income. There is a choice between a) regular deposits are made monthly @ 7.2% interest (compounded monthly) or b) regular deposits annually @ 7.6% interest (compounded annually). Which is the better option and why? What would be the total of all payments made in each case?

8 Finance – Special Topics

Section 8.1: Payout Annuities

The purpose of a payout annuity is to provide an individual with regular income, often as a supplement to other income. For example, people who win a large sum of money in the lottery may receive all of it up front, or they can elect to receive it as an annuity. An individual, upon reaching retirement age, may have a retirement fund that has matured. This can get reinvested into an annuity type account, from which the retiree receives a regular income. Payments are made to the individual until the account has a $0 balance. It is designed to end after a fixed amount of time.

eamesBot/Shutterstock.com

Definition: Savings annuities and payout annuities have key similarities and key differences. These are

1) With savings, P = \$0. With payout, P = \$full amount
2) With savings, A = \$full amount. With payout, A = \$0
3) With savings the individual is making regular payments. With payouts the individual is receiving regular payments.
4) With savings, the value increases over time. With payouts, the value decreases over time (as money gets withdrawn).

The result is basically a reversal of time. Let us see what happens in an account with *present value, P*. For purposes of demonstration, we will let the interest rate be annual, though this pattern can be generalized for a periodic rate of $^r/_k$. We will let $r = 0.03$, $t = 12$ years and the withdrawal amount (which is still our regular payments variable) $p = \$2.00$. The amount is not important so long as we can see the pattern that emerges. In these problems, $A = 0$.

Payment amount	Year Count	Time in account	Present Value (column 4)	Multiply by 1.03 (column 5)
\$2.00	1	1 y	$2 \div (1 + 0.03)^1$	2
\$2.00	2	2 y	$2 \div (1 + 0.03)^2$	$2 \div (1 + 0.03)^1$
\$2.00	3	3 y	$2 \div (1 + 0.03)^3$	$2 \div (1 + 0.03)^2$
\$2.00	4	4 y	$2 \div (1 + 0.03)^4$	$2 \div (1 + 0.03)^3$
\$2.00	5	5 y	$2 \div (1 + 0.03)^5$	$2 \div (1 + 0.03)^4$
\$2.00	6	6 y	$2 \div (1 + 0.03)^6$	$2 \div (1 + 0.03)^5$
\$2.00	7	7 y	$2 \div (1 + 0.03)^7$	$2 \div (1 + 0.03)^6$
\$2.00	8	8 y	$2 \div (1 + 0.03)^8$	$2 \div (1 + 0.03)^7$
\$2.00	9	9 y	$2 \div (1 + 0.03)^9$	$2 \div (1 + 0.03)^8$
\$2.00	10	10 y	$2 \div (1 + 0.03)^{10}$	$2 \div (1 + 0.03)^9$
\$2.00	11	11 y	$2 \div (1 + 0.03)^{11}$	$2 \div (1 + 0.03)^{10}$
\$2.00	12	12 y	$2 \div (1 + 0.03)^{12}$	$2 \div (1 + 0.03)^{11}$
Column adds up to:			$1P$	$1.03 \cdot P$

Subtract column 5 – column 4. Everything connected with an arrow will subtract and become zero (0). Anything not connected remains. Also, instead of dividing by powers of (1 + 0.03), we will use the negative exponent rule and multiply instead. Recall the rule looks like this when the exponent is 5, though this rule works for any exponent.

$$\$ \div (1 + 0.03)^5 = \$ \times (1 + 0.03)^{-5}$$

We end up with the equation $1.03P - 1P = 2(1) - 2 \times (1 + 0.03)^{-12}$

Combine terms on the left side and factor out 2 on the right and we have:

$$0.03P = 2 \times [1 - (1 + 0.03)^{-12}]$$

Now divide by 0.03 $\quad P = 2 \times [1 - (1 + 0.03)^{-12}] \div 0.03$

We can generalize a formula for payout annuities.

Definition: For an annuity with regular withdrawals, p, until the balance is zero (0), and P, r, t, k as in compound interest formulas the value of the annuity can be written as

$$P = p \times \left[1 - \left(1 + \frac{r}{k}\right)^{-kt}\right] \times \frac{k}{r}$$

To solve for p: Calculate the $[\dots] \times \frac{k}{r}$ expression first, divide by P, then raise to the (–1) power.

Solving a payout annuity problem is nearly identical to a savings annuity problem, with a few minor differences. When using a calculator, we need to recall how to evaluate negative exponents. We had experience with this when solving for present value in compound interest situations. The steps for solving on a calculator will not be shown. Instead, we will use the spreadsheet functions.

As usual, if the compounding periods are not stated, we assume it is the same as the payment periods.

Example: Francesca will be getting a check for \$500 every month for 20 years from her retirement account. The account earns 3% interest. How much is needed in the account at retirement?

Solution: In this example, we know p = \$500, $t = 20$, $k = 12$, and $r = 0.03$. We need to know the present value, that is we are solving for P.

We use the PV() function and input the appropriate numbers.

```
PV(rate,nper,pmt,fv,type) <-- leave blank
=PV(0.03/12,20*12,-500,0,)
```

The amount needed in the account is \$90,155.46

Example: Michael won the lottery where the pot was \$562,325. He decides to take it as an annuity for 30 years at 4.2% interest. How much can Michael expect to receive every two months?

Solution: Here we know the present value P = \$562,325. We also know $t = 30$, $r = 0.042$, and $k = 6$.

We will use the PMT() function in a way that gives us a positive result.

```
PMT(rate,nper,pv,fv,type)<-- leave blank
   =PMT(0.042/6, 30*6, -562325, 0,)
```

Michael will receive \$5,504.52 every two months.

Try This: A parent wishes to set up a scholarship fund for their local high school. The fund starts with \$75,000. They want to award scholarships each year for 40 years. If the interest rate is 3.5% annually, how much in scholarships can be awarded each year?

Try This: For a scholarship fund to last indefinitely, the annual payout needs to be completely paid by interest. Construct a problem that asks what the present value of a fund needs to be to provide an annual scholarship of an amount you choose. Decide what interest rate the fund receives. Then solve for the present value.

Introwiz1/Shutterstock.com

SECTION 8.2: LOANS

If there is a single word that makes financial markets, individual investors, and private equity companies nervous, it is the word *uncertainty*. When there is uncertainty there is risk. When there is risk, higher fees are imposed as a sort of insurance policy against the failure of the investment.

Photo by Mike Petrucci on Unsplash

Here is a simple example to illustrate this concept. A private equity firm is looking at four opportunities. These are small businesses that will need to file for bankruptcy and close unless they receive an infusion of cash to keep going.

All four have a 70-75% chance of getting back to healthy business operations once receiving the funds. But this means there is a 25-30% chance they will fail. For simplicity of the illustration suppose each one requires \$50,000. Due to the risk of failure, the private equity firm is willing to invest with the stipulation that the companies each pay back \$130,000 in five years. What is the annual interest rate on that loan?

Since this is a matter of simple interest, A = \$130,000 and P = \$50,000. This means I = 80,000 and r = 80000 ÷ (50000 × 5) = 32%. Also, each agreement requires that the businesses return to health. If a business fails, it will not be obligated to pay back anything. So, the private equity firm loses \$50,000.

The high interest rate provides insurance against one of the companies failing. Let us look ahead 5 years. Suppose one of the businesses out of the four ***does*** fail. The private equity firm invested 4 × \$50,000 = \$200,000. Since three of the businesses succeeded the firm receives in return 3 × \$130,000 = \$390,000. The difference is \$390,000 – \$200,000 = \$190,000. The private equity firm gained r = \$190,000 ÷ (\$200,000 × 5) = 19% return on their investment.

This may seem like a lot to pay, perhaps even a bit unfair. But when a business owner is facing certain bankruptcy, the choice is between going out of business versus the (very good) chance of regaining momentum and having the business thrive. To avoid private equity taking advantage of people in desperate situations, the industry needs to be well-regulated as well.

As private citizens, individuals may need to borrow money for lots of reasons. Essentially there are two categories of loans – secured and unsecured. Secured loans generally have better interest rates, and the borrower offers some asset as collateral on the loan. If the borrower defaults on the loan, the lender may seize the asset as payment. Unsecured loans generally have higher interest – such as a payday loan, student loan, or deferred interest loan (furniture and appliance stores offer these), or debt consolidation loan. Most mortgages fall under the category of secured loans, and the property is the collateral.

Conversation starter: Lenders consider multiple factors when offering loan terms (how much of a loan a person qualifies for, interest rate, and length in time). These are: credit history, capacity to make payments, collateral, other assets (capital), and conditions (what is the loan for). List some specific ways a person's habits and behavior can help or hurt their ability to secure a loan in the amount needed at a reasonably low interest rate.

A piece of good news is that we do not need a new formula when making regular loan payments on a schedule. The reason is a loan amount or principal can be treated the same as the present value of a payout annuity. In a spreadsheet we would still assign a negative value to present value in both instances. If we had a balance sheet with a debit column and credit column, we would need to be careful which column we put the regular payments. Our goal when problem solving is not the accounting aspect. We are generally interested in the amount itself.

Definition: For an amortized loan with regular payments, p, until the balance is zero (0), and P, r, t, k as in compound interest formulas the value of the loan (remaining balance) can be written as

$$P = p \times \left[1 - \left(1 + \frac{r}{k}\right)^{-kt}\right] \times \frac{k}{r}$$

To solve for p: Calculate the $[\square] \times \frac{k}{r}$ expression first, divide by P, then raise to the (−1) power.

As usual with present value calculations, the exponent is negative. The remaining balance on the loan follows an exponential decay pattern.

Try This: Here are two problems to try. Use the same procedures that were followed when solving payout annuity problems.

1) If an individual has a monthly car payment of $290, and the loan rate is 4.5% for 72 months (6 years) what was the car loan amount?
2) Tyree is approved for a $165,000 mortgage. The interest rate is 6.1% for 30 years. What will the monthly payments be? Assuming Tyree already paid 20% of the sale price of the home, what was the sale price?

One reason mortgages may involve more risk for banks, and why they insist on 20% down payment (unless there is a program the buyer qualifies for that allows less money up front) is that for the first couple years of the loan not a lot of the monthly payment goes toward the principal. If the homeowner can no longer make payments and is forced to sell, the value of the home may have decreased in two years. When a seller is forced to sell a home for less than the remaining balance on the loan, it is called a short sale. The seller must demonstrate the ability to pay the portion of the mortgage that will not be covered in the sale.

To see what portion of monthly payments goes to interest and what portion goes to principle we need to create an amortization schedule, a table that shows the split for each payment. This schedule is for a mortgage of $200,000 with an interest rate of 6% paid monthly for 30 years. Formulas are shown with " " around them for display purposes. The formulas we see in row 11, corresponding to the 7th payment, are correct given where information is located on this sheet. Any gold cell is just a number, not a formula.

	A	B	C	D	E
1	Loan Amount	Interest Rate	Time (in Years)	Payments Per Year	Monthly Payment
2	$200,000	6%	30	12	$1,199.10
				=PMT(B2/D2,C2*D2,-A2,,)	
3	Payment Number	Payment	Interest Charged	Portion to Principal	Balance Due
4					$200,000.00
5	1	$1,199.10	$1,000.00	$199.10	$199,800.90
6	2	$1,199.10	$999.00	$200.10	$199,600.80
7	3	$1,199.10	$998.00	$201.10	$199,399.71
8	4	$1,199.10	$997.00	$202.10	$199,197.60
9	5	$1,199.10	$995.99	$203.11	$198,994.49
10	6	$1,199.10	$994.97	$204.13	$198,790.36
11	7	"=E$2"	"=E10*B$2/D$2"	"=B11-C11"	"=E10-D11"

Notice that with each payment, the portion that goes to interest goes down by a bit and the portion that goes toward principal (what is still owed) goes up by a bit.

Conversation starter: Recreate the spreadsheet just shown and find out how many payments it takes for principal and interest to be about the same. Discuss the significance of this to the homeowner. If payments are monthly, how long into the mortgage is this?

In the definition of present value of a loan with regular payments, the phrase *remaining balance* was used. This was intentional. The present value formula can be used to calculate the remaining balance at any point. This can also be determined from the spreadsheet amortization schedule as well. With each payment we see what the remaining balance is. To do this we would need to know the original mortgage amount. If we do not know the original mortgage amount, then we can simply use the PV() function on the annuity spreadsheet.

But it might be fun and instructive to practice calculator skills, especially given a problem for which we know the answer, or we can check it using a spreadsheet function.

Example: Suppose a mortgage has a 7% interest rate with payments of $1436 each month for 30 years. What will the balance be with 12 years left on the loan?

Solution: To use the calculator, we do not need to know what was the original mortgage amount. We have $p = 1436$, $r = 0.07$, $k = 12$, $t = 10$. We are solving for P. We need $k \cdot t = 12 \cdot 10 = 120$.

Description of Step	Result of Calculation
1. Calculate $(.07 \div 12 + 1)^{-120}$	0.497596267508631...
2. Make it negative and add 1	0.502403732491369...
3. Multiply by p: $\times 1436$	721.451759857606593...
4. Multiply by $\frac{k}{r}$: $\times 12 \div .07$	$123,677.44 or .45 if we round up

SECTION 8.3: CONTINUOUSLY COMPOUNDED INTEREST

We effectively have four unique formulas for calculating present value and future value of any conventional monetary product.

- compound interest under a lump sum amount and interest is compounded annually
- compound interest under a single lump sum amount and interest is compounded multiple times a year
- compound interest with multiple payments and interest is compounded multiple times a year (at the time payments are made)
- simple interest where interest is calculated in advance and paid all at once or spread evenly over the repayment term

What distinguishes them is a) how interest is accrued and b) when money is paid out (lump sum versus multiple payments). We have seen what happens when the number of compounding periods increases, from annually to perhaps quarterly to monthly and then daily. Is it possible to compound interest hourly? or even by the minute? by the second? by the nanosecond? The answer is... yes, especially given that we have such fast computer processing speeds.

For the record, there are 3.1556952×10^{16} or 31 quadrillion, 556 trillion, 952 billion nanoseconds in a non-leap year of 365.2425 days. We can do the calculation ourselves, but why bother...

Definition: As the number of compounding periods (k) gets very large, approaching infinity, something interesting happens. For extremely large values of k,

$$\left(1+\frac{r}{k}\right)^k \approx e^r$$

This means there is such a thing as *continuously* compounding interest. Because the bigger k is, the better the above approximation gets. This leads us to a fifth unique formula for calculating present value and future value of a financial product.

Definition: When a lump sum amount has a present value P and future value A and the interest rate, r, is continuously compounded we have

$$A = P \cdot e^{rt} \quad \text{and} \quad P = A \cdot e^{-rt}$$

In fact, there are so many benefits to continuously compounded interest that we can take any account that is compounded and convert it to continuously compounded interest.

Definition: When a lump sum amount is subject to an interest rate, r, compounded k times a year we can calculate the equivalent continuous rate R

$$R = \ln(1 + r \div k) \times k$$

Caution: Rounding before the final answer can lead to errors.

Let us demonstrate this with an example.

Example: \$200 is deposited into an account at 6% interest compounded monthly. What is the equivalent continuous compound interest rate? How much is in the account in 8 years?

Solution:

$$R = \ln(1 + .06 \div 12) \times 12 = 0.059850498\ldots$$

Without rounding, multitply by 8: 0.478803985…

$$A = 200 \times e^{0.478803985\ldots} = \$322.83$$

PRACTICE EXERCISES

1. At retirement, money goes from a savings account to one that provides regular income. If a person wants to take $35,000 out of the account each year for 25 years and the account earns 4% interest, a) how much needs to be in the account at the start of the 25 years? b) What is the total of all payments made to the individual? c) How much interest was earned during that time?

2. There is $50,000 available to a student going into college on a 5-year master's degree program. It is put into an annuity that earns 6% interest. How much can the college student take out each semester (twice a year) for 5 years?

3. This is a two-part question. First, an individual wants to withdraw $35,000 each year for 30 years when they reach retirement. They need to know how much to deposit each year for 25 years at 4.75% interest now so that there will be enough money in the account when the savings annuity switches to a payout annuity. Same interest rate for both.

4. A person bought a home for $215,000. They put 20% down and will take out a 30-year fixed rate mortgage at 6.5% interest for the remaining 80%. a) what is the present value of the loan? b) what will the monthly payments be? c) how much interest (total) will be paid? Create an amortization table showing how much of each payment goes to interest and how much goes to principal.

   Five (5) years later... the person has an opportunity to refinance to pay off the mortgage in 15 years (at 6.5% rate). What will the new monthly payment be? How much will the person save in interest payments by doing this?

5. If $2000 is borrowed in an account subject to 6% interest compounded continuously, how much needs to be paid back in 2 years? Compare that with an account subject to 7.5% interest compounded twice a year. Which is the better deal?

6. A consumer bought furniture on a credit card for $5,250. The APR is 16.9%. If they want to pay off the furniture in 4 years, how much $ per month do they need to pay to the credit card company? What is the total of all payments? How much interest was paid over this time?

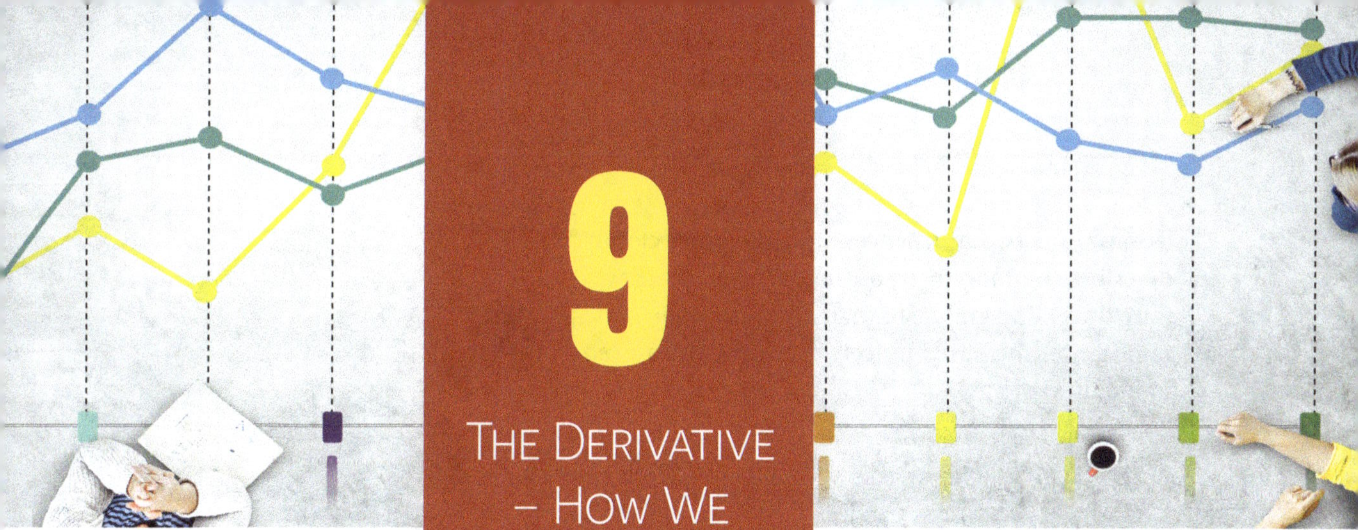

9

The Derivative – How We Measure Change

Section 9.1 Rate of Change on an Interval

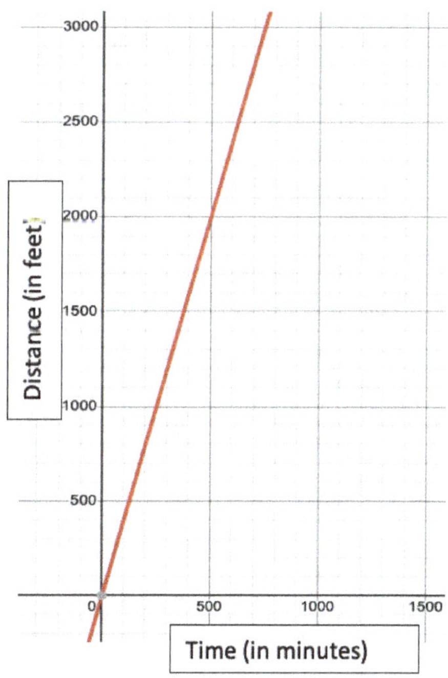

In this chapter we will explore the meaning of the phrase "change of y with respect to x." How one quantity changes with respect to the other is at the heart of calculus. This is an informal introduction to one-variable calculus of the derivative. Our goal is to define what we mean by "the derivative," how it relates to slope, and apply what we learn to business concepts. We will develop the concepts starting with what we know and build on those until we can apply what we have learned to problems involving making business profitable.

It all starts with the idea of slope as rate of change when we have a linear relationship between two quantities. This was studied in a previous chapter.

Consider the fable *The Tortoise and the Hare* as a basis for understanding the relationships between time, distance, and speed. Speed is the measure of the **rate of change** of distance over time, after all. In a previous chapter we learned that when the relationship between two quantities is linear, there is a constant **slope** (rate of change). In the fable, the straight-line relationship between distance and time most closely describes the movement of the tortoise, so we will start there. The graph shows us the steady increase in distance (measured in feet) over time (measured in minutes).

Dolimac/Shutterstock.com

When we graph, the point (0,0) is on the graph because at the beginning of the race time = 0 and distance = 0. Another point that can be identified rather easily is the point (500, 2000).

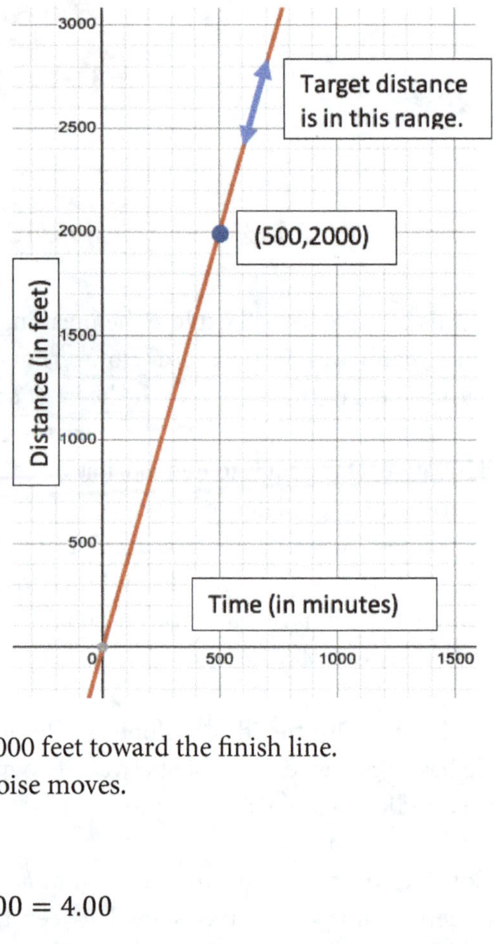

Example: Using the graph provided, answer the following questions about the tortoise.

1. Locate the point (500,2000) on the graph and make a statement about what the numbers 500 minutes, 2000 feet mean.
2. Calculate the speed of the tortoise from two points on the graph. (0,0) is a handy one. Give your answer in feet per minute.
   Hint: $slope = \frac{\Delta y}{\Delta x} = \frac{rise}{run} = \frac{vertical\ change}{horizontal\ change}.$
3. Determine how long (in minutes, and then in hours/minutes) it takes for the tortoise to finish the race. (How many feet is ½ mile?) Make use of the graph, a table of values, or an equation… or all three… to understand the race from the tortoise's point of view.

Solutions:

1. Locate that point on the graph. (see graph) What it means: In 500 minutes, the tortoise has moved 2000 feet toward the finish line.
2. Calculate the speed in feet per minute that the tortoise moves.

   Speed of the tortoise
   $$\frac{2000-0}{500-0} = 2000 \div 500 = 4.00\ feet/minute$$
3. How long to finish?
   Since 5,280 feet = 1 mile, we take ½ of that. So ***½ mile = 2,640 feet.***

We also know that distance = rate · time. Rate is the same thing as speed.

Distance (y) = 4 ft/min · time (x). Write this as an equation. $y = 4x$.

To find out how long it takes for the tortoise to travel that distance, we first see that it must be greater than 500 minutes because at that time the tortoise will have traveled 2,000 feet. The tortoise still has to go another 640 feet. Let us start there and use the equation for distance as a function of time (now that we know the slope). We now know $y = 4 \cdot x$, so we will make a table. From the graph, we can also ***estimate*** that the distance of 2,640 will fall *somewhere between 600 and 700 minutes.*

If needed, we can narrow down the values of x if the target distance is in between two numbers on our table. The solution is there, however. When x = 660, y = 2640, our target distance. 660 minutes converted to hours is 660 ÷ 60 which gives us 11 hours! What a marathon!

x	y	$y = 4 \cdot x$
600	2400	600 · 4
620	2480	620 · 4
640	2560	640 · 4
660	2640	660 · 4
680	2720	680 · 4
700	2800	700 · 4

There is a pattern in the table!
Whenever x goes up by 20, y goes up by 80. Why?
From the table, $\Delta x = 20$ and $m = 4$. Using the slope formula in solving for change in y we have $\Delta y = 20 \cdot 4 = 80$.

The values of y increase by 80 each time x increases by 20!

Definition: The ratio for slope $\frac{\Delta y}{\Delta x} = m$ of a linear function can be rewritten as a formula for **change in y**, if we know the change in x.

$$\Delta y = m \cdot \Delta x$$

We now have a very clear picture of the race from the point of view of the tortoise. The hare, on the other hand, took off like a sprinter. But then something happened. In the story, we know that the hare stopped to take a nap, eat, nap some more, eat some more. How is this behavior reflected on the graph of the hare's distance over time? We can make a graph that tells the story of a sprinter taking off, then stopping for a long time, then resuming the race at a reduced speed. ***The steeper the line, the greater the speed.*** Horizontal line means no progress (no speed). The hare stopped at 2,000 feet with only 640 feet to go. Meanwhile, the tortoise passed the napping hare at 500 minutes. The hare did not start trying to catch the tortoise until 600 minutes into the race. Will the hare be able to catch up in time?

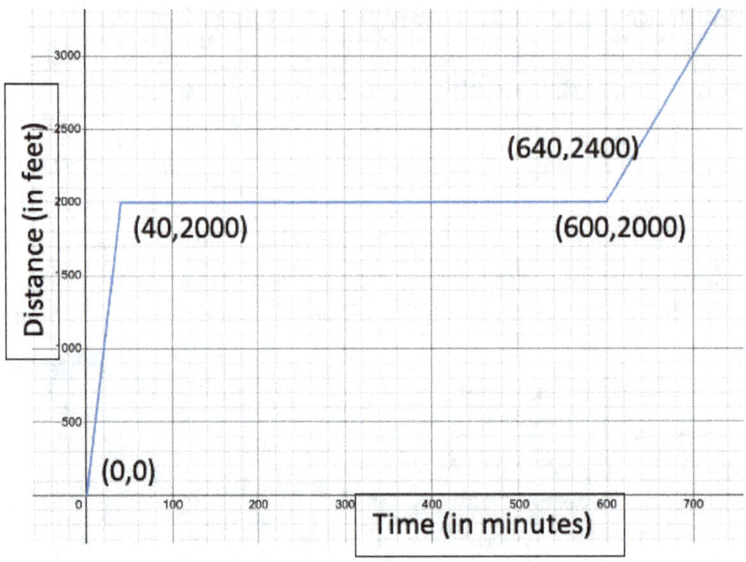

This graph shows the race from the hare's perspective. What we can tell is that the hare wasted a lot of time. Then when it did start racing again, it wasn't nearly as fast.

Questions to consider and for understanding:

1. What was the time and distance at which point the hare stopped to relax (feeling overconfident)?
2. How fast had the hare been moving until that moment?
3. At what time did the hare realize that the tortoise might win, and started to race again?
4. After all the napping and eating, the hare could not run quite as fast. What was the speed on that final part of the race?
5. Who won? How long was it before the hare crossed the finish line?
6. Summarize the hare's race in the following statement:
   For the first ____ minutes the hare ran at a constant speed of ____ feet per minute. Then, for ____ minutes the hare made no progress (speed = 0). The hare then ran at a speed of ____ feet per minute to finish in ____ minutes, which is _____ hours and _____ minutes.

Answering these questions will give us a complete mathematical picture of what occurred in the race.

Solutions:

1. What was the time and distance at which point the hare stopped to relax (feeling overconfident)?

Answer: (40,2000) *which means* 40 *minutes, at* 2,000 *feet*

2. How fast had the hare been moving until that moment?

Answer: (2000 – 0) ÷ (40 – 0) = 50 feet per minute

3. At what time did the hare decide to join the race again? Answer: At 600 minutes into the race, or 10 hours. The amount of time that the hare wasted was 600 – 40 = 560 minutes
4. After all the napping and eating, the hare could not run quite as fast. What was the speed on that final leg of the race? Answer: We need to calculate the slope between the points (600,2000) and (640,2400). Slope = speed:

$$\frac{\Delta y}{\Delta x} = \frac{2400-2000}{640-600} = (2400 - 2000) \div (640 - 600) = \mathbf{10} \text{ feet per minute.}$$

5. Who won? How long was it before the hare crossed the finish line?

x	y	$\Delta y = 10 \cdot \Delta x$
600	2000	
620	2200	$2000 + 10 \cdot 20 = 2000 + 200$
640	2400	$2200 + 200$
660	2600	$2400 + 200$
664	2640	$2600 + \mathbf{40}$

Use a table to increment x by 20 and y by 200 until we reach 660. At the 660-minute mark, the hare managed to narrow the gap but did not catch up. 2600 feet was 40 feet behind the tortoise, who was at the finish line.

We can confidently state mathematically that the tortoise won.
To get the time for the hare crossing the finish line, we start at the point (660,2600) and since we need 40 more feet distance, we will solve for Δx

a) use $\Delta y = 40 = 10 \cdot \Delta x$
b) which means $40 = 10 \cdot 4$
c) $\Delta x = 4$
d) *Add 4 to the time* for a race time of 664 minutes, or 11 hours + 4 minutes

6. Summarize the hare's race in the following statement:
For the first 40 minutes the hare ran at a constant speed of 50 feet per minute. Then, for 560 minutes the hare made no progress (speed = 0). The hare then ran at a speed of 10 feet per minute to finish in 664 minutes which was 11 hours and 4 minutes.

Since the hare was inconsistent, going from 50 feet per minute to 0 feet per minute, and then finishing at 10 feet per minute, we might be interested to know what the hare's ***AVERAGE*** rate of speed was throughout the entire *664 minutes* of the race.

By making a straight line from (0,0) to the finish (664,2640) we can see how the hare's race would have looked at an average rate of speed the whole way.
The average speed of the hare was:

$$slope = \frac{\Delta y}{\Delta x} = 2640 \div 664 \approx 3.9759$$

Notice that the average speed of the hare was a ***hair*** less than the tortoise's speed of 4 feet per minute. This graph shows the progress had the hare run the entire race at 3.9759 feet per minute.

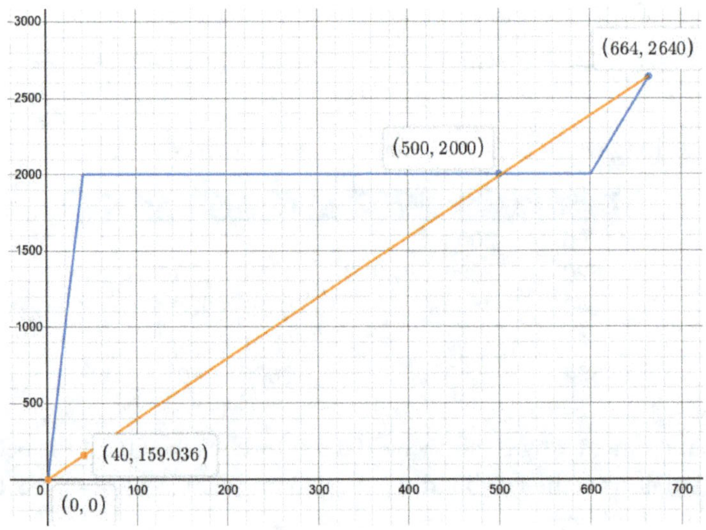

Useful results of this investigation:

1) If we know two points on a line and the slope, we can get more points on the line by increasing x by a certain amount (Δx) and then increase or decrease y by multiplying the slope times the change in x: $\Delta y = m \cdot \Delta x$. (If slope is negative, then y would decrease)
2) When the change of one quantity with respect to another varies over an interval, we can use a straight line to find the AVERAGE rate of change over that interval.

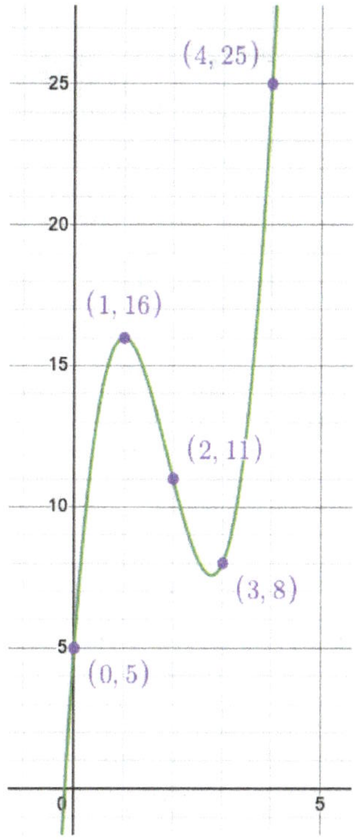

We need to consider this idea of average rate of change a bit more. Here we have a graph that shows typical ups and downs we might see in places like the stock market, job growth, prices of a certain commodity, etc. Fluctuations happen over time. When we do not have a linear relationship between two quantities, we need a different definition for slope *at a point.*

Later in this chapter we will be learning how to use information called the ***derivative***, which is a measure of slope on a curve at any point. The derivative is ***instantaneous rate of change***, like the current speed on a car's speedometer shows your speed at a moment in time. When you are driving, your actual speed changes based on traffic, speed limit, and road conditions.

We will define instantaneous rate of change by exploring **AVERAGE** rate of change over a small interval, letting the intervals of x get smaller and smaller until we begin to see a pattern. In chapter 1 we learned about average rate of change of any function, linear or not, over an interval.

On this graph, what is the AVERAGE rate of change between **x = 0 to x = 4**?
What information do we need? Once we have all the numbers we need, what do we do with those numbers?

The first thing we need is to recognize that "**x–0 to x=4**" is an ***interval*** on the x axis. Average rate of change occurs between two given x values.
What we need is to identify the two points (x,y) for the formula. These two points are (0, 5) and (4, 25).
Using a straight-edge instrument helps with that because the curve is very steep.
Now we calculate the slope between the two points (0,5) and (4,25).

$$Average\ rate\ of\ change = \frac{\Delta y}{\Delta x} = \frac{25-5}{4-0} = \frac{20}{4} = 5$$

The conclusion then is to say, "**the average rate of change between x = 0 to x = 4 is 5**".

This means that ***on average***, y increases by 5 whenever x increases by 1. This is what market analysts mean when they say that fluctuations in the market average out over time. What happens minute by minute, or hour by hour is not as important as what happens over a specific time interval on average.

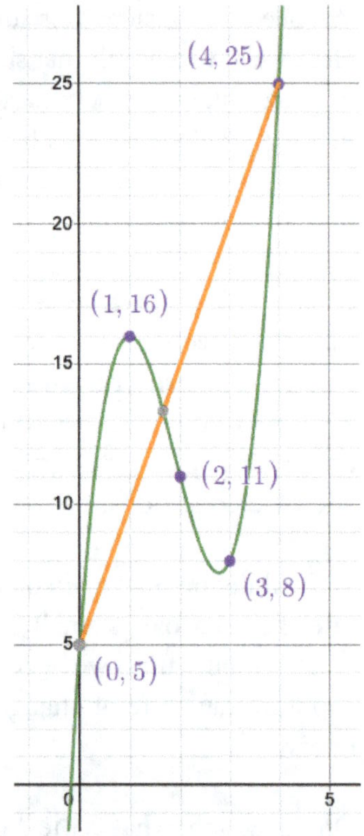

Try This: Make a graph of the curve, and on the same graph show the straight line from (0,5) to (4,25) that models the average rate of change.

Solution: (see graph) The straight line from (0, 5) to (4, 25) has a slope of 5. Here is a follow-up question to consider. Suppose we keep the orange line anchored at (0, 5) but move the other end to another point on the curve.

1) What is the average rate of change on the curve for x in [0,1], ie from (0,5) to (1, 16)?
   Answer: 11
2) What is the average rate of change on the curve for x in [0, 2], ie from (0, 5) to (2, 11)?
   Answer: 3
   What if we move both ends of the straight line?
3) What is the average rate of change on the curve for x in [1, 3], ie from (1, 16) to (3, 8)?
   Answer: – 4

Section 9.2 Toolkit Functions and Tangent Line to a Curve

For the purposes of our investigations, there are some useful equations that describe different kinds of relationships between two quantities, which we designate x and y. In previous chapters, we have learned about five of these: linear, quadratic, polynomial, exponential and logarithmic. As we go forward with different applications, it will be necessary to introduce a few more, and to name them. Here are the toolkit functions that we will be using throughout the remainder of this course. Keep in mind that new functions can be created by adding, subtracting, multiplying, or dividing any of these by any other. There are infinite possibilities, especially when we consider different coefficients.

Toolkit Function Name	Formula
Constant	$f(x) = 1$
Identity	$f(x) = x$
Power—Square	$f(x) = x^2$
Power—Cubic	$f(x) = x^3$
Rational—Reciprocal	$f(x) = \frac{1}{x}$
Rational—Bump Function	$f(x) = \frac{1}{x^2 + 1}$
Square Root	$f(x) = \sqrt{x}$
Exponential	$f(x) = e^x$
Natural Logarithm	$f(x) = \ln x$

Proceed with caution when any of these is involved.

Toolkit Function	Values of x to be assumed unless stated otherwise
$f(x) = \frac{1}{x}$	$x > 0$ (x is positive and not zero) ***or*** $x < 0$ (x is negative and not zero)
$f(x) = \sqrt{x}$	$x \geq 0$ (x is positive and also zero)
$f(x) = \ln x$	$x \geq 1$ (x is 1 or larger)

Graphs of All Toolkit Functions (with the two newest on the bottom)

Linear	Quadratic	Cubic
$y = x$ 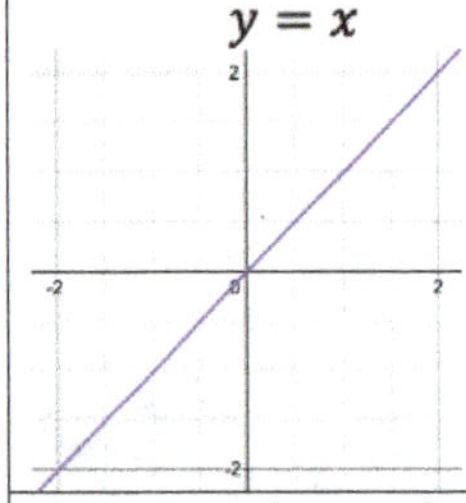	$y = x^2$ 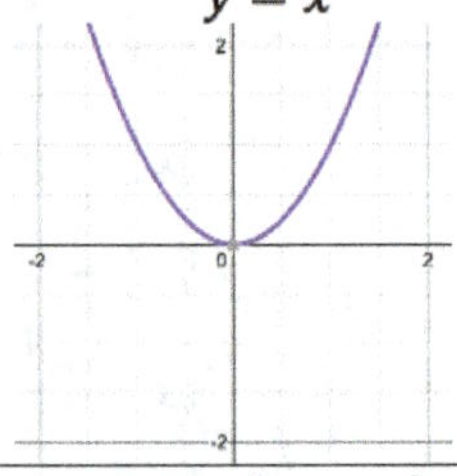	$y = x^3$ 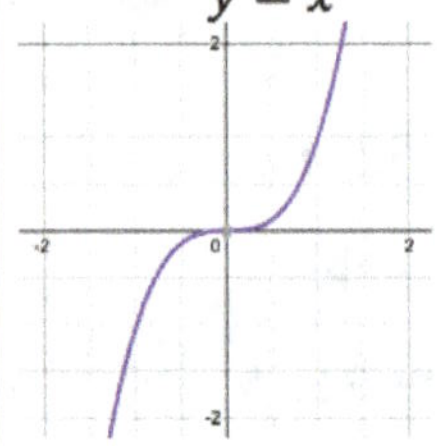
domain x: $(-\infty, \infty)$ range y: $(-\infty, \infty)$	domain x: $(-\infty, \infty)$ range y: $[0, \infty)$	domain x: $(-\infty, \infty)$ range y: $(-\infty, \infty)$
Radical (Square Root)	**Exponential**	**Logarithmic**
$y = \sqrt{x}$ 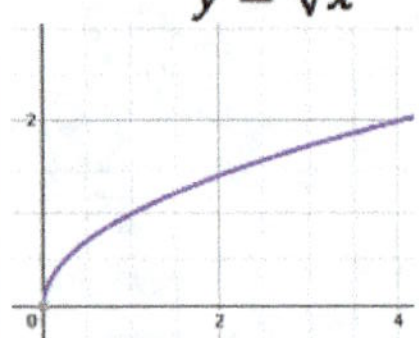	$y = e^x$ 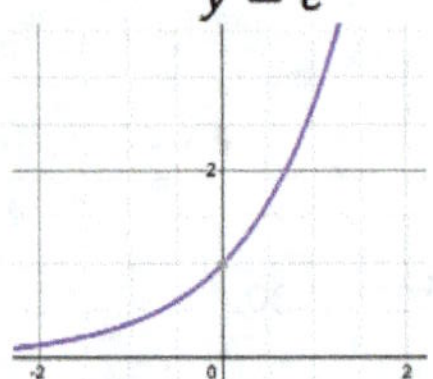	$y = \ln x$ 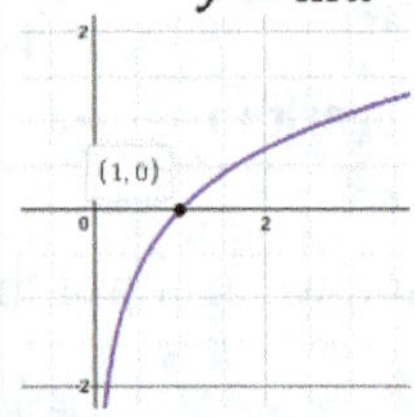
domain x: $[0, \infty)$ range y: $[0, \infty)$	domain x: $(-\infty, \infty)$ range y: $(0, \infty)$	domain x: $(0, \infty)$ range y: $(-\infty, \infty)$
Reciprocal	**Bump Function**	
$y = \frac{1}{x}$ 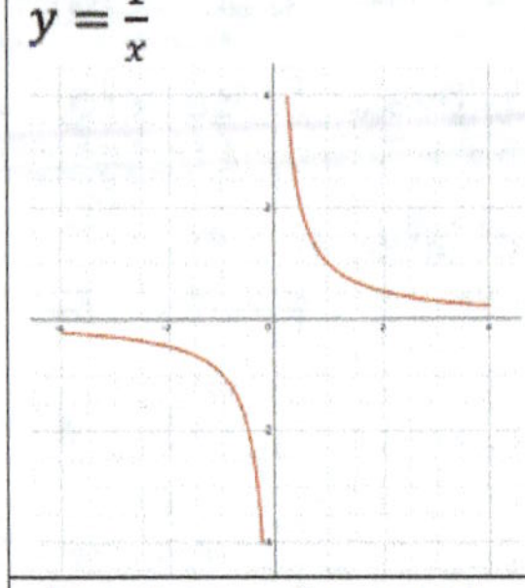	$y = \frac{1}{x^2+1}$ 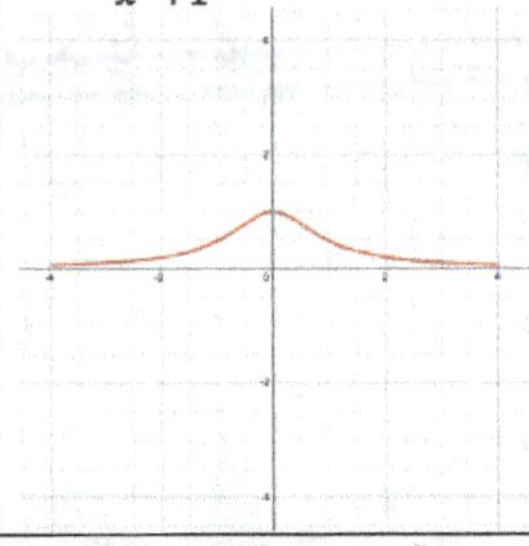	
domain x and range y: $(-\infty, 0) \cup (0, \infty)$	domain x: $(-\infty, \infty)$ range y: $(0,1]$	

Try This: Make your own graph of each of the 8 toolkit functions. Use graph paper (preferred). Make a second, smaller graph that can be cut out and pasted to an index card. On one side of the index card, put the graph. On the other side, put the equation. Use these to drill yourself until you can answer all of them with no errors. Make sure you can do both – identify the equation from the graph; identify the graph from the equation.

If this were a traditional Calculus course, we would be concerning ourselves with function operations, composition of functions, and limits and continuity. But all of our models will be based on data; we will assume that the functions are well-behaved and are basic variations on the toolkit functions.

Let us consider motion again, but this time we have a projectile. A person throws a baseball up in the air. The height of the ball is dependent on three things: the force of gravity (which is acceleration), the speed at which the ball is thrown, and the initial height of the ball above the ground. Also, the ***units of measure matter*** in this situation because we will use the force of gravity as –9.81 *meters/sec*^{2}. So height is measured in meters and speed is measured in meters/second.

Here is what we know: The speed of the ball when thrown is 27.2 m/s and the height above the ground is 0.5 meter. Let the variable "x" be time in seconds. Then by Newton's Second Law of Motion

$$h(x) = 0.5 + 27.2x - 4.9x^2$$

[–4.9 is half gravity].

x	y
0	0.5
1	22.8
2	35.3
3	38
4	30.9
5	14

We can use technology to graph that function. We will start with a table of values. It does not make sense to choose negative numbers for x. We are stopping at 5 because when x = 6 we get a negative number. The ball cannot go below ground. Ground level is y = 0. These y values are measured in meters, so we have a general idea that the ball is going up, then coming back down.

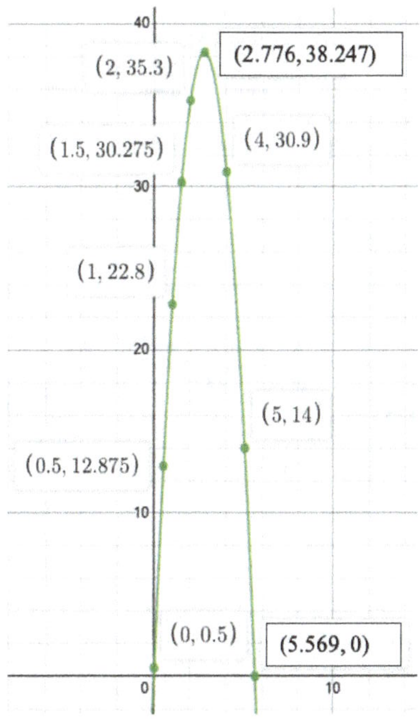

The relationship between height in meters and time in seconds can be seen on this graph. We can label points that come from our table of values, and points that appear to be important to the situation.

The type of function is a quadratic function and belongs to the family of "square" functions.

Given the equation, the graph, and the known positions of the ball that are labeled here, what can we say about this situation?

1) We can say that the ball reached a maximum height of 38.25 meters above the ground.

2) We can say that the ball reached its maximum height at approximately 2.8 seconds after being thrown.
3) We can say that it took a total of 5.6 seconds to fall back down to the ground.

What we cannot say (yet) is what the ball's speed was at any of these points.

Suppose we wanted to know exactly ***how fast the ball was going at the 2 second spot***. We would need to be able to determine the slope of the curve at that point, which is difficult because this is not a straight line. Also, we must contend with the fact that slope is sometimes negative. Speed will be the absolute value at these points.

Now is the time to introduce the *two special lines* that help us determine what the slope is on a curve. These two lines need to be drawn at or near the point of interest.

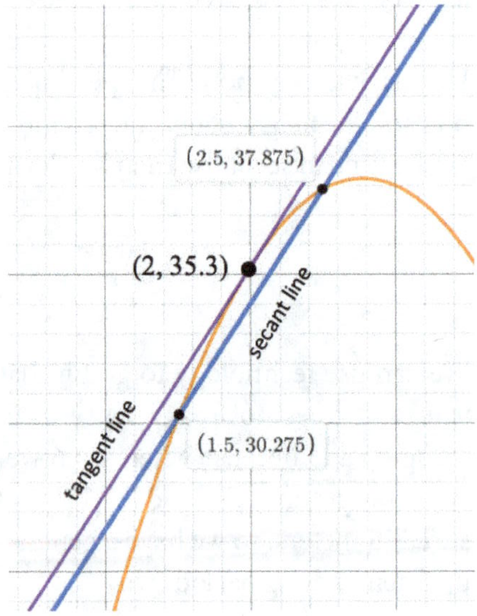

To help our understanding, we will visualize the problem using a closeup of the graph of our projectile, concentrated on the part that is near x = 2.
The point (2, 35.3) is labeled. This is where we want to know the speed of the ball, which is the slope at that point.

The first straight-edge line we need is called the ***tangent line*** to the curve at a point. It is the line that passes through (2, 35.3) and *only touches the graph at that point (shown here in purple.)* The tangent line is like a ruler balanced on the surface of a ball.

The second line is called the ***secant line***. There are lots of secant lines, but here we see one that **appears to be parallel to the tangent line** (which is important!) *and* it crosses through the curve in two points (also important!)

Definition: Let a curve with equation $y = f(x)$ be given. The **tangent line** to the curve at a point (x_0, y_0) is the straight line with slope equal to the slope of the curve at the point. [$y_0 = f(x_0)$ perhaps goes without saying.]

We are going through a lot of effort just to find the speed of the baseball at 2 seconds. Part of the difficulty is with the tangent line. We only have one point. We do not know the slope because that is what we are solving for. The secant line will come to the rescue. Secant lines are useful because they

intersect with the curve in ***TWO points***... which means we can calculate the slope! Notice the two values of x that were chosen have an x coordinate that happen to be ½ unit from 2.
2 + ½ = 2.5 and 2 – ½ is 1.5.

This is exactly what we want:

If the ***tangent line and the secant line are parallel***, then they have the same slope. We can calculate the slope of the secant line, and that will tell us what the slope of the tangent line is, which in turn tells us the speed of the ball at x = 2 seconds. Remember parallel means two lines are not the same line and will never intersect because they remain the same distance apart.

So far, we have accomplished quite a bit:

1) a closeup on our graph of the curve near the point (2, 35.3).
2) we have drawn to the best of our ability the **tangent line** to the curve that passes through our point
3) we have drawn to the best of our ability a **secant line** that passes through two nearby points on the curve and ***appears to be parallel*** to the tangent line!
4) We have identified the two points that the secant line passes through on the curve: (1.5, 30.275) and (2.5, 37.875)

Now we have enough information to calculate the speed of the baseball.

Slope of the secant line is:

$$slope = \frac{\Delta y}{\Delta x} = \frac{(37.875 - 30.275)}{(2.5 - 1.5)} = \frac{7.6}{1} = 7.6 \div 1 = 7.6$$

This is the slope that matches the slope of the tangent line, which is the speed of the ball at x = 2.

The summary statement is that 2 seconds after being thrown, the ball is traveling at an approximate speed of 7.6 meters per second.

Since we are talking about estimating slope at a point on a curve, there is another way we can do this via the graph. Instead of finding a secant line that is parallel to the tangent line, sometimes we can extend the tangent line to one of the axes. Without technology, it can be difficult to pinpoint the exact spot where a line crosses with either the x or y axis.

This is why we have options. When one approach does not work, try another. Also, we are looking for a reasonable estimate. Let us see an example.

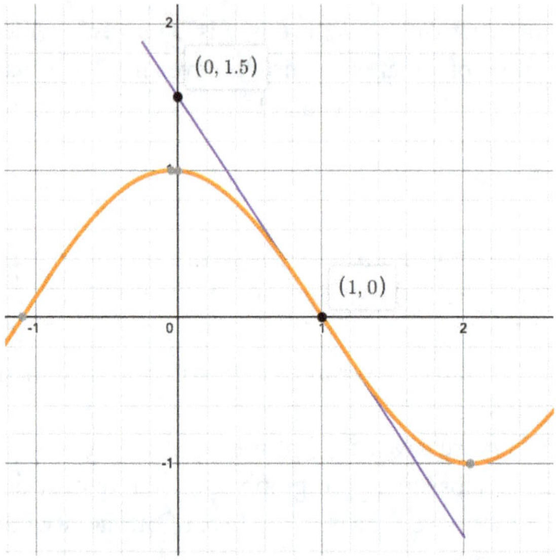

We have a curve but no equation. We only have the graph. The goal is to estimate the slope of the curve at the point (1, 0).

The tangent line to the curve passing through (1, 0) is drawn and extended so that we can see clearly that it crosses the y axis at the point (0, 1.5).

Since we have two points, there is no need for a secant line. In this example, finding a parallel secant line would be very difficult anyway.

The slope between the points (0, 1.5) and (1, 0) is $m = {}^{\Delta y}/_{\Delta x} = -1.5$

That result is our estimate of the slope of the curve at the point (1, 0).

Definition: The slope on a curve at a point is called the **derivative** at a point. Instead of using the symbol $\frac{\Delta y}{\Delta x}$ (which is slope between two points), we use the symbol $\frac{dy}{dx}$ at (x_0, y_0).

Finally, we can estimate slope at a point using a table. We select x values closer and closer to the desired x until we see a pattern emerging when we calculate the slopes of the secant lines. We can do this without graphing at all if we have the equation.

Example: For the function $f(x) = \sqrt{3x + 16}$, find the derivative at $x = 3$.

Setting up the table. We need three columns, one for our x's, the second for the y's, and the third for the slope between two points. Use headings as shown for calculations. We ***have a choice of values for x***. It was decided to start with 0 and creep closer to 3. We will start with these and see if we can determine a pattern.

x	y = f(x)	Calculate the slope between (3, 5) and a **second point**
3	**$5 = \sqrt{3 \cdot 3 + 16}$**	
Second point		
0		
1		
2		
2.5		

A blank table is provided for you to complete for practice. Next we will calculate all the y values from the function. Once we have the y values, calculate the slopes for each new point with the original (in this example, the original is (3, 5).

x	y = f(x)	Calculate the slope between (3, 5) and a second point
3	$\mathbf{5 = \sqrt{3 \cdot 3 + 16}}$	
Second point		
0	$4 = \sqrt{3 \cdot 0 + 16}$	$\frac{(5-4)}{(3-0)} = 0.333$
1	4.36	$\frac{(5-4.36)}{(3-1)} = 0.32$
2	4.69	$\frac{(5-4.69)}{(3-2)} = 0.31$
2.5	4.85	$\frac{(5-4.85)}{(3-2.5)} = 0.30$
We probably need one more, perhaps two more, rows because so far the slopes keep going down by 0.01. ***We need the numbers to get closer together.***		
2.8	4.94	$\frac{(5-4.94)}{(3-2.8)} = 0.30$
2.9	4.97	$\frac{(5-4.97)}{(3-2.9)} = 0.30$

When we calculated the slope of the last three secant lines from the table, accurate out to two decimal places, our slopes were identical. We were better off including at least one more calculation than was necessary because it allows us to check our work better.

Conclusion: The derivative of $f(x) = \sqrt{3x + 16}$ at $x = 3$ is about 0.30.

Try this: For the function $f(x) = \sqrt{2x + 12}$, find the derivative at the point (2, 4). Use a table and select values of x that are: 0, 1, 1.5, 1.8, 1.9, and 1.99. These will be the "second point" for slope calculation.

Solution:

x	y = f(x)	Calculate the slope between (2, 4) and a second point
2	**$4 = \sqrt{2 \cdot 2 + 12}$**	
Second point		
0	$3.464 = \sqrt{2 \cdot 0 + 12}$	$\frac{(4-3.464)}{(2-0)} = 0.268$
1	3.74	$\frac{(4-3.74)}{(2-1)} = 0.26$
1.5	3.87	$\frac{(4-3.87)}{(2-1.5)} = 0.26$
1.8	3.95	$\frac{(4-3.95)}{(2-1.8)} = 0.25$
Keep going to be sure...		
1.9	3.975	$\frac{(4-3.975)}{(2-1.9)} = 0.25$
1.99	3.9975	$\frac{(4-3.9975)}{(2-1.99)} = 0.25$

What is your conclusion?

SECTION 9.3 THE DERIVATIVE AS A FUNCTION

In Lesson 2 we explored how to find the slope of a curve at a point using secant lines or by extending tangent lines to approximate the derivative. Let us summarize the different descriptions of this, and the vocabulary:

Start with y = f(x) as a function of x. Assume it is "well-behaved" on an interval so that it has a ***derivative (slope)*** at the point (a, b).

Each of these is the same thing:

1) The slope of f(x) at the point (a,b)
2) The slope of the tangent line that passes through (a,b)
3) The instantaneous rate of change of y with respect to x at the point (a,b)
4) The derivative of f(x) at the point (a,b)
5) The slope of a specific secant line, which is (on a graph) *parallel* to the tangent line at (a,b) and passes through two points on the graph of y = f(x).

We go from defining the derivative at a specific point to a definition of the derivative at ANY point, which means that the derivative can be understood as a function of x, as a companion function.

Definition: Start with **y = f(x)** as a function of x, and it **has a slope** at all points (x,y) in its domain, except any end points.

The ***derivative of f(x)*** is its companion function which we call $f'(x)$. In words, we say "***f-prime of x***". We can use the formula for the derivative to calculate the slope at any point.

We also say that $f'(x)$ is the "**rate of change of f with respect to x**".

Notation: $f'(x) = \frac{dy}{dx}$ [These are two ways of writing the same thing.]

Example: For $f(x) = x^2$ its derivative function is $f'(x) = 2x$. Consider the point (3, 9) which is on the graph of f(x). Then we can find the derivative (slope) at the point (3,9) using the formula for the derivative.

Solution: The *slope at* (3, 9) $= f'(3) = 2 \cdot 3 = 6$

Example: Find the derivative at the point (4, 16) for $f(x) = x^2$

Solution: The derivative at (4, 16) is $f'(4) = 2 \cdot 4 - 8$

Let us look at the derivative functions for all the toolkit functions. It should be noted that there are rules associated with finding derivatives of functions. These rules involve a level of mastery of advanced algebra that is not necessary when accomplishing the goals and objectives of the study of this book. Toward that end, consider the questions that follow this chart.

Toolkit Function Name	Formula	Companion Function (Derivative)
Constant	$f(x) = c$	$f'(x) = 0$
Identity	$f(x) = x$	$f'(x) = 1$
Power—Square	$f(x) = x^2$	$f'(x) = 2x$
Power—Cubic	$f(x) = x^3$	$f'(x) = 3x^2$
Rational—Reciprocal	$f(x) = \frac{1}{x}$	$f'(x) = -\frac{1}{x^2}$
Rational—Bump	$f(x) = \frac{1}{x^2 + 1}$	$f'(x) = \frac{-2x}{(x^2 + 1)^2}$
Square Root	$f(x) = \sqrt{x}$	$f'(x) = \frac{1}{2\sqrt{x}}$
Exponential	$f(x) = e^x$	$f'(x) = e^x$
Natural Logarithm	$f(x) = \ln x$	$f'(x) = \frac{1}{x}$

Conversation starter: By looking at the graph of each toolkit function, can you predict whether the derivative should be positive or negative

a. to the right of x = 0
b. to the left of x = 0

Now look at the function equations for $f'(x)$. Is $f'(x)$ positive for x values that we expect? Is it negative for x values that we expect?

INTERPRETATIONS OF THE DERIVATIVE:

What the derivative *measures* depends on the context, and the units of "x" and "y". Some of the words associated with the derivative are as follows: velocity, speed, acceleration, marginal cost, marginal revenue, and marginal profit, inflow rate, outflow rate, evaporation rate, or rate of increase/decrease.

In business settings, the use of the word "marginal" is used to describe how much of the y quantity is needed to increase x by ONE unit. We will see this in many examples involving cost, revenue, profit, and price. This is the focus of the next chapter.

Example: Suppose the number of pounds of beef that the market demands is given by the function $y = f(x) = \frac{1}{x}$. Y is measured in thousands of pounds and x is price in \$. The companion function $f'(x) = -\frac{1}{x^2}$

1. In this context, what is $f'(x) = \frac{dy}{dx}$ a ***measure of***?

   Solution: $\frac{dy}{dx}$ *measures* $\frac{\textit{thousands of pounds}}{\textit{dollar in price}}$ which can be interpreted as "thousands of pounds (of beef) per dollar in price".

   In other words, $f'(x) = \frac{dy}{dx}$ measures how much demand ***changes*** for every increase of \$1 in price.

2. What is the demand for beef when price is *\$3.00*?

   Solution: $f(3) = ⅓ = 0.333$ thousand pounds
   = 0.333 x 1,000 pounds
   = 333 pounds

3. Find and interpret the *derivative of f(x) with respect to x* at $x = \$3.00$.

   Solution: $f'(\$3.00) = f'(3) = -\frac{1}{3^2} = -\frac{1}{9} \approx -0.111$ which we interpret as "demand decreases by 0.111 thousand pounds if the price goes up from \$3 to \$4"

   As before we can convert that number to pounds:
   – 0.111 thousand pounds per dollar
   = – 0.111 x 1,000 pounds per dollar
   = – 111 pounds per dollar

Try this: Answer questions 2 and 3 but when $x = \$5.00$

Solution: When x = \$5.00 the demand is 0.200 thousand pounds of beef, or 200 pounds. The derivative when x = \$5.00 is – 0.040 which is – 40 pounds of beef per dollar. We interpret that using a summary statement:

"When the price of beef is \$5.00 per pound, the demand is decreasing at the rate of – 40 pounds of beef per dollar of increase in the price."

COMBINATIONS OF TOOLKIT FUNCTIONS AND THEIR DERIVATIVES:

Functions and derivatives behave the way we expect. When we add or subtract two functions, we add or subtract their derivative (companion) functions. When we have a coefficient with a function, we have a coefficient with the derivative function.

Things get a bit more complicated when the x variable is multiplied by a constant *inside* the function. In each of our toolkit functions, it is possible to rewrite the function so that the constant coefficient of x becomes a coefficient of y.

Example: Suppose $g(x) = \sqrt{3x}$. What is the derivative then?

Solution: Rewrite $g(x) = \sqrt{3} \cdot \sqrt{x}$ and since $\sqrt{3} \approx 1.732$, $g(x) = 1.732 \cdot \sqrt{x}$ is acceptable.

Now we can establish derivatives of functions with a coefficient, and sums/differences of functions.

Definition: Suppose $f(x) = x^2$ and $g(x) = x$ are two toolkit functions. Suppose we have constant a not equal to 0.

If $h(x) = a \cdot f(x) = ax^2$.
Then $h'(x) = a \cdot f'(x) = a \cdot 2x = 2ax$.

In words, coefficients get passed from the function to the derivative.

Let $h(x) = f(x) + g(x)$
then $h'(x) = f'(x) + g'(x)$

Let $h(x) = f(x) - g(x)$
then $h'(x) = f'(x) - g'(x)$

Example: $h(x) = x^2 + x$
then $h'(x) = 2x + 1$

Example: $h(x) = x^2 - 3x$
then $h'(x) = 2x - 3$

Continuing a previous example, find the derivative of $g(x) = 1.732\sqrt{x}$

Solution: The toolkit function here is $f(x) = \sqrt{x}$ and $f'(x) = \frac{1}{2\sqrt{x}}$.

$$g'(x) = 1.732 \cdot \frac{1}{2\sqrt{x}} \text{ which simplifies to}$$

$$g'(x) = \frac{1.732}{2\sqrt{x}} = \frac{1.732}{2} \cdot \frac{1}{\sqrt{x}} \text{ and } 1.732 \div 2 = 0.866$$

so, we have $g'(x) = 0.866 \cdot \frac{1}{\sqrt{x}} = \frac{0.866}{\sqrt{x}}$

It is not necessary to simplify. But when looking at an answer key, often the solution is simplified. It is nice to see where the 0.866 came from.

PRACTICE EXERCISES:

1. Here we see the number of designated living wage jobs in a city per 1000 working age adults over a 5-year period.

Year	1997	1998	1999	2000	2001
Jobs	665	720	770	805	825

What is the average rate of change in number of living wage jobs from 1997 to 2000? Give your answer in jobs/year.

2. Here is a graph of a function f(x). Use the graph to find the average rate of change of y = f(x) with respect to x for x = 2 to x = 4. Give your answer first as a fraction. Then write it as an integer or decimal.

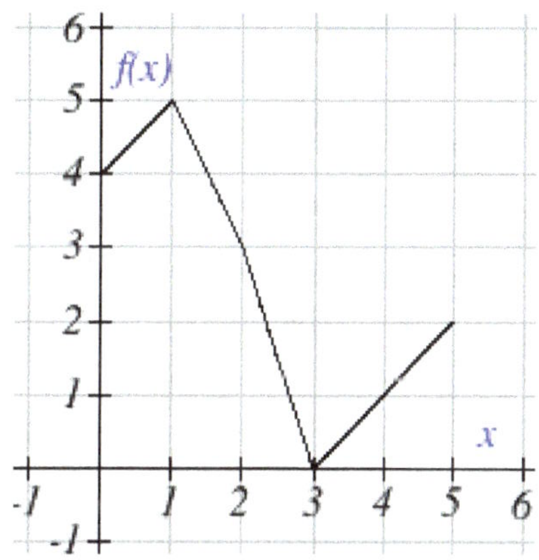

3. For $f(x) = 2x^2 + 6x - 5$ find the average rate of change on the given interval for x: [-1, 3].

4. Create a "Table of Values" for each of the toolkit functions using at least 5 values of x. Then construct your own graph. Does your graph resemble the ones in this section? Make sure to select both positive and negative x values ***when appropriate*** in order to practice calculator operations with negative numbers. [When are negative values of x not appropriate?]

5. Given a ball thrown vertically upward according to the formula

$$h(x) = 0.5 + 27.2x - 4.9x^2$$

a) A line is ***tangent*** to the curve at x = 0.5 seconds. What is the y coordinate of the point where the tangent line and the curve intersect?

b) A line is ***secant*** to the curve and passes through (1, _____) and (0, ______). What are the y coordinates of the two points?

c) Find the slope of the secant line in b)
d) Use this number to estimate the speed of the ball at 0.5 seconds.
e) Is this a "reliable" estimate, given that the actual speed of the ball is 22.3 meters/second, 0.5 second after being thrown?

6. What is the slope of the secant line through the given two points for $y = x^2$, where the two points are
   a) the point (3, 9) and a second point with x = 2.97
   b) the point (3, 9) and a second point with x = 3.02

   Use this information to estimate the slope at x = 3

   Sketch the graph of for x between 2 and 4

7. Here we see a temperature graph on a certain day in May in Boston.
   a) What was the average change in temperature from 9 am to 3 pm?
   b) Estimate how the temperature was changing (in °F/hour) at 10 am?
   c) Same question but at 6 pm?

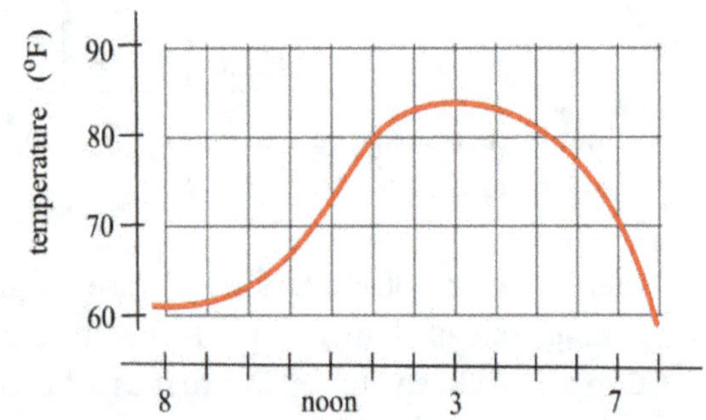

8. A person standing at the side of a road was measuring the distance between themselves and a car that was traveling on a straight road.

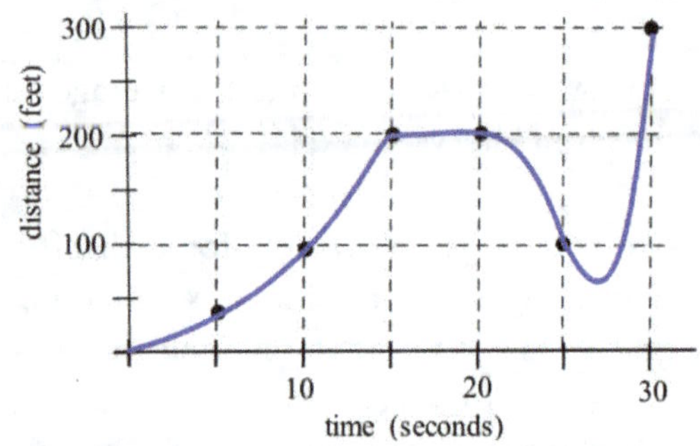

   a) Where was the car in relation to the person at the start?
   b) What are the units of velocity/speed on this graph?
   c) What was the average velocity of the car from 0 seconds to 30 seconds?
   d) What was the average velocity of the car from 10 seconds to 25 seconds?
   e) Estimate how fast the car was traveling at
      i. 10 seconds?
      ii. 18 seconds?
      iii. 25 seconds? (Hint: slope will be a negative number. To get speed, make it positive)
   f) What is happening between 15 seconds and 20 seconds?
   g) Velocity is negative, while speed is positive between 20 seconds and about 27 seconds. Why? What does this mean? Hint: Look at how the distance between the car and the observer is changing.

9. Fill in the table with appropriate units for $\frac{dy}{dx} = f'(x) = slope$.

Units for x	Units for y = f(x)	Units for $f'(x)$
hours	miles	
vehicles	people	
dollars	bottles of water	
days	birds (migrating)	
hours	miles per hour	
minutes	gallons	
ounces	dollars	

For each function in **exercises 10 to 13**, find its companion derivative function. Then answer these three questions about each: (Round as needed to 2 decimal places)

a) What is $f(a)$?
b) What is $f'(x)$?
c) What is the derivative at $x = a$?

10. $f(x) = x^3$ and $a = 4$

11. $f(x) = x^2 + x - 2$ and $a = 3$

12. $f(x) = -0.98x + 24.5$ and $a = 7.1$

13. $f(x) = 230e^x$ and $a = 11$

14. A ball is thrown upward, and its height is given by the equation $f(x) = -4.9x^2 + 27.2x + 2.5$. A graph of the function is shown as well, with points graphed. y is in meters; x is in seconds.

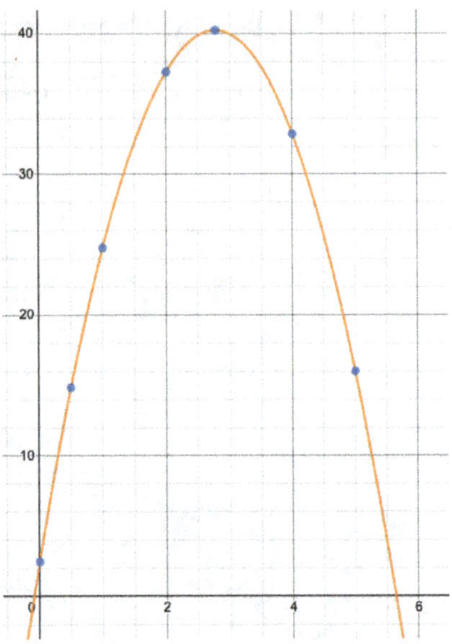

Find $f'(x)$.

What is the velocity (derivative) of the ball at the points that are labeled?

x = 0 x = 0.5

x = 1 x = 2

x = 2.776 x = 4

x = 5

Describe what is happening with the ball. What is the initial velocity? What is happening to the velocity before the ball reaches its maximum height? What is the velocity at the maximum height? On its way back down, what is happening to the velocity?

10

Applications of the Derivative

Section 10.1 Cost, Unit Cost, and Marginal Cost

Now that we have established the existence of a function and its derivative (which is also as a function) we will explore two scenarios in which the derivative helps us answer questions about a phenomenon.

Example: Our first function pair concerns memory. Specifically, it deals with how much content a person tends to recall after several days. The variable "x" again is a measure of time, this time in days. The variable "y" is a measure of the portion of material that is recalled at that time. The y variable can be interpreted as a percentage since the portion at the beginning, at x = 0, is 100. It should also be noted that this equation (formula) has no proven experimental basis in science, except that it is within the realm of what is possible. We use it for illustration purposes only. The decline of recall is represented by an equation, and we will make use of the assumption that recall is not linear. It starts with a function, a model for the relationship between time (x) and how much material is recalled (y).

Gustavo Frazao/Shutterstock.com

Our "recall function" model is:

$$y = f(x) = 0.082x^4 - 1.97x^3 + 15.75x^2 - 52.5x + 100$$

and is valid for x between 0 and 10. The domain is [0, 10]

The derivative function is $\frac{dy}{dx} = f'(x) = 0.328x^3 - 5.91x^2 + 31.5x - 52.5$

The domain of the derivative cannot include the endpoints. We only have rate of change for x in $0 < x < 10$. Up to 9.999… but not 10.

We will need a graph of f(x): (After 10 days, or x = 10, the function no longer applies)

We include a table of values for clarity and support of multiple representations of data. We use "> 0" when we want to get as close to 0 as possible, and we use "< 10" when we want to get as close to 10 as possible.

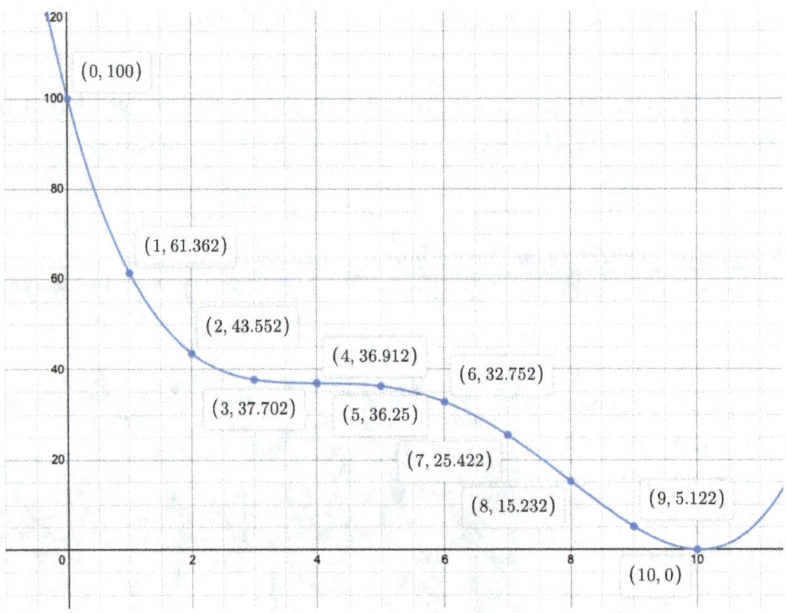

We will complete a table of (x,y) values that represent the relationship between *amount of recall over x days*. That is f(x). We will also complete a table of derivative (slope) values which will show *how fast or slow the rate of decline in memory is over x days.*

x	y=f(x)
0	100
1	61.4
2	43.5
3	37.7
4	36.9
5	36.25
6	32.75
7	25.4
8	15.2
9	5.1
10	0

x	$\frac{dy}{dx} = f'(x)$
> 0	-52.5
1	-26.6
2	-10.5
3	-2.3
4	0*
5	-1.75
6	-5.4
7	-9.1
8	-10.8
9	-8.6
< 10	0*

*Two places where the derivative of 0 are approximated

But what do all these numbers mean? What insights can be gained?

Some questions we can ask to help understand what is *mathematically* significant in this situation involve ***interpreting*** what we see on the graph and the numbers in these two tables. We will ask and answer some relevant mathematical questions about this situation.

1. Where does the ***greatest rate of decline*** in recall occur?
   This question asks about "rate of decline" which is measured by the derivative. Looking at the slopes at the various points, and taking their absolute values, we could conclude that the greatest rate of decline occurs at or very near x = 0. The slope of – 52.5 is the steepest and gives us the "greatest rate of decline".

2. What are the ***units*** for $\frac{dy}{dx}$?
   The units are the units of y ***per*** unit of x. In this situation that means we are measuring change in "amount of recall per day".

3. Why is the derivative (slope) negative? Why is it never positive?
   The derivative is negative any time the y values are decreasing. We can only assume that memory continues to fade over time, which is why the derivative is never positive.

4. What does it mean when the derivative is zero?
   The derivative (slope) is zero at an instant when no change is happening. In this situation the rate of decline slowed down to zero and then started to speed up again. In math terms, we call this a "saddle point". What might be more descriptive is to call it a brief, momentary pause, or leveling of the y variable before it started to decline again. This seems to happen at x = 4.

5. At what point does the amount of recall get cut in half? (50% is retained)
   We do not know the exact time, but it happens when y = 50. That would place it between days 1 and 2. We can approximate the time to be 1.5 days.

6. Why does the graph stop at x = 10?
   The amount of recall reaches zero. In other words, whatever content was memorized is all gone. Without further study, or something else entering the situation, day 10 is when this model ceases to be useful.

Conversation Starter: Think of one or two additional questions to answer about the situation that can be answered from the $y = f(x)$ equation and one or two that can be answered from the $\frac{dy}{dx} = f'(x)$ equation.

Here is a graph of the derivative function:

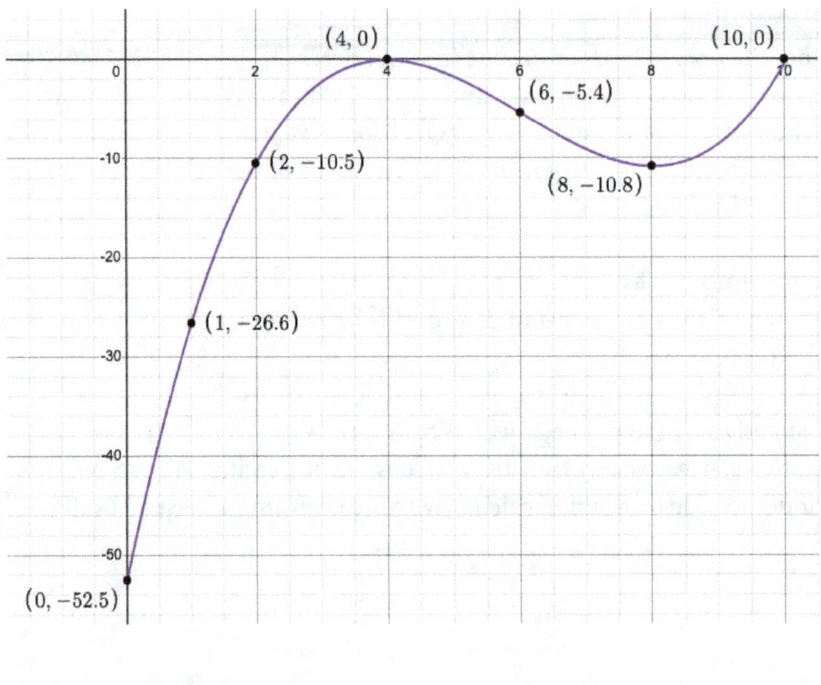

The derivative function is quite distinct from the recall function. That is because now the coordinates of each point are not (x, y) but $(x, \frac{dy}{dx})$. Both equations are polynomials, but the derivative is one degree less than the degree of the original function. Also worth noting is that the derivative graph is completely in the 4th quadrant, where the first coordinate is positive, and the second coordinate is negative. This occurs because the slope at any point on the original function is negative. We also see the two places when the derivative becomes zero, where the loss of memory is not as severe.

Example: The second exploration in this lesson has to do with cost to produce or manufacture a product. To make it interesting we will be manufacturing ceramic teapots. The cost function in business is often written using the variable "q" which represents the quantity of items in production. The reason for this is that quantity is tied to demand. But for purposes of clarity and mathematical consistency, we will continue to use the "x" variable as the input, or independent variable in our equation/model.

Solution: Let "x" be the quantity of teapots produced each week and y = C(x) is the overall (total) cost to produce "x" teapots. We know from a previous chapter that $C(x)$ = *Fixed Cost* + *Variable Cost*. Keep in mind that our cost function will have a "fixed cost" amount and the rest is the "variable cost". Let the fixed cost be \$38 and the variable cost is $14\sqrt{x}$. We will write a formula for the cost:

The Total Cost function is $C(x) = 38 + 14\sqrt{x}$. Variable Cost is $VC(x) = 14\sqrt{x}$.

Before we look at the graph of this, what do we expect to see (is it increasing or decreasing?) Does it ever reach a maximum? or a minimum? The more we produce, the more it is likely to cost to produce the items, therefore it is our expectation that the graph of C(x) will be increasing. The minimum is likely to occur when we are producing nothing (x = 0) and the maximum is only affected by our materials, equipment, and available labor. In theory, if we had unlimited supplies, equipment, and personnel there would be no maximum.

We will see if our expectation is verified by the graph.

Our total cost function is a variation of one of our toolkit functions, $y = \sqrt{x}$. Compare the graph of that function to our total cost graph. The shapes are the same, with only a few minor differences!

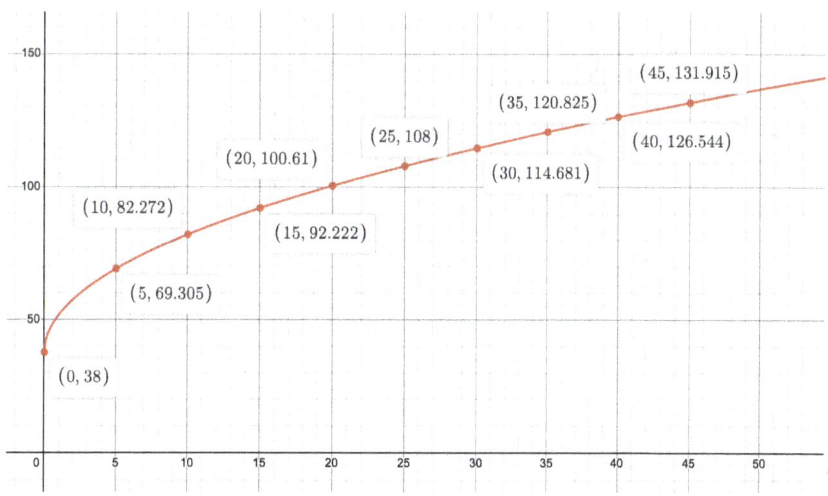

Try this: Make a table of values for C(x) choosing x to be multiples of 5 from 0 to 45.

There are in fact two more functions that we will be using in this example. The first is the "unit cost" or cost per teapot. Unit cost is a measure of how *efficient* our production is. Do we expect the **cost per item** to increase or decrease the more items we make?

Definition: The **unit cost function**, which we will designate *UnitC(x)* is found by dividing the total cost to make x items by x:

$$UnitC(x) = C(x) \div x$$

In this example then we have $UnitC(x) = \frac{38 + 14\sqrt{x}}{x}$. Notice that x cannot = 0.

Before we see the graph of this unit cost, what do we expect to see? Is it increasing? decreasing? Should the ***cost per teapot*** to make 10 teapots be more or less than the ***cost per teapot*** to make 20? Are there any clues in the information provided so far that might give us insight? In general, the answer here can vary greatly. Materials and supplies may be cheaper in bulk when making more of something. Then again, more production may mean more labor requirements. Our model (equation) will tell us the situation.

First we will generate a table of values starting with x = 1 and then use multiples of 5 up to 50.

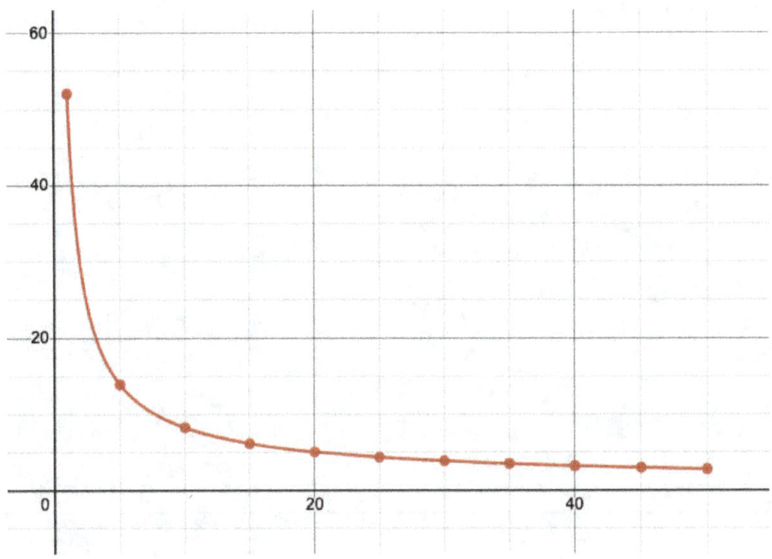

x	*UnitC(x)*
1	52
5	13.86
10	8.23
15	6.15
20	5.03
25	4.32
30	3.82
35	3.45
40	3.16
45	2.93
50	2.74

Now can we answer the question about cost per teapot? It would be unrealistic to believe that the unit cost will continue to go down. There must be a limit.

In fact, there is! We have additional information. Models like this are generally only applicable ***for specific values of x***. It turns out that we do not have the capacity to make more than 45 teapots. This means that our unit cost has both a ***minimum and a maximum***. The most it costs to make a single teapot is \$52.00 (when we make only one). The least cost to make each teapot is \$2.93, when we are making all 45 of them (full production).

In our teapot factory, as the total cost goes up, the unit cost goes down. This tells us that overall, the efficiency of our manufacturing process is such that making more teapots (at least up to a certain point) saves money in the combined overhead, labor and materials required per teapot.

We will tackle some questions we could ask about this situation (before we talk about the derivative). Each one of these questions is answered from the cost and unit cost functions since *none* of them involve a *rate of change*.

1. Our operating budget is \$125.00. If we wanted to minimize unit cost ***and*** stay within budget, what would our production be? What would be the unit cost?

   Solution: Start with the total cost graph. We want a production amount where the total cost is \$125. We can use the formula to help as well. When $x = 38$, $C(38) = 38 + 14\sqrt{38} \approx \$124.30$. If we increase production to 39, we have $C(39) = 38 + 14\sqrt{38} \approx \$125.43$ which is over budget. Our production would be 38.
   Using the Unit cost function, we can calculate the unit cost when $x = 38$. $UnitC(38) = (38 + 14\sqrt{38}) \div 38 \approx \$3.27$ per teapot to produce.

2. At what production level is the total cost between \$120 and \$121?

   Solution: From the graph, we see the point (35, 120.825). Since 120.825 is between \$120 and \$121 our production amount is 35.

3. At what production level (approximately) is the unit cost \$7.00? \$4.00? \$3.00?

   Solution: For a unit cost of \$7.00, the production is between 10 and 15. From the graph, we estimate $x = 13$.

The point (27,4) is a good estimate for the \$4.00 unit cost. The production level would be about 27 teapots.

The point (44,3) is a good estimate for the \$3.00 unit cost. The production level would be about 44 teapots.

How would we verify these answers? Calculate them using the equation.

In a production setting, we also have a quantity called the "marginal cost" function. This is the derivative of the cost function, and it approximates the ***cost to produce one more item*** if currently producing "x" items.

Definition: Given the total cost C(x) to produce x items, the **marginal cost** is the amount it costs to increase production by a **small amount** from x to x + h. It is given by the average rate of change formula:

$$\frac{\Delta C}{\Delta x} = \frac{C(x+h)-C(x)}{h} = [C(x+h) - C(x)] \div h.$$

When $C(x)$ is given by an equation that has a derivative, **marginal cost** is $C'(x) = \frac{dC}{dx}$.

In this example, $C(x) = 38 + 14\sqrt{x}$ which means that $C'(x) = \frac{7}{\sqrt{x}} = 7 \div \sqrt{x}$. We will make a table using x values 1, 2, and then multiples of 5:

x	$C'(x)$
1	\$7.00
2	4.95
5	3.13
10	2.21
15	1.81
20	1.57
25	1.40
30	1.28
35	1.18
40	1.11
45	-----

1. When x = 20, how much would it cost to produce one more teapot?

   Solution: $C'(20) = 7 \div \sqrt{20} \approx \$1.57$. Notice this is not the same as the unit cost when making 20 teapots!

2. How many teapots are being made if the cost to produce one more is \$1.18?

   Solution: In other words, what is x when C'(x) = 1.18? Looking at our table, we can say x = 35

SECTION 10.2 AVERAGE VARIABLE COST AND REVENUES

In the previous lesson we explored what insights can be gained when we know both a function and its derivative function. We asked and answered questions about memory and recall using the two functions. That example set us up to explore the Total Cost function, how it is written as a sum of Fixed Cost and Variable Cost. Then we introduced two new concepts related to cost: Unit Cost and Marginal Cost, which was used to estimate the Cost of producing one more item than the current production level.

Our goals in this lesson are:
1) Determine what fixed costs and variable costs are from the cost function.
2) Calculate the Average Variable Cost (Unit Cost) function.
3) Compare Average Variable Costs at different production levels and interpret the results.
4) Write the Revenue function given an equation for price (demand).
5) Calculate the Marginal Revenue function.
6) Compare Marginal Revenue at different production levels.

We need one more definition before continuing our investigation of cost to produce, given ***x*** is the **quantity** in production.

Definition: Given $C(x)$ = *Fixed Cost* + *Variable Cost* and *Variable Cost* = $VC(x)$ for producing x units of a product, **Average Variable Cost** is the average cost per item on the interval $[0, x]$.

Average Variable Cost on the interval $[0, x]$ =

$$\frac{\Delta y}{\Delta x} = \frac{C(x) - C(0)}{x - 0} = \frac{(Fixed + Variable) - Fixed}{x} = \frac{Variable\ Cost}{x}$$

which we are calling $AVC(x)$.

$$AVC(x) = \frac{VC(x)}{x}$$

Conversation Starter: Compare $AVC(x)$ to $UnitC(x) = \frac{C(x)}{x}$. How are they different? What makes them different?

We will be concerned with questions involving average variable cost and average revenue in a business setting. In our previous lesson we were introduced to a function that we called "Unit Cost". We need to distinguish between these two concepts. First and foremost, we always want to think of "average" as something that is **calculated over an interval**. The interval *[0,x]* is used to define "Average *Variable* Cost". The key difference is that the Unit Cost includes the fixed cost when calculating cost per item. Average Variable Cost subtracts out the fixed cost, as seen in the definition.

Example: Given the cost function for production of *cell phone cases* is $C(x) = 750 + 0.01x^2$, find a) Fixed cost, b) Variable Cost, c) Unit cost, d) Average Variable Cost. Find e) the marginal cost $C'(x)$ using one of the toolkit function formulas.

Part 1: Calculate all 6 function values when x = 150.

Part 2: Give a sentence or two describing what each of these calculations is telling us about cost when production is 150.

Solution:

a) Fixed cost is the part of C(x) that is constant.

$$Fixed\ cost = 750$$

b) Variable cost is the part of C(x) that contains x.

$$VC(x) = 0.01x^2$$

c) Unit cost is C(x) divided by x.

$$UnitC(x) = \frac{750 + 0.01x^2}{x} = (0.01x^2 + 750) \div x$$

d) Average variable cost is VC(x) divided by x. Note that $x^2 \div x = x$.

$$AVC(x) = \frac{0.01x^2}{x} = 0.01x$$

e) Finally, we will write the marginal cost function.
Marginal cost $C'(x)$ uses the toolkit combo $[C(x) = x^2, C'(x) = 2x]$. We multiply in front by 0.01. (The derivative of 750 is zero.)

$$\mathbf{C'(x) = 0.01 \cdot 2x = 0.02x}$$

Part 1: When $x = 150$, $C(150) = 750 + 0.01 \cdot 150^2 = 975$

$Fixed\ cost = 750$ (does not depend on x),

$VC(150) = 0.01 \cdot 150^2 = 225$

$UnitC(150) = (225 + 750) \div 150 = 6.50$

$AVC(150) = 0.01 \cdot 150 = 1.50$

$C'(150) = 0.02 \cdot 150 = 3.00$

Part 2: Write a sentence or two telling what each of these calculations says about cost when production is at 150.

The total cost to produce 150 cell phone cases is $975

The fixed cost of production, regardless of how many cell phone cases are produced, is $750.

The variable cost for producing 150 cell phone cases is $225, which it the total variable cost for all 150 in production.

The unit cost for producing 150 cell phone cases is $6.50, which means at the production level of 150 it costs the company $6.50 per case, which includes the fixed cost (overhead and basic operations).

The average variable cost for producing 150 cell phone cases is $1.50. At the production level of 150 without considering fixed cost, it costs the company on average $1.50 per case.

The marginal cost at the production level of 150 cell phone cases is $3.00. This means it would cost the company an additional $3.00 to make one more cell phone case and increase production to 151.

Conversation Starter: When is unit cost preferred over average variable cost when looking at numbers? Same question but reverse it. When should average variable cost matter more than unit cost?

Try this: For $C(x) = 750 + 0.01x^2$, find the total cost, unit cost, average variable cost, and marginal cost when x = 200, 250, 300, and 350. We already calculated for x = 150. Put your answers into a grid or table. What do these numbers tell us? Complete this sentence: Marginal cost is _______ as much as average variable cost.

If we knew that our information is applicable for production up to 420 (for example), we could enter the equations into a spreadsheet and calculate for all multiples of 10 or 20 starting with x = 0 all the way up to 420. If multiples of 10, there will be 21 additional rows. Use the Fill...Down feature to calculate these formulas all the way down. What are the advantages/disadvantages of using a spreadsheet?

	A	B	C	D	E	F	G
1	x	Fixed Cost	Variable Cost	Total Cost	Unit Cost	Average Variable Cost	Marginal Cost
2	0	750	=0.01*A2^2	=B2+C2	These do not apply when x = 0		
3	20	750	=0.01*A3^2	=B3+C3	=D3/A3	=C3/A3	=0.02*A3
4	40	750					
5	60	750					
...	...	...	...	...	...	...	...
23	420	750					

Now we will talk about revenue. We have already learned that revenue is a product of price with quantity. Price is determined by the demand function, and x is quantity. So, we will start there.

In our cell phone case manufacturing company, the demand equation is given by $price = f(x) = 15 - 0.018x$. What is the revenue function, $R(x)$?

$$R(x) = x \cdot (15 - 0.018x)$$

Since $R(0) = 0$, we have an interesting situation when it comes to Unit Revenue and Average Variable Revenue. The Unit Revenue is the price per unit. That price is dependent on the amount in production, which we assume to be equal to the amount in demand. If production = demand, then we have a perfectly competitive situation. This concept can get more complicated, but for the purposes of our investigation we will assume that production = demand.

Definition: When production (supply) = demand, then the average revenue per unit sold is equal to the price.

$$AR(x) = price(x)$$

We also can derive meaning from the idea of marginal revenue. In the same way that we can discover how cost would increase if production increased by a small amount, we could also discover how revenue would increase if production/sales increased by a small amount.

Definition: Given total revenue, $R(x)$, **marginal revenue** for increase in production by a small amount from x to x + h is given by:

$$\frac{\Delta R}{\Delta x} = \frac{R(x+h)-R(x)}{h} = [R(x+h) - R(x)] \div h.$$

When $R(x)$ is given by an equation that has a derivative, marginal revenue is $R'(x) = \frac{dR}{dx}$.

In general, *price* = $b - mx$, where the slope is $-m$ and b = *price when x* is 0.

The choice of $-m$ is to signify there will always be a negative sign with the x term. This means our revenue equation will always be in the form of

$$R(x) = x \cdot (b - mx)$$

We do this so that we can have a formula for R'(x) based solely on the values of *b and m.*

Definition: The pair of functions $R(x)$and $R'(x)$ will typically be as seen here, when *price* = $b - mx$.

$$R(x) = x \cdot (b - m \cdot x)$$

$$R'(x) = b - 2 \cdot m \cdot x$$

In our cell phone case manufacturing business, $b = 15$ and $m = 0.018$.

$$R(x) = x \cdot (15 - 0.018x) \text{ and}$$

$$R'(x) = 15 - 2 \cdot 0.018x = 15 - 0.036x$$

Example: For $R(x)$ as given above, calculate average revenue and marginal revenue when x = 20, 30, and 60. Then write a sentence or two explaining these results.

Solution: When asked to repeat the same calculation for more than one input, it is always a good idea to make a table. It is easier to visualize the results that way.

Here we see that the average revenue per item sold is the same as the price. But just because the average revenue goes down, does not mean that profits will also go down. The marginal revenue shows us what the revenue would be if we produced and sold one additional item at the given production level (x). It makes sense that these numbers would also decrease as x increases because if production is increasing, so is demand... which means the price is going down as will our marginal revenue also go down.

x	Average Revenue	Marginal Revenue
	15-0.018x	15-0.036x
20	14.64	14.28
30	14.46	13.92
60	13.92	12.84

Conversation Starter: Why is marginal revenue decreasing at a faster rate than average revenue?

Hint: The answer has to do with the fact that marginal revenue seeks to increase production and increase demand at the same time, which means lowering prices. Average revenue is about what has happened up to the current level of production/demand.

Section 10.3 Optimization with the Derivative

In these two chapters we have focused primarily on **five** relevant calculations on functions. We will list them now, and note what we **expect**, what we **need**, and how it is **used**.

The first two apply to a **specified value**, or values of x and result in a number result.

1. *Average rate of change* of a function on an ***interval*** $[x_1, x_2]$. We also called this the *slope of the secant line* that passes through two points on the graph of the function.
   a. we **expect** to get a number for an answer, because both x_1 and x_2 are numbers.
   b. we **need** the x and y coordinates of the two points: (x_1, y_1) and (x_2, y_2) either from the graph of the function or calculate the "y's" from the equation/formula.
   c. we **calculate** the slope using $\frac{\Delta y}{\Delta x} = \frac{y_2 - y_1}{x_2 - x_1} = \frac{change\ in\ y}{change\ in\ x}$.
   d. we **can use** this to estimate slope at a point on a curve if the secant line appears to be a good representation of the slope at a specific point on the curve.
2. *Instantaneous rate of change* of a function at a point. We call this the slope or derivative of the function at a (specified) point. It is the *slope of the tangent line* to the graph that passes through only one point (x_1, y_1).
   a. we **expect** to get a number for an answer, because we are given a specific value of x (the value of x is a number).
   b. we can **estimate** this from the graph by sketching the tangent line which passes through (x_1, y_1). Identify a second set of coordinates (another point) and calculate the slope—OR—

  c. we **need** the equation of the derivative for a more accurate answer.
  d. we **calculate** it from the equation of the derivative if known (plug in numbers): Evaluate it using x_1.

The last three involve the creation of a ***new function*** or formula using x as the variable, which then in turn can be used to calculate one of these: unit values, average over [0,x], marginal amount, or a rate of change, *at any value of x.*

3. *Unit function*, which in Economics measures $ per unit of production/sales.
   a. we **expect** to get a new function from the one that is given.
   b. we **need** the equation/formula of the quantity that we want to express as a unit quantity.
   c. we **write** the expression from a given function $f(x)$. The unit function is defined to be $Unit_{f(x)} = \frac{f(x)}{x} = f(x) \div x$.
   d. we **use** the new formula/function to calculate the unit cost/revenue/profit at a specified value of x.
4. *Average of a function* on **[0,x]** which itself is a new function of x.
   a. we **expect** to get a new function from the one that is given.
   b. we **need** the equation/formula of the quantity that is being averaged.
   c. we **simplify** this expression $\frac{f(x) - f(0)}{x}$. When $f(0) = 0$ this becomes $\frac{f(x)}{x}$ and looks like the unit function.
   d. we **use** the new formula to **calculate** the average at a specified value of x.
5. *Derivative of a function*, which in Economics is called "*marginal*" equation, measuring the change in a cost, revenue, or profit with respect to production quantity. In a physical application it might be called "*velocity*" or "*speed*" at which a measurable unit is changing with respect to time.
   a. we **expect** to have the companion function, which we call "f-prime".
   b. we **need** to have a means of finding the derivative formula, or it is given along with the function that represents the quantity in question.
   c. we **use** the new formula to **calculate** derivatives at a specified value.

In Calculus we refer to the process of optimization when we are looking for either a minimum or maximum of a quantity over its domain or a portion thereof (on an interval of x). Any potential maximum or minimum is called an ***extremum***. The plural of that word is ***extrema***, from Latin. Suppose we are looking for the maximum and minimum value of a function f(x) on an interval .

This means $f(a)$ and $f(b)$ both exist. The function exists everywhere in between $x = a$ and $x = b$ as well.

Consider this graph of a function on the interval [0,7].

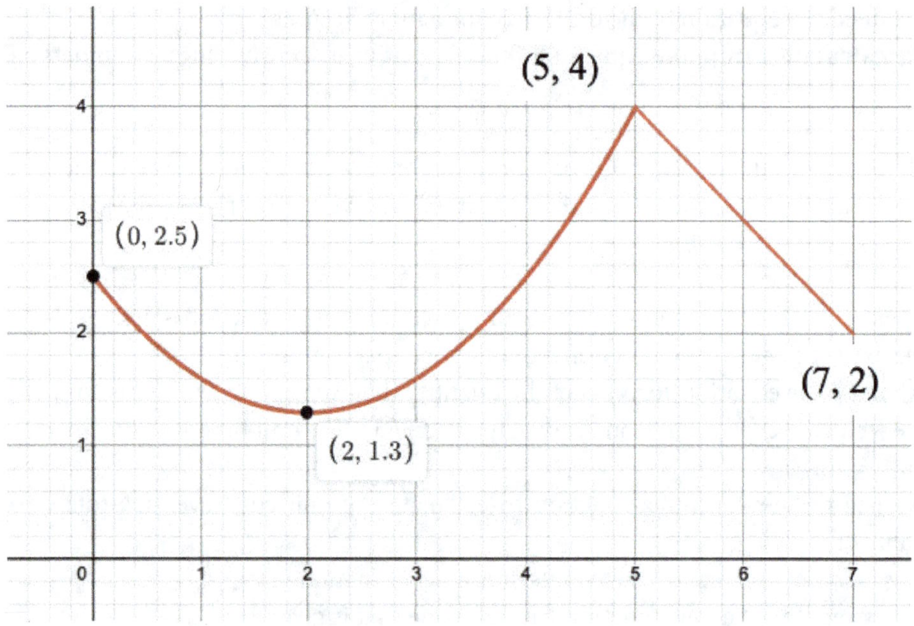

The Extreme Value Theorem in Calculus *guarantees* that *f(x)* has both an absolute minimum and an absolute maximum somewhere between $x = 0$ and $x = 7$. We do need the function to be continuous (unbroken). Not only do we have a guarantee, but we know where they must be. Extrema MUST occur at

a) one or both endpoints, or...
b) a place on the interior where the derivative does not exist, but the function is continuous (like a cusp), or...
c) a place where the derivative is zero.

From the graph, we will identify the endpoints. These are (0, 2.5) and (7, 2)

State or list any point(s) where the derivative does not exist. (5, 4)

State or list any point(s) where the derivative is zero. (2, 1.3)

Now the absolute maximum will be the one with the highest y value. Here it is the point (5, 4). The absolute minimum will be the one with the lowest value. Here it is the point (2, 1.3). In general, absolute min/max can occur at more than one point. Our concern is to identify only the ones we care about, on a specified closed interval of x.

In a business production setting, we have several functions that qualify for both optimization and for marginal analysis. Two of these we have already seen. Marginal cost and marginal revenue functions have been introduced to calculate how revenue and cost would be impacted if production/sales were to increase by a small amount.

In a previous example, we considered a business production setting in which teapots were made. The cost function was given as $C(x) = 38 + 14\sqrt{x}$ and its companion function (the derivative) is $C'(x) = \frac{7}{\sqrt{x}} = 7 \div \sqrt{x}$. We will take another look at a table for $C'(x)$ using x values 1, 2, and then increment "x" by multiples of 5. Values of x do not go past 45.

Orlova_Anna/Shutterstock.com

We will now use the marginal cost to answer some questions about ***optimizing*** production:

x	*C'(x)*
1	$7.00
2	4.95
5	3.13
10	2.21
15	1.81
20	1.57
25	1.40
30	1.28
35	1.18
40	1.11
45	-----

Is C'(x) = 0 anywhere? No.

On the interval [0,45] not including the endpoints, is there a place where the derivative does not exist?

No because our formula works for any x value in this interval. In fact, the derivative is always positive, which supports the data that total *cost increases* as production increases.

Where are the extrema for cost on x in [0, 45]?
The only extrema for cost occur at the endpoints.

What is the maximum cost? What is the minimum cost? The extrema for cost occur at the endpoints, with the minimum occurring at x = 0 when total cost = $38. The maximum occurs at x = 45 with total cost = $131.915

Optimizing for total cost may not be the goal anyway. Perhaps instead the goal is to optimize unit cost, or cost per unit. This should have the effect of increasing the gap between revenue and cost, which has to do with profit. We will take another look at the graph of unit cost in the teapot factory.

We saw this graph before, and we see that the unit cost is decreasing on the interval [1, 45].

Unit cost does not make sense for anything less than x = 1. And the operation is most efficient when at full production of 45 teapots.

We will now look at revenue, and then introduce the profit function in our teapot manufacturing business.

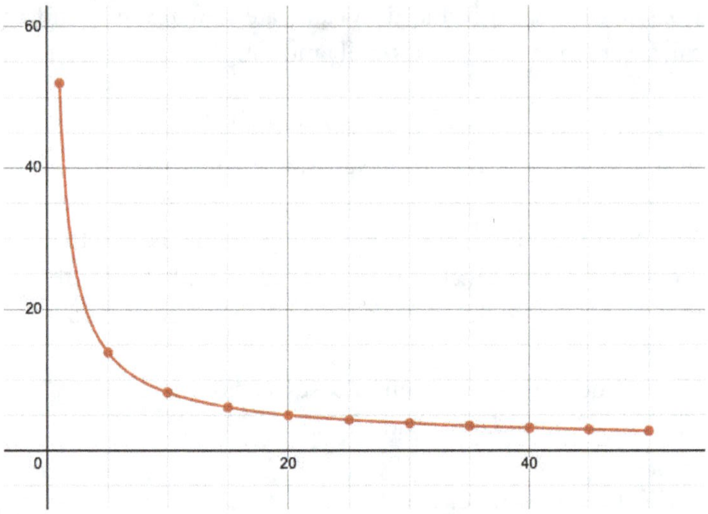

Suppose that demand for our teapots is such that

$$price = 10.5 - 0.16x$$

What are $R(x)$ and $R'(x)$? From the price equation, b = 10.5 and m = 0.16.

$$R(x) = x \cdot (10.5 - 0.16x)$$

$$R'(x) = 10.5 - 0.32x$$

x	*C(x)*	*C'(x)*	*R(x)*	*R'(x)*
0	$38.00	---	0.00	---
1	$52.00	$7.00	10.34	10.18
2	$57.80	4.95	20.36	9.86
5	$69.305	3.13	48.50	8.90
10	$82.27	2.21	89.00	7.30
15	$92.22	1.81	121.50	5.70
20	$100.61	1.57	146.00	4.10
25	$108.00	1.40	162.50	2.50
30	$114.68	1.28	171.00	0.90
35	$120.825	1.18	171.50	-0.70
40	$126.54	1.11	164.00	-2.30
45	$131.915	---	148.50	---

Not far from the place where our unit cost is minimized we seem to have a maximum revenue in the vicinity of production x = 35. We see that in two ways. On the table the largest value of R(x) occurs at x = 35, *AND* R'(x) goes from a positive number to a negative one. Another theorem in Calculus called the Intermediate Value Theorem (IVT) guarantees that the derivative function will hit all the values between two values on our table. Why is this important? Because extrema occur where the derivative is zero (0). And *zero is between 0.90 and —0.70.* So, there is an x between 30 and 35 where R'(x) = 0... which makes that either a maximum or minimum revenue! We will state that another way.

Observation #1: On the table, we noticed that revenues increased up to \$171.50, then started to go down again. This was our first clue that there may be a maximum right at $x = 35$, or at least nearby.

Observation #2: We know from the Extreme Value Theorem that if there is going to be a maximum or minimum, it will occur at one of the endpoints or at a place where the derivative is zero. It seems rather obvious that the smallest revenue occurs when $x = 0$. But the other endpoint has a revenue of \$148.50, which is smaller than the revenues at $x = 30$ and $x = 35$.

Observation #3: If we were to graph the revenue function, we could see that the shape of the graph is a quadratic, and that the vertex occurs at $x = 32.813$.

Recall that the vertex of a quadratic occurs where the derivative (slope) is zero.

Observation #4: We have further evidence of a place where the derivative is zero and a potential maximum. R'(x) went from a positive number to a negative number. We know from IVT Calculus that there must be an x where $R' = 0$.

Our manufacturing operation requires that we choose a whole number for production, so we will complete the table filling in all values of x between 30 and 35. We can see that $x = 33$, which is the nearest whole number to 32.8, is where we would maximize revenue.

x	*C(x)*	*C'(x)*	*R(x)*	*R'(x)*
10	\$82.27	2.21	89.00	7.30
15	\$92.22	1.81	121.50	5.70
20	\$100.61	1.57	146.00	4.10
25	\$108.00	1.40	162.50	2.50
30	\$114.68	1.28	171.00	0.90
31	115.95	1.26	171.74	0.58
32	117.20	1.24	172.16	0.26
33	118.42	1.22	172.26	-0.06
34	119.63	1.20	172.04	-0.38
35	\$120.825	1.18	171.50	-0.70
40	\$126.54	1.11	164.00	-2.30
45	\$131.915	---	148.50	---

We have just *optimized* revenue. We found the maximum.

But the goal of any business is to maximize profit. This brings us to the last two equations that we will need in this chapter.

Definition: Let profit = P(x) and the marginal profit is P'(x).

$$P(x) = R(x) - C(x)$$

$$P'(x) = R'(x) - C'(x)$$

Maximum profit occurs when $P'(x) = 0$ which means we want to find the value(s) of x where

$$R'(x) \cong C'(x)$$

This gives us two options for optimizing profit. We will look at both. The first option is to work from the table. Look down the column and see if we can find a place where $R'(x) \cong C'(x)$.

We will not give up just because we do not see it right away, either. Using previously calculated values, we do not immediately see where this may occur. We should include all values between 25 and 30 as we suspect the solution will be in that range. As close to zero as possible is what we are looking for.

x	*C'(x)*	*R'(x)*	*R' – C'*
10	2.21	7.30	5.09
15	1.81	5.70	3.89
20	1.57	4.10	2.53
25	1.40	2.50	1.10
26	1.37	2.18	0.81
27	1.35	1.86	0.51
28	1.32	1.54	0.22
29	1.30	1.22	-0.08
30	1.28	0.90	-0.38
31	1.26	0.58	-0.68
32	1.24	0.26	-0.98
33	1.22	-0.06	-1.28
34	1.20	-0.38	-1.58

Again, the Intermediate Value Theorem comes in handy. In the $R'(x) - C'(x)$ column the value goes from a positive number to a negative one between x = 28 and x = 29. Comparing the two values, *—0.08 is closest to zero*. We maximize profit when we are only producing and selling 29 teapots at the price of *price* = 10.5 – 0.16 · 29 = $5.86 to retailers.

Spreadsheets are one way to see everything everywhere all at once. But sometimes it can be too much. Using a tool of our choice, we can graph the profit function and locate the maximum on the graph.

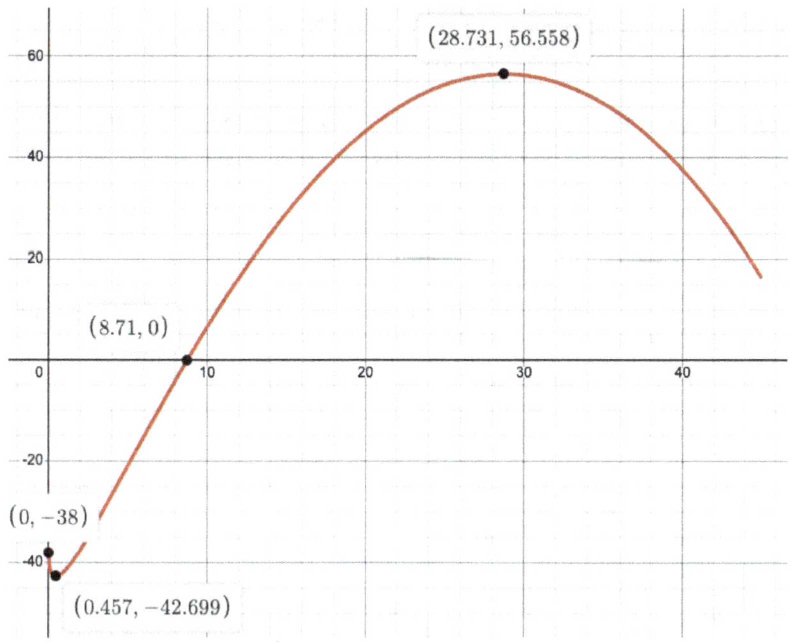

Profit from production and sales of between 0 and 45 ceramic teapots is shown here. The precise maximum occurs when x = 28.731 and y = 56.558. When x = 29 the profit is 56.548.

Try this: Go back and gather all information we have concerning the "cell phone case" business. Using a spreadsheet (or table of values), make columns for ***x*, *price***, ***C(x)***, ***C'(x)***, ***R(x)***, ***R'(x)*** and then two more columns for ***P(x)*** and "***R'(x) – C'(x)***". There should be eight columns in all. Assume x in [0, 420]. Do not go past 420.

Find the maximum revenue and maximum profit. Write a sentence or two about what is required – in terms of production, sales, and price, to maximize profit.

Practice Exercises

1. Let the recall function be given by $y = \frac{100}{x^2+1}$. Compare this with the toolkit function $y = \frac{1}{x^2+1}$. Name two ways they are basically "the same". Name two ways they are different.

2. Given that $y = \frac{100}{x^2+1}$, its derivative is $\frac{dy}{dx} = \frac{-200x}{(x^2+1)^2} = -200x \div (x^2+1)^2$.

   What is the slope at x = 3? Interpret this number in the "recall" function context.

3. The total cost to produce "x" items is given by $C(x) = -0.2x^2 + 20x + 120$ and the marginal cost is $C'(x) = -0.4x + 20$; we also know that the maximum number of items that can be made is 50.

   a. What is the fixed cost?
   b. What is the variable cost equation?
   c. What is the unit cost equation?
   d. What is the unit cost if the current production amount is 30?
   e. If the current production amount is 30, what would it cost to make one more?
   f. At what production amount would you be if it cost $2.00 to make just one more?

4. The cost to produce backpacks is given by the equation $C(x) = 22 + 2.7x - 0.01x^2$

   a. What is the fixed cost?
   b. What is the unit cost function?
   c. What is the variable cost function?
   d. Find the Average Variable Cost function.
   e. Use the answer in d) to find the average variable cost for x = 10; x = 25; x = 50; x = 75
   f. What do the numbers mean?

5. The demand for backpacks is given by: *price* $(p) = 12 - 0.11x$

   a. Write the revenue function R(x)
   b. What units are the "y" variable for R(x)?
   c. Write the average revenue function.
   d. Write the marginal revenue function.
   e. Use the answer in c) and d) to find average revenue and marginal revenue when x = 10; x = 25; x = 50; x = 75
   f. Explain these results.

6. The cost to produce a certain video game is given by the equation $C(x) = 15000 + 3.1x - 0.008x^2 + 0.004x^3$ [x is in thousands of video games produced]

   a. What is the fixed cost?
   b. What is the variable cost to produce "x"?
   c. Find the Average Variable Cost function.
   d. Use the answer in c) to find the average variable cost for x = 50; x = 100; x = 150; x = 200

   What do the numbers mean?

7. Consider the graph of a function f(x) Answer the following questions. Of the points that are labelled, can you identify the endpoints? ______________

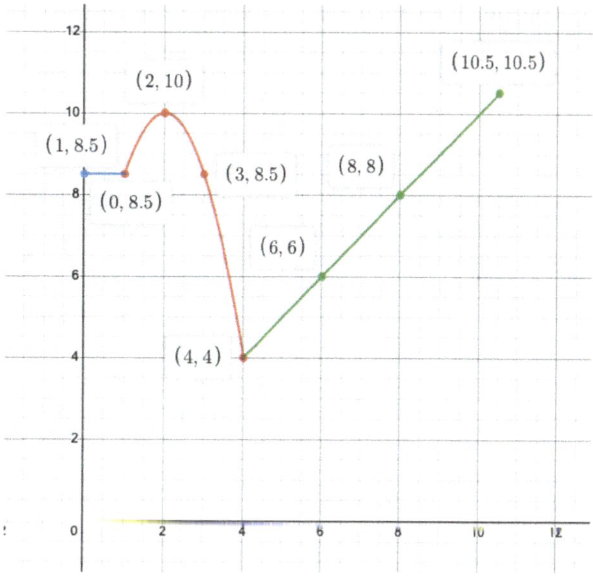

   Name the place(s) where the derivative does not exist. ______________

   Is there a place where the derivative is zero? ____________

   Name an interval where the derivative (slope) is zero ______________

   List all extrema:

   ____

   Where is the absolute maximum? __________ Absolute minimum? __________

8. For the following questions, please use the same cost function as in question #6 and the price function *price* = 500 – 1.2*x*. Try to get the derivatives of cost and revenue on your own and see if you can do it. We are also considering the interval $0 \le x \le 225$. For the purposes of exercises, the derivatives are

$$C'(x) = 3.1 - 0.016x + 0.012x^2$$
$$R'(x) = 500 - 2.4x$$

   a. Where is the "Break Even" point? At what production level will revenue = cost?
   b. On what interval of x do we see revenue exceeding cost?
   c. Use any of the techniques we have used in this course (including graphing in Excel) to find the maximum cost for $0 \le x \le 225$

d. Use any of the techniques we have used in this course (including graphing in Excel) to find the maximum revenue for $0 \leq x \leq 225$

e. Write a formula for the profit function. Make a graph of profit for $0 \leq x \leq 225$ and make note that it could sometimes be negative. (Feel free to use Excel for the graph).

f. What is the maximum profit? Solve the equation $\boldsymbol{C'(x)=R'(x)}$ using any of the techniques that we have learned. Explain your reasoning.
Hint: Maximum profit occurs at the point (127.107, 194.942)

Questions for reflection: What topic did you find the most challenging and least challenging? What was most enjoyable? least enjoyable?

For topics that were challenging, how could you approach new learning that might make it easier?

Did you study with a partner? Did you like it? How could you make group study or study with a partner better?

What did you discover about yourself as a learner?

Remember, learning is a journey not a destination.

www.ingramcontent.com/pod-product-compliance
Lightning Source LLC
LaVergne TN
LVHW080048210926
848481LV00011B/3305
9798385112906